AMERICAN EDUCATION

Its Men

Ideas

and

Institutions

Advisory Editor

Lawrence A. Cremin
Frederick A. P. Barnard Professor of Education
Teachers College, Columbia University

Student Life and Customs

Henry D. Sheldon

ARNO PRESS & THE NEW YORK TIMES
*New York * 1969*

Reprint edition 1969 by Arno Press, Inc.

*

Library of Congress Catalog Card No. 70-89233

*

Manufactured in the United States of America

Editorial Note

AMERICAN EDUCATION: *Its Men, Institutions and Ideas* presents selected works of thought and scholarship that have long been out of print or otherwise unavailable. Inevitably, such works will include particular ideas and doctrines that have been outmoded or superseded by more recent research. Nevertheless, all retain their place in the literature, having influenced educational thought and practice in their own time and having provided the basis for subsequent scholarship.

Lawrence A. Cremin
Teachers College

Student Life and Customs

INTERNATIONAL EDUCATION SERIES

STUDENT LIFE
AND CUSTOMS

BY

HENRY D. SHELDON, Ph. D.

PROFESSOR IN THE UNIVERSITY OF OREGON

NEW YORK

D. APPLETON AND COMPANY

1901

EDITOR'S PREFACE.

A BOOK on Student Life in Universities and Colleges has to deal chiefly with the way and manner in which students react against the regular work of the institution and its rules and regulations in order to preserve their individuality.

The discipline of the institution, both as to the learning which it teaches and as to the regulations it imposes, tends to efface the independence of the student and to make him in some sense a mere automaton. But, on the other hand, the learning taught at the university, although it is remote from the present life of the student, is of such a character as to give him confidence in himself by enlarging his survey of the world in which he lives. In this aspect the student finds his individuality stimulated and developed. He feels that he is enlightened as compared with the prosaic ordinary citizen, or as compared with his former self.

Goaded by the contradiction between his growing individuality and his sense of the slight done to his likes and preferences by the requirements of the school, the student reacts against the established order in which he finds himself, and endeavours to recover his internal equilibrium by proving his personal ability to destroy the social might that manifests itself in his community, and more especially in the school of which he is a member.

Education involves two wills: an individual will and an institutional will. The state and the family are institutions, and they may be so strict in their *régime* as to crush out the individual will unless it saves itself by reaction.

The earliest and most rudimental of national forms are likest to the family. Simple, implicit obedience to the will of the parent is the part of the child. The symbol of the dragon which appears so frequently in the art of China and Japan embodies this idea of unreasoning obedience to authority. Merely external authority is a dragon.

Spontaneity and freedom are by all means desirable, but they must conform to reason. Modern civilization far more than ancient seeks to harmonize the will of the individual with the will of the social whole. It seeks to make obedience rational by giving to the student an insight into the necessity of its rules of order for public safety and prosperity. With this insight the authority of the state and the family is not any longer an external affair: it becomes the inward guiding principle of the individual.

The opposition between the individual will and the will of the social whole has produced what is called by a recent writer the isolation of the school. The school breaks the continuity of the home life of the pupil by setting tasks of its own and by requiring of the child a somewhat rigid conformity to the regulations that it adopts. When pedagogical theory teaches that it is wholly the fault of the school that it is isolated from the home life of the child, it goes too far.

One could say that all education, whether in the school, the family, the state, the church, or civil society—that all education is an attempt to overcome the isolation of the undeveloped individual, the immature specimen of the human race—i. e., the infant or the savage, for the child or the savage is isolated from the rationality of his true being. His thought is feeble

because he can not re-enforce it by the thought of the
race. His action is feeble because it is not re-enforced
by the action of all mankind. Education strives to
emancipate the individual child from his isolation. It
is the child, and not the school, that is self-estranged.
In the school the child recovers his true self. But self-
estrangement, as a principle, helps one understand many
things in education that are otherwise enigmatic: for
example, how that the culture of all races proceeds by a
mastery of a classic literature—the study of Confucius
and Mencius in Chinese education, the study of the code
of Manu, the Vedas, the Hitopadesa, among the East
Indians, the study of the Koran among the Moham-
medans, and the study of the Bible and of Greek and
Latin classics among modern Christian nations. It
is a sort of vicarious living over again of the far-off
world—far off from the present and offering an earlier
epoch of the nation's civilization.

The child cradled in his immediate present takes it
for all in all, and for an isolated, complete whole; but
his education teaches him that it is not isolated, but
that it is in causal relation with all its past, and in a
causal reaction with all that is distant from it in space.
Finding himself mistaken as to the completeness of his
present life in this isolation, the youth begins to take
his steps with increasing wonder and delight at finding
new worlds that were before invisible to him, but which,
when once seen, help explain to him what is here and
now. The intellectual nations of the world, take as
examples the Persian or East Indian, the Egyp-
tian or the Greeks and Romans, have studied not only
their own classics, but also such elcments as they possessed of abstract science like mathematics and astron-
omy, and have undertaken foreign travel as an element
of education. The school is wont to symbolize its
isolation, or its difference from the every-day life of

the immediate present, by the adoption of certain formal usages, the wearing of some special garb to distinguish the order from the rest of the community, the adoption of some mode of life different from that of the family of the average citizen. The student perhaps has been aided in, rather than hindered from mastering the strange and far-off phases of the life of his people by these matters of peculiar garb and the community life in the school or college. He takes some pride in thus celebrating his arrival at a step removed from the commonplace life which he lived as an immature youth. In the school where he is he expects to be enlarged in his life by the addition of the will and intellect of the race. He takes some pleasure in making this distinction of his new life from his old life visible by a cap and gown, and by a college life in a system of barracks (college dormitories) rather than in the family life adopted by his civilization.

All culture begins with this first estrangement of the immature individual toward his immediate surroundings, material and spiritual, and with the effort to make himself at home in what is at first strange and different, but which he will soon render familiar by study and practice.

He will begin to see, step by step, his own rationality as realized in civilization, and identify it with the purpose of the life of his race. He will make over for himself a second nature in these other stages of rational life, isolated by time and space from him.

He will increase proportionally in his ability to think and to do. He will not be surprised at the discovery of a difference from the manners and customs of his family or neighbourhood. He will not be astonished at the habits of doing and thinking which he sees among foreigners, but will explain them in the light which he has obtained from the comparative study of manners and customs, and modes of doing things; he will be able to criticise his own manners and customs and methods of doing, and will see how to reform them in such a manner as to bring about a better conformity with what is rational.

It is in connection with this process of self-estrangement that the series of phenomena arises which takes on the character of reaction against the ordinances of the institutions of culture—phenomena of student life treated in this book. It is marked in the entire history of the race that the culture world, the world of self-estrangement, as organized in the school, the church, the state, and especially in the family, always assumes the attitude of authority and demands implicit obedience on the part of the child or the individual citizen. This obedience—more in ancient times than now—has been insisted upon to such an extent as to threaten to produce the effacement of the individual. It was thought that the individual must be effaced before he could become a participator in the intellect and will of the social whole.

It sounds paradoxical to say that the pupil must be effaced before he can be re-enforced. All the improvements and reforms in pedagogy from the beginning have made it a point of effort to correct this defect and prevent the complete effacement of the pupil, for the more one can save of the strength of the pupil in will and intellect the better, provided it is turned in the direction of conformity to the will and intellect of the social whole. Insight, as I have before stated, emancipates the person from authority. When insight is obtained there is no longer any blind authority; for the person does his deed freely and intentionally through insight into its rationality. He does not do it to oblige some other person merely, but because he sees that it is in itself reasonable.

During the entire history of the civilization of man there have been special reactions against blind obedience to authority, and these we find to continue down to the present. It appears that there were great riots and mobs from the earliest times in universities. Students were obliged to renounce the manners and customs that they brought with them from their homes and neighbourhoods and put on other forms and customs that were strange to them. In a certain sense they had to lose their individuality. But they reacted against this: they resorted to secret societies, in which they mocked the forms and ceremonies of the venerable institution, and ridiculed one after another all of the studies which they pursued with so much diligence in their daily tasks. They went so far as to caricature their teachers.

And especially they delighted in outraging the sense of propriety of the people of the community in which their school was situated. They had escaped from the world of productive industry and daily duties and home life into the university; now they wished to express their sense of freedom by attacking the public order, and outraging the citizens of the town in which they lived, by assaults upon person and property.

Again, they sought to give objectivity to their new feeling of individuality by forcing the members of lower classes into absurd rites and ceremonies. The hazing of students, the initiation of them into the societies of upper classes—in such mad performances as these they preserved in some sense their native spontaneity and individuality. They protected themselves against the all-effacing authority of the institution by insane pranks and capricious action. They attacked rationality in the name of irrationality, and in this way they preserved their self-activity and sense of personality.

There is an illustration of this in The Abbot, where

Walter Scott describes a revelry as taking place at Melrose Abbey. It was an annual mask, a species of insurrection conducted by an Abbot of Misrule, in which the stately ceremonial of the abbey is mocked. The surrounding community, year in and year out, obeyed the stern and unyielding authority of the abbot of the monastery, but on the occasion of some feast-day of the church it recovered its sense of independence by mocking the institutional forms.

In ancient times the Saturnalia was celebrated in Rome, and on that day especially the slave might masquerade as his master, or any private citizen might masquerade as the king or emperor. The slave on that festal day alone of all the year wore the pileus or badge of freedom, and was indulged in license of speech. In some cases the menials were allowed to partake of a banquet, attired in the clothes of their masters, who waited on them at the table. In modern times the carnival at Venice and other European towns, and its counterparts in the Mardi Gras of New Orleans, the Veiled Prophets of St. Louis, and similar revelries in other cities of the United States founded by French or Spaniards, belong to the same reaction by which the sense of personality is retained in the midst of a general life of conformity to use and wont.

The student in college loves nothing else so much as to march in a torchlight procession disguised in a mask. At Yale he used to celebrate the completion of the study of geometry by burying with funeral ceremonies a copy of Euclid, the text which he used.

It makes an interesting book to collect in one volume a history of student life at colleges and universities. As before said, nearly all that has to be written in such a book concerns in one way or another the reaction of the student against the strict life imposed upon him by authority and against his continuous occupation with

Greek and Roman life and with abstract mathematics—
a *régime* that threatens to efface his individuality and
make him into a puppet.

This theory of self-estrangement also explains why
secrecy has so much to do with the student's social life
in the college and the university. In his reaction
against the requirements of college, which are blazoned
before him and forced in upon his attention at every
turn, he feels a heart-hunger which can be gratified
only by the utmost self-abandon. He must ridicule all
that is sacred and rational, and assert himself in his
most irrational form of activity. For this he requires
the cloak of secrecy. Besides, secrecy gives him a sense
of personal dominion as opposed to public order.

The great object of student life is to be able to overcome the isolation of the immature individual, whether
child or savage. The uncultured individual who has
been living a life of use and wont is called by the student a Philistine. The student acquires a quasi-savage
appetite to torment the individual who is contented
with the life of the present in its shallow immediateness. He himself is sacrificing all this immediateness in
order to acquire the power to be at home in the remote
past and in the life of people far distant in space. That
the Philistine should be so contented arouses his ire.
He takes the poor farmer's load of hay, left on the public square, and during the latter part of the night trans-
fers it piece by piece and wisp by wisp to the top of
the college chapel. In the morning the farmer is
guided to his vanished load of hay by the gaze of the
populace at the unusual spectacle of a cart that has
been removed to the top of the chapel and its load re-
placed upon it. The university is a great power organized, if it is reasonable. It is also a great power when
organized in the name of unreason.

The student lays great stress on whimsical secrets—

such, for example, as the words to which the Greek letters in the name of his fraternity stand. The countersign to be repeated by each student who attended the burial of Euclid was some line from Homer's Iliad with which he had been familiar in his recent classroom studies.

Where this reaction is not found in student life two causes may be looked for: either the life of the college does not stimulate individuality enough by its course of study, and in this case the students are and remain Philistines; or, in the other case, the daily life of the student affords its hours of respite from the institutional life—as happens where there are no commons or large boarding-houses, and the students are scattered over a large city and are resident in their own families or in small boarding-houses, where they form social relations with the population outside college.

It is interesting to investigate the educative effect of the intense college life in the barracks system of dormitories and commons, as compared with the college life which exists where the students are nearly all " day pupils."

W. T. HARRIS.

WASHINGTON, D. C., *September 10, 1901.*

AUTHOR'S PREFACE.

THIS volume aims to be a general introduction to
the subject of student life, and as such presents only the
main outlines. The lack of an extensive monographic
literature treating critically of student societies in the
different colleges and universities, prevents, for the
present, any more pretentious and exhaustive work. If
the present study shall stimulate others to fill the serious gap which exists in the literature of the subject, it
will have accomplished one of its main purposes. It
is hoped that the facts herein collected will be of service to that group of pedagogical thinkers, which since
the days of Froebel has made spontaneity the touch-
stone of educational progress.

The author wishes to express his sense of obligation
to all those who, either in private letter or by answer
to printed *questionnaire*, have in any way contributed
material. To Dr. G. Stanley Hall, of Clark University,
he is particularly indebted for criticism and stimulation.
Among numerous friends who have been of essential
service, special mention should be made of Drs. W. H.
Burnham and E. C. Sanford, of Clark University; Dr.
E. B. Huey, Prof. W. H. Chambers, of Moorhead Normal School; Dr. Frederic E. Bolton, of the University
of Iowa; Dr. H. C. Moreno, of the Leland Stanford Jr.
University; and Mr. Arthur M. Cathcart, of Colorado
Springs.

EUGENE, OREGON, *September 29, 1901.*

B

CONTENTS.

CHAPTER I.

STUDENT LIFE IN EUROPE.

CHAPTER II.

STUDENT LIFE IN COLONIAL COLLEGES.

CHAPTER III.

STUDENT LIFE DURING THE REVOLUTIONARY PERIOD,
1775–1840.

CHAPTER IV.

STUDENT SOCIETIES DURING THE TRANSITION PERIOD, 1840–1870.

CHAPTER V.

STUDENT SOCIETIES IN MODERN PERIOD, 1870–1900.

CHAPTER VI.

STUDENT SOCIETIES IN SECONDARY SCHOOLS.

APPENDIX—BIBLIOGRAPHY.

STUDENT LIFE AND CUSTOMS.

CHAPTER I.

§ 1. STUDENT LIFE IN THE MEDIÆVAL UNIVERSITIES.

FROM the fifth to the tenth centuries culture in western Europe was on the defensive. The invasions of the fierce northern barbarians, by destroying the material basis of civilization, made the independent pursuit of science and philosophy impossible. Learning was confined to the rudiments of knowledge necessary for church services; education became a mere instrument of the ecclesiastical *régime*. The monasteries and cathedral schools were the chief centres of instruction. The so-called educational revivals of this period, in England under the Northumbrian kings and Alfred, and in Gaul under Charlemagne, are more properly conceived as church reformations. There could be no real student life, because no student class as separate from the clergy existed, and because the spirit of freedom was wholly absent from the scholastic centres.

By the beginning of the eleventh century the positive forces of society, government, law, order, gained the ascendancy, and there followed a reawakening of the European mind, which was as true a Renaissance as the more brilliant movement of the fifteenth century. In northern Europe, the seat of theological interest, the new spirit of speculation busied itself in

1   1

examining the foundations of current beliefs. Peter Abelard originated the dialectical method of inquiry and teaching which in the course of a century shifted the basis of thought within the Church from mysticism and authority to rationalism. In southern Europe, particularly in the communes of northern Italy, the traditions of the old empire still possessed the imaginations of men. The awakened interest in consequence took a secular rather than a rationalistic tendency, civil law supplanted theology as the chief subject of interest.

During the early stages of the awakenment fixed curricula and standard institutions of learning were equally lacking; scholars wandered from master to master and from subject to subject at will. They were not bound to spend a fixed number of years on any one branch of knowledge, or in any one city. By degrees, however, the most famous teachers, like Abelard or Irnerius, gathered their pupils about them in some central location, which in time necessitated regulations between master and scholar, student and townspeople. The fame of the educational centre or " *studium generale* " grew, its rules from mere regulations became rigid laws, and eventually the recognition of Pope or sovereign constituted the institution a university. Thus the universities of the twelfth and thirteenth centuries were the natural products of a popular thirst for knowledge, and were democratic in their organization and conception. Such were Bologna and its daughter universities in Italy, Paris and Montpellier in France, Oxford and Cambridge in England. In the later mediæval period, the fourteenth and fifteenth centuries, universities owed their foundation to authority, usually to kings or bishops. Among the institutions of this class may be enumerated the universities of Scotland, Spain (chiefly), Scandinavia, Germany, and eastern Europe.

While the mediæval universities were the outgrowth
of a free spirit of inquiry which tended to be either
secular or rationalistic, they were at the same time
Church institutions, and their students clerks or priests.
Placed in such intimate relations with the Church at a
time when the latter dominated the spiritual life of
man, the universities were greatly influenced by the
ideals of mediæval Christianity. Nowhere is this influence more apparent than in their student life. Asceticism was the professed rule of life of the priest and the
monk, so it was the prevailing theory in the discipline of
those they trained. Other-worldliness demanded the
subjection of the flesh, and so the mediæval school
starved and flogged its students into submission. A celebrated college of the University of Paris, in the time of
Erasmus, deliberately aimed to crush the spirit of its
students by inflicting upon them almost impossible sanitary conditions. Not infrequently the iron discipline
provoked outbreaks which cost the teachers their lives.
The physical conditions of life were hard. The student's quarters were devoid of comfort and in winter
scarcely tenantable. There was no fireplace or stove in
his room, and the wind whistled through the loosely built
casement. Students were not permitted to go beyond
the walls of their colleges without official attendance,
and if convicted of an infringement of the rules they
were soundly birched. This description applies only to
the later, more organized period of university life (fourteenth and fifteenth centuries). During earlier centuries the students were left to themselves, with no attempt at discipline, and the wildest license prevailed.

The strength of the ascetic ideal is seen in the absence of authorized or respectable amusements. Athletic games were not only absent, but they were absolutely prohibited, and violations of this rule were more
severely punished than actual crimes. Playing with the

bat and ball, chess, the use of musical instruments,
dancing, the keeping of unclean birds and beasts, were
all forbidden by college statutes. Only at rare intervals
do we find an exception to the general practice, such as
the rule at the University of Cambridge, which required
each student to take a daily walk with a single companion in imitation of the apostles. The sports and
pastimes of the small minority of the students who indulged themselves were of a lawless character, and in
direct contravention of the statutes—such, for instance,
as cockfighting, the use of the crossbow, the keeping
of falcons, and fishing in streams belonging to other
corporations. The only source of legitimate enjoyment
was derived from what Professor Rashdall has characterized as " ecclesiastical dissipation "—that is, story-
telling and feasts on saints' days.

From the absence of the ordinary means of enjoyment it must not be imagined that the mediæval students were a mild-mannered and law-abiding class. On
the contrary, the violence and lawlessness which characterized mediæval life in general reached its highest
expression in the university. Under the protection of
their clerical tonsure, the students of 'Paris attacked
and slew passers-by, carried off the women, ravished the
virgins, committed robberies, and broke into houses.
Over and over again at Oxford occurs the dismal record
that certain jurors swear that a monk or clerk killed A
or B, citizen or clerk, with a sword, poleaxe, or knife,
and has fled. Such violence was not confined to turbulent freshmen and young aristocrats, but masters of arts,
monks, friars, beneficed clergymen, and heads of colleges were involved in street brawls and assaults.

Such turbulence culminated in systematic conflicts
between the students and the population among whom
they were situated, known as town and gown rows. The
dimensions and nature of these collisions may be seen

from the following typical cases: In the thirteenth century a long-standing feud existed between the Parisian scholars and the monastery of St. Germain concerning the ownership of a piece of ground. On one occasion the provost of the monastery, surrounded by his armed retainers, set upon the unarmed and defenceless boys and masters and belaboured them with clubs, swords, and iron-tipped staves. Many of the students were badly wounded, some mortally, but were nevertheless dragged off to the horrible dungeons of the abbey. In 1345 a party of Oxford students, disliking the wine set before them at an inn, hurled a pewter mug at the head of the innkeeper, who thereupon appealed to his fellow-townsmen for redress. The bells of the city are sounded, both sides appear on the streets fully armed and fight during the remainder of the day without seriously injuring each other. The next day a horde of two thousand rustics enter the city, overcome opposition, pillage the halls of the students, killing and wounding the scholars, tearing their books to pieces, and in some instances firing the buildings. The countrymen manifested their hatred of the clergy by flaying off the crowns (all the skin as far as the tonsure) of their victims and by mutilating their bodies. The fugitives were beaten and wounded clinging to the very altars of the churches. For its share in this uprising the king deprived the city of Oxford of the most important of its civic rights. Affairs of this type were of frequent occurrence in the history of the mediæval university. At times the feeling of animosity between town and gown reached such a pitch that the students migrated to another locality.

The more jovial side of student life is seen in the drinking customs and initiation ceremonies. No important event could take place without being made the occasion of a drinking bout. Nearly all the minor steps of advance in the career of a university man were celebrated by parties and feasts given by the successful and elated candidates. During the longer disputations, the need of refreshment was likely to be felt during its progress as well as at the conclusion.

The custom of initiation has been one of the most widespread and popular student usages in all ages. It " gratified the bullying instinct, the social instinct, and the desire to find at once the excuse and means of a carousal " (Rashdall). During this period the loose custom grew into a stereotyped form. In the quaint allegory of the time, the freshman is a wild beast who must be tamed before he is permitted to enter refined circles. Dressed to represent a wild boar, the bejaunus (yellow-bill), as the newcomer was nicknamed, meets two students who are investigating the sources of certain abominable odours. They chaff the victim about the wild glare of his eye, the length of his ear, and the ferocious aspect of his tusks. Then comes the deposition (middle Latin *depositio*, or laying off, of the animal attributes) or taming : the freshman's face is smeared with soap, his ears are clipped, his beard cut, and his tusks removed with a saw. Finally, he makes a mock confession of sins, and receives absolution only on condition that he provides a magnificent banquet for his tormentors. In southern France the initiation of the bejauni took the form of a criminal trial, and was marked by drunkenness and immorality. At first the academic authorities endeavoured to suppress the initiation ceremonies, but later the custom gained their sanction and support.

The student organizations of the middle ages differ from those of the modern period in being to a very slight extent the manifestation of the play instinct. They grew out of the actual material needs of their constituency. The typical organization of the first spontaneous, democratic period of student life is the " nation," which, in its essentials, may be conceived of as a guild of students. The rise of the nation may be accounted for in the following manner: Numbers of young men of good position found themselves in a strange city without political rights—a serious condition of affairs in the twelfth century. The authority of the empire was so uncertain that each city or district exercised the powers of life and death over its inhabitants. To be deprived of citizenship meant a serious menace to life and property, so the students associated themselves together in order to create an artificial citizenship to take the place of the natural citizenship which they had relinquished in leaving their own cities. The contemporary guild movement favoured the legal recognition of such a claim, and the students' power of migration secured the consent of the locality. At Bologna the students, owing to the narrow commercial policy of the masters, gained the upper hand and exercised great authority, as they were able to subject disobedient members to public infamy. The two great divisions of Bologna were the cismontanes with seventeen nations and the ultramontanes with sixteen nations; the political functions belonged to the two great divisions, while the smaller national associations were clubs for the mutual assistance and recreation of the members. Each nation elected two proctors, who tended the sick, supported the needy, managed funerals, and settled all quarrels which threatened to become serious. The nation, in the institution of its origin and greatest strength, may be described in modern terms as a trades union of students.

The national organization was stronger in Italy than elsewhere; in no other European country were the students able to wield the same influence. At Paris the nations originated 1219–21 A. D., but membership was confined to the masters of arts. Here there were four chief divisions—the French, Normans, Picards, and English (afterward called Germans). In the faculty of arts all voting was by the natural units. The nations of Oxford were much less important than those of Paris. At a very early date Oxford may have had a fourfold division in imitation of Paris; the archives, however, record only two nations during the historic period, the northerners and southerners, Boreales and Australes. By 1274 the two divisions had become amalgamated, and the two proctors of the University of Oxford are the only reminder of their existence. The nations remained in Scotland until the nineteenth century (Aberdeen), and even to the present day exhibit considerable vigour at the University of Helsingfors in Finland.

Another instrumentality of student self-government, particularly important at Oxford and Paris, were the *hospitia* or inns. Early in the history of the universities it became necessary to set apart certain houses or halls exclusively for student use. With large numbers of boys and youths, packed together in a very narrow space, the exigencies of the case imperatively demanded some sort of control. At first, the body of scholars in the hospitia formed an independent democratic community, which elected a principal and invested him with certain limited powers. In the course of time the university authorities stepped in and supported the authority of the principal. The government of the hospitia from a republic became first a limited and then an absolute monarchy. The interference of the chancellor in the internal affairs of the hospitia seems, however, to have been necessary to guarantee their financial integrity. The early regulations respect the independence of community life, and merely provide that each inn shall give security for rent in advance to the chancellor and empower that official to choose between rival candidates for the principalship. Gradually the chancellor assumed the authority of removing offending principals and forbade the hospitia to receive students under the ban of the university. Finally, the principalship of the hospitium was restricted to graduates. Under the name of halls, a few survivals of the old hospitia survive at Oxford and Cambridge. Since the civil war of the seventeenth century they have been an unimportant element in the life of the English universities. The facts relating to them during the mediæval period are so few that one is unable to estimate their influence on the student life of the times.

The early colleges of Oxford and Paris were simply endowed hospitia; their founders aimed to secure board and lodging for poor students, who were unable to support themselves, and adopted the common life of the hospitia as the best means of securing this end. The dependence on the endowment deprived the collegian of the freedom before exercised and made strict discipline possible. The college offered unusual pedagogical advantages to the student in the form of opportunities for Latin conversation and disputations, and in equipping libraries for his use. Because of these advantages, it came to pass that by the fifteenth century the colleges at the University of Paris and the English universities gave most of the instruction. From their inception, however, the English colleges were independent, self-perpetuating corporations, while the colleges of Paris were subject to the inspection of university authorities. The early Oxford colleges inherited much of the free democratic spirit of the hospitia, the students participating in the government to a considerable degree.

§ 2. STUDENT SOCIETIES AT THE GERMAN UNIVERSITIES.

The earliest German universities, Prague and Vienna, were founded in the fourteenth century, and reproduced many features of the University of Paris, including the division of the students into four nations. This national organization was the cause of an important migration of students and professors from the University of Prague. In Bohemia, then as now, the Czech and German were arrayed against each other. In three nations the German element predominated and was able to outvote the Bohemians on questions of university policy. Restive under such a condition of inferiority in their own seat of learning, the Bohemians in 1409, under the leadership of John Huss and Jerome of Prague, petitioned the king to so alter the constitution of the university that in the future the position of the two factions would be reversed, the Germans possessing one vote, the Bohemians three. Fearing the royal decision, five thousand German students deserted Prague for Leipsic, where the division into four nations was continued. From this time on, however, the national organization was discouraged in the German universities because of the factional quarrels and disturbances which it provoked.

In the fifteenth century the college (or boarding house for students) succeeded the nation as the chief unit of student organization in the German universities. Inaugurated, as in England and France, to extend aid to needy students, the German colleges or *bursæ* rapidly degenerated and came to be considered mere hives of drones. The great power vested in the authorities for disciplinary purposes degenerated to tyranny, and was bitterly resented by the students. So strong was this popular antagonism in Germany that the first breath of humanism at the beginning of the sixteenth century was sufficient to overthrow the colleges.

During the fifteenth and sixteenth centuries the habits of the German students were—if we can judge from the statutes—fully as bad as those of the Parisian pupils. The early Vienna laws forbade the student from spending more time in drinking, fighting, and guitar-playing than in physics, logic, and the regular lectures. All persons in the university convicted of drunkenness, of following lewd women, of insulting citizens, or habitual gambling, were condemned to lose their academic privileges. It was found necessary to insert an express provision against ribaldry and indecent gestures at the disputations. In the sixteenth century laws almost identical with these were found necessary. The statutes denounce the folly of youths who imagine the university a " place of unbridled license, and who by bad example ruin others; who destroy quiet and studious industry, disobey the rector, do not attend church; wander about by day and night, stirring up disturbances, breaking into houses, robbing gardens, committing thefts, and wantonly insulting and injuring others." The words of Melanchthon verify the testimony of the laws: " Never were youth so hostile to the laws; they are resolved to live according to their own decrees and not to regard the will of God "; they should know " that universities were not intended to assemble young men of leisure for the purpose of amusing themselves and gambling."

Pennalism (*pennal*, German, from middle Latin *pennale*, a box of pens carried at the belt of the freshman student; a name for the newly entered students and for the humiliating servitude (fagging) to which they are subjected by the men of the upper classes), that greatest of the perversions of German student life, which systematized all the degrading elements in previous conditions, came in with the seventeenth century, and flourished in the confusion and savagery of the Thirty Years' War. It grew out of the custom, innocent in itself, of student initiation or "deposition" which we have previously described in the section on mediæval student life. In the sixteenth century the deposition was not merely a piece of buffoonery invented by the students, but was an officially authorized ceremony. A statute of the University of Erfurt required the deposition for matriculation. The chief Protestant reformers participated in the celebration of the rite. Said Luther on one occasion, " This annoyance accustoms children from their youth to endurance, and he who can not endure and listen to anything will not do for a preacher or a governor." At another initiation, " This deposition of ours is only a figure and a picture of human life in all manner of ill fortune, trouble, and discipline." To the mind of Melanchthon it was a reminder of the continuous necessity of patience; to another the aim of the ceremony was the admonishment of conceited students in such a way that they might realize " how trifling their learning is and how much they have yet to learn."

The perversion of the "deposition" came from its connection with the new nations, organizations which had nothing in common with the mediæval nations except the name and the principle of membership by locality. The mediæval nations were openly established and recognised corporations which elected officials and took part in the government of the university. The seventeenth century nations were secret societies of irresponsible students, formed in the teeth of the authorities. The new system of secret societies was the common possession of all the German universities; the nations in the different academic centres were in league with each other; a notorious member expelled from one university was immediately welcomed by his brethren elsewhere. The nations developed a peculiar code of honour which considered all those dishonourable who revealed any portion of their proceedings to the authorities, and visited heavy punishment on all such offenders. Each nation was regularly organized with its seniors, directors, fiscal department, and even beadles, who held office some for a longer some for a shorter term. Newcomers were cited to appear before the court of the nation, and were fined for their offences in money and entertainment.

Taking advantage of the apprenticeship which the freshmen were supposed to serve before deposition, the older students, or schorists (because they cut off the hair of the freshmen), inveigled the unfortunate strangers into their organizations, where they were reduced to a state that bordered on penal servitude. On arriving at the university the freshmen were waited on by representatives of the national brothers and asked: " Will you come to the *magnificus* and promise to obey him in all proper things? We advise you to arrange matters so that you will thank us for your lives. Follow our advice with cheerfulness, or you will have to follow it in sorrow; join yourselves to the nation—a year soon goes by—lest they treat you so that you will have cause to curse them all your lives." If threats fail to make the desired impression, the new students are told of the love and friendship to which, after the manner of the ancient Epicureans, the nations are devoted. The members speak of the vows of eternal obligation which they have sworn to each other. Such was the pressure brought to bear on newcomers that few were able to escape this year of penal servitude.

Once a member, the unfortunate pennal, as the freshman was called, soon had his visions of Epicurean happiness rudely shattered. He was attached to some

older student, whose behests he was compelled to obey.
The seniors forced the pennals to copy all sorts of writing, to wait on their master's guests, to go on errands
ten and twenty miles and even farther. If the master
became stupidly drunk, the novice must not flinch or
budge from him, but must remain close at hand and
serve him, helping him along the street if need be.
Should the senior be ill, the juniors wait on him by
turns, so that he need never be alone; should he desire
music, the junior must play all night long to please his
idle whim. The pennal must suffer blows and shameful
personal abuse without protest, and " let the other work
his entire will upon him as if he were nothing but a
dog." The juniors must preserve silence, or they will
never be absolved and permitted to become students;
this prospect terrifies them into submission. At the
end of the pennal year an absolution feast was served
which often took the little hoard which had been designed by frugal care to carry the student through the
university. After one generation of older students had
established complete authority over the freshmen and
kept them for a year in servitude, the custom was difficult to break up, because the degradation was only en-
dured in the hope that after the pennal year was over
the sufferers might have their turn in tyrannizing over
the new freshmen.

The greatest evil of pennalism lay in the fact that
it made all sorts of excesses possible by uniting the students in a close league against the authorities. A writer
of the time has left us a vivid description of the sad state
of affairs which resulted from student license: " Mean-
while I saw a great chamber, a common lodging room
or museum, or study, or beer-shop, or wine-shop, or ball-
room, or harlot's establishment. In truth, I can not say
what it was, for I saw all these things. It was swarming
full of students. The most eminent of them sat at a

table and drank to each other until their eyes turned in their heads like those of a stuck calf. One drank to another from a dish, out of a shoe; one ate glass, another dirt, a third drank from a dish where there were all sorts of food—enough to make one sick to see it. One gave another his hand; they asked each other's names and promised to be friends and brothers forever, with the addition of this clause, ' I will do what is pleasant to you and avoid what is unpleasant.' So each would tie a string off his leather breeches to the many-colored doublet of the other. But those with whom another refused to drink acted like a madman or a devil, sprang up as high as they could for anger, tore out their hair in their eagerness to avenge such an insult, threw glasses in each other's faces, out with their swords and at each other's heads, until here and there one fell down and lay there; and such quarrels I saw between close friends and blood relatives with devilish rage and anger. Others drank to each other off seats and benches, or off the table or the floor, under their arms, under their legs, with the cup under them, over them, behind them, or before them. Others lay on the floor and let it be poured into them as into a funnel." * Such disorders were not always confined to any one such feast, but were continued for days together at meals and lectures, publicly, privately, and even in the public streets. Occasionally there were bolder outbreaks with all sorts of outrageous howls, the breaking into houses and windows and the like.

During the Thirty Years' War the prevailing confusion prevented any effective legislation against pennalism. The action of any one state simply resulted in

---

* From the pseudonymous Philander von Sittewald, quoted by Karl von Raumer, and translated in Barnard's Journal, vol. vi, pp. 44, 45.

driving students from its universities into the neighbouring territories. In 1660 all the Protestant kingdoms and duchies united in an effort to crush the practice. They succeeded in driving the evil below the surface, and in putting a stop to any open manifestations and to its most flagrant violations. The nations, although forbidden by edicts, still existed under an altered name, and with them many of the usages and the code of honour engendered by pennalism. Throughout the eighteenth century outcroppings of pennalistic practices appeared from time to time. They were specifically forbidden at Göttingen in 1757, and Kiel in 1774. It was not until the great uprising of German students which followed the War of Liberation that pennalism was finally extinguished on German soil.

The important student organizations of Germany in the eighteenth century were the *Landsmannschaften* (clubs of students from the same province), lineal successors to the nations of the previous century and the secret student orders which were fashioned on the rites of freemasonry. As all such organizations of students were strictly forbidden, it is impossible to trace their development, although we have abundant evidence of their subterranean existence at the different German university centres. At intervals they come to light through connection with some student prank or outrage, and are forthwith forbidden by law. Such rescripts against the Landsmannschaften appeared at Leipsic in 1680, Halle 1717, Rostock 1730, Jena 1765, Göttingen 1762, Kiel 1774, and Erlangen 1794, but were absolutely without the results expected. In fact, the Landsmannschaften flourished on prohibitions and official opposition; decrees of abolition were probably one of the great sources of their strength, because they gave additional zest to the enterprise. On entering a Landsmannschaft, the candidate promised never to reveal what at any time happened within the society, to be always watchful against the *renoncers* (students belonging to no society), and to conceal the existence of the society. If questioned by the authorities, a society man must lie stoutly and give up, if need be, his existence at the university for the sake of the society.

Without making a further attempt to trace the history of the separate organizations or of the societies at particular universities, the writer will sketch the salient features of the Landsmannschaften as they existed at the end of the eighteenth century. At each university there existed a group of societies bound together in a loose sort of federation through participation in a common code of laws known as the *Komment*. This constitution provided that no society could be organized without the consent of those already existing, or could a society be extinguished without the unanimous consent of all the remaining Landsmannschaften. Turning aside from the Komment for a moment, we will now give our attention to the organization of the separate societies.

Each Landsmannschaft took its name from one of the principalities or subdivisions of Germany, such, for example, as Thuringia, Swabia, Westphalia, etc., and also selected for itself a colour or colours by which it was known. The Landsmannschaften admitted two classes of members—*Burschen*,* or full members, who formed the nucleus of the organization, and the *Renoncen*, or associate members, who attached themselves to the society for the sake of its protection and influence. The foxes, or freshmen, were compelled to serve

---

* Latin *bursa*, purse, common purse (Judas bore the purse), and hence a member of the club or class that had a common purse ; in the fifteenth century it came to be applied to the members of the higher classes at the German universities.

2

a novitiate before they were admitted as full members. During the period of apprenticeship they are expected to obey orders implicitly, and are trained in fencing, drinking, and the laws of the Landsmannschaft. Admission to full membership was attended with certain ceremonies, frequently with a catechization on the Komment and the principles of the association, the attaching of a ribbon, the communication of the cipher of the association, and the kiss of brotherhood. The officers of the Landsmannschaft were a senior, a *consenior*, a secretary, and a number of special committeemen proportioned to the members. These officials together constitute the council which resolves absolutely on all matters connected with the society, attends to its connections abroad, and presides at regular festivals. To this senior council the unconditional submission of every member is due; to withstand its decisions is to incur the condemnation of infamy. This arrangement placed the management of the society in the hands of its oldest and most hardened members, and was responsible for much of the recklessness and dissipation which characterized the Landsmannschaften.

The Komment treats chiefly of honour—how it may be preserved, attacked, and regained when lost. The sword is the great talisman of honour. Much of the Komment in consequence discusses the duel—how it may be occasioned and fought. At its inception the Komment was probably modelled upon the ceremonial of the later chivalry and court life as developed at the court of Louis XIV. Most of the technical terms employed in the duel are evidently from this source. Such words, in part distorted forms, are numerous, including such terms as comment (suspendu), satisfaction, avantage, touche, secundieren, renommieren, renonce, maltraitationen, and others.

The Komment separates students into classes: (1)

according to their place of residence, and (2) according
to the length of their residence at the university. A
pavement-beater (Pflastertreter or Quark) is one whose
parents live in the university town, and a cummin-Turk
(Kümmelturk) is one whose parents live within four
miles of a university town. During the first half year
of a student's residence he is a fox; the second half year
makes him a brander fox. At the beginning of the second year he becomes a young Bursch, six months later a
Bursch, and then at the beginning of his third year an
old Bursch. The end of the promotion process is not
reached until the second half of the third year, when
our hero—if he survives so long—is known as a mossy-
head.

The honour of the Bursch was a highly artificial
and intricate product. A man might be declared dishonourable on sixteen different counts, many of them
extremely frivolous from the standpoint of rational
ethics. For example, a man might become dishonourable by allowing himself to be called so by a member of
another society without resenting it or by returning
only a verbal insult when the other party was prepared
to fight. To give information to the authorities or to
declare one's self free from the obligation of the Komment was as great an offence as to break one's word of
honour or to steal. The code regulated duels and intercourse between the societies with a nicety worthy of the
Chinese imperial court, but left a man free to lie, to
cheat at cards, or to recognise no obligation whatever to
a Philister or outsider. The most common verbal insult was to call another " *Dumme Junge* " (stupid
youth). Under article D of the Komment of the societies of Altdorf the dishonoured one who has violated
the code has no claim to the satisfaction of a Bursch,
and any advantage may be taken of him. The stigma
" dishonourable " could be removed either by the ac-

cused fighting with a member from each of the societies, or by the unanimous vote of the deputies of all the societies.

The Landsmannschaften were a great stimulus to quarrelling and duelling. No man could be a jolly reputable Bursch unless he had already fought many duels and was known as a keen and powerful swordsman. Quarrelling, insults, a provoking conduct carried so far as to be ridiculous, and innumerable duels, were the consequence. To make up the full number of a hundred duels was the ambition of many students. Learned studies suffered under such conditions, and social life was an unpleasant existence on a continued war footing in which those unacquainted with weapons were wholly defenceless. Societies were in a state of constant excitement and irritation against each other. The privilege of changing from one side to another availed nothing, for a man who had insulted one was obliged before he entered another to fight duels with all his former colleagues; nor could a new society establish itself on a received footing except by fighting itself into recognition.

National animosities, however, did not prevent the Landsmannschaften from combining for riots and other excesses. In Fichte's time at Jena (1793–1798) violent riots were of common occurrence; houses were broken into and robbed of their contents to supply the marauders with the means of sensual indulgence. The arm of the law was powerless to restrain such outbreaks; so bold had the students become that upon one occasion, when the house of a professor at Jena had been attacked, five hundred students openly demanded of the duke amnesty for the offence. As the Landsmannschaften were responsible for these uprisings, the authorities endeavoured at various times to suppress them, but such attempts only caused the students to break out anew and raise fresh disturbances. The philosopher Fichte, however, by his personal influence, persuaded two of the most reprehensible societies to disband and turn over their documents to him for safe-keeping. Owing to the jealousy of his colleagues, his praiseworthy attempt was without permanent effect. The Landsmannschaften of this period were instrumental in demoralizing their members by inordinate drinking and by making popular dangerous forms of vice.

The secret orders which appeared in the German universities about the middle of the eighteenth century were bitter rivals of the Landsmannschaften, and in their origin were offshoots of the contemporary Masonic movement. They were prohibited at Göttingen in 1748, at Erlangen in 1762, at Tübingen and Jena in 1765. By the year 1816 they had completely disappeared from the German universities. Some of the most famous orders were the Order of the Cross, founded in 1762 with all the rites of freemasonry; the Order of the Coopers, which exerted a destructive influence; and the Black Order, or Order of Harmony, which arose in 1771 at Erlangen. This last organization was not confined to students, but possessed lodges among the citizens of Nuremberg and Coburg. The orders differed from the Landsmannschaften in admitting members without regard to nationality and in adopting an elaborate ritual after the manner of the Masons. The resemblance in ritual was particularly close in the case of the Black Knights with the Masons: they named Pythagoras as the founder of their order. In their hall stood a basin full of water, the symbolical meaning of which was explained to those initiated, together with a statue of Virtue and one of Friendship, a cross of the order with the sun, moon, and stars emblazoned upon it, a crucifix, and several skulls. In the middle of the eighteenth century there were few students who did not belong to one of these secret orders.

The heroic struggle of the north Germans against Napoleon, terminating with the War of Liberation, created a strong feeling in favour of German unity and the constitutional forms of government. In the absence of free political institutions, these sentiments found a home in the universities. The thousands of students who had enlisted at the summons of the king and fought honourably in the great battles of the campaign, returned home filled with a noble enthusiasm. To quote words of a German writer: " The youth, enchanted, as it were, previously by the chains of ignoble and even vulgar academical habits, now felt themselves released by the most lofty experiences. They were delivered from the tyranny of false honour, and saw the Komment in its true light. True honour and courage devoted to the cause of country alone was substituted for that imp, point of honour." While predominantly political, the new movement had a religious side; there was a feeling —strong, although indistinct and undeveloped—that Germany without Christianity was hopeless and lost. The Landsmannschaften or Corps, as representatives of local divisions and at enmity among themselves, and with strong tendencies to dissipation, could not meet the needs of the new movement, and so a new type of student organization, the *Burschenschaften,* was formed.

The first society of the new order was organized at Jena in 1816; others were founded soon afterward. The Burschenschaften first came prominently before the public in connection with the so-called Wartburg festival, held in October, 1817, the three hundredth anniversary of Luther's defiance of the Pope. Five hundred students, representing all the students of Protestant Germany, gathered together at Eisenach. The keynote of the celebration was struck by the orator of the occasion, Riemann, of Ratzeburg, Knight of the Iron Cross, a distinction gained for bravery on the bloody day at Belle Alliance. After showing that the young men must hold fast to the good already obtained of German freedom, with rising enthusiasm he invoked the shades of Luther and all the noble heroes who had fallen in the contest for freedom and right to be invisible witnesses of the vow which he offered in the name of the assembly: " That which we have acknowledged we will maintain as long as a drop of blood remains in our veins. The spirit which has brought us hither—the spirit of truth and justice—shall lead us through our whole life; that we, all brothers, sons of the one and same fatherland, shall form a brazen wall against every outer and inner enemy of that fatherland; that the death of open battle shall not terrify us from standing in the heat of the battle when the invader threatens; that the splendour of the monarch's throne shall not dazzle us from speaking the strong free word when truth and right demand it; and that we will never pause in the endeavour after every human and patriotic virtue."

The ceremonies of the day consisted of a grand procession in the morning, a vast banquet at midday with gay songs and festive healths, and the celebration of the sacrament of the Lord's Supper in the afternoon, all of which was carried out without confusion or disturbance. The crowning episode of the festival occurred in the evening, when, without previous notice, twenty-eight books noted for their un-German views were burned in a huge bonfire. The works of the Russian court chancellor, Von Kotzebue, were on the proscribed list. This affair created great excitement throughout Germany. Opposition to the Burschenschaft began to show itself, compelling almost every one to take sides.

The general German Burschenschaft was organized

by representatives of the local societies in October, 1818, one year after the Wartburg festival. To borrow the words of its preamble, it was " the free union of all German youth engaged in learned studies at the university, based upon the relations of the German youth to the coming union of the German people." To hasten and facilitate this union, the Burschenschaft declared the unity, freedom, and equality of all Burschen among each other, the equality of all rights and duties, and the German, Christian education of every mental and bodily faculty in the service of the fatherland. The freedom and unity of the students were to present a picture of the unity of a prosperous nation; the orderly, common life of the Burschenschaften was to prepare its members for national life, " so that each of them may be raised to such a grade of self-knowledge as in his own pure individuality to display the brightness and glory of the German national spirit."

The general or central Burschenschaft maintained no continuous executive organization. Its only organ was an assembly of delegates, three from each university, which met yearly. Some one local society was chosen to transact the necessary business for the remainder of the year. The assembly of delegates decided controversies, passed upon the constitution of the local societies to insure that they contained the true principles of the order, and recommended alterations in the constitution, which required the ratification of the local societies before taking effect. The central Burschenschaft required the local chapters to settle internal disputes, not by duel, but amicably by appeal to the general assembly. Each society must likewise recognise as just the penalties of the others. In their relations with the Landsmannschaften, which were still a power in the universities, the Burschenschaften should first attempt to gain over their opponents by persuasion; this

feeling, they must resort to the most efficient means of opposition which the situation permitted. So fundamentally different were the underlying principles of the two orders that their reciprocal attitude was that of bitter antagonism and hostility.

The local Burschenschaften (or unions of matriculated students) promoted common life by two instrumentalities—systematic physical exercise, usually taking the form of fencing and gymnastics, and the Burschenhaus. The founders of the order considered the latter the most important means of promoting closer union and social intercourse, and made it incumbent upon the members to frequent it as much as possible. Every one of the large number of festivals provided for in the constitution were held in the Burschenhaus. The constitution of the Jena Burschenschaft placed the administrative control in the hands of a committee of nine managers and three candidates for managership, all of whom were elected every half year. This board wielded the entire executive, legislative, and judicial authority of the society; it decided quarrels and points of honour, and supervised external business, such as fixing the time of meeting. As a check on the board of managers, another committee of twenty was appointed to see that the laws of the society were obeyed. The constitution of the local society was long and intricate, and showed the evidence of experienced legal hands in the framing.

For two years the Burschenschaften held possession of the universities, for, although they were unable to exterminate the Corps or Landsmannschaften, they so far overshadowed the latter in importance that all eyes were focused upon them. While they met with the greatest opposition from the political conservatives, their most bitter enemies existed within their own ranks. The great majority of the members held to the

principles enunciated in the constitution, and believed
that the preparation of the German people for unity and
freedom should come through a lofty moral life. A
small faction, however, known as the Blacks, began to
separate themselves from the main body of the party;
these radicals were not content to abide the slow influence of education and time, but discarded constitutional agitation in favour of an immediate armed movement against existing authorities.

Karl Follen,* the leader of the Blacks, was a disciple
of Fichte, and carried the views of that philosopher in
regard to the supremacy of the moral ego to their logical conclusion, and applied them to the state. His
cardinal principle of action was the doctrine that all
which is recognised by the human reason as good,
beautiful, and true, should immediately be accomplished by means of the moral will. He asserted with
great boldness that his own life was such as reason required. " With an indescribable expression of contempt in his features, he accused those of cowardice
and weakness who imagined that a knowledge of truth
and beauty, and especially of their highest ideals, could
be disjointed from living them out, practising them,
realizing them to their widest extent." His own character was one of boldness, austerity, and rectitude, and
his worst enemies could accuse him of nothing worse
than want of humility.

According to Follen's logic, the identity of reason
and action was carried into politics, and the state must
correspond to the reason of its constituent members.
Reason demanded unconditionally the acceptance of
the republican form of government. His outline of a
future " constitution for the empire of Germany " was

---

* Karl Follen came as an exile to America in 1835, and was
professor in Harvard College till his death in 1840.

the last of the paper constitutions of revolutionary times. It embodies a complete disregard for every existing right. Follen's intolerance is seen in the provisions which confine the franchise to those who had partaken of the sacrament, and forbade the Jewish form of worship within the boundaries of the empire. Follen himself admitted that such a constitution could only be established by the shedding of blood. The harshness with which Follen enforced his views drove many of his friends into opposition. His personal supporters were entirely out of sympathy with the Burschenschaften, which, in their opinion "contained at least twenty rascals to one good fellow."

One of the most devoted of Follen's followers at Jena was a theological student, Karl Ludwig Sand. Sand fell a victim to Follen's logic and resolved to assassinate August von Kotzebue, a German of conservative tendencies, in the pay of Russia, who opposed the Burschenschaften. For months after this resolve was made, Sand attended lectures regularly, as if preparing himself for future years of usefulness. On March 19, 1819, however, he called on Von Kotzebue, stabbed him fatally, and then attempted unsuccessfully to commit suicide. No exception could be taken to his behaviour during imprisonment, which was sane and praiseworthy; without troubling the keepers, he thankfully received all the services which were rendered for the alleviation of his suffering. Sand undoubtedly considered himself a martyr to the cause of freedom, and accepted death with quiet heroism. A searching investigation failed to discover any conspiracy, or to implicate any one as Sand's accessory.

Notwithstanding this conclusion of the court, the reactionary governments of the German states were so alarmed at the murder, which they considered the legitimate outcome of the liberal movement, that Metternich had no difficulty in securing their consent to resolutions passed by the Bundestag (September 20, 1819), which abolished the general German Burschenschaft, provided government inspectors for each university, decreed the removal of dangerous professors, and declared that no student expelled from one university should be permitted to enter another. The members of the Burschenschaften, as loyal citizens of their respective states, obeyed the commands of their sovereign. The Jena Burschenschaft at its last meeting presented an address to the grand duke, which proudly stated that, owing to the society a free and virtuous mode of life had grown up; trustful publicity had taken the place of creeping secrecy; and its members could, without shame, display to the eyes of the world what they meditated in their inmost hearts.*

Karl von Raumer, who had watched the Burschenschaften from their origin, and had been on terms of intimacy with their leaders, speaks in the following strain of the reforms which they brought about: " They

---

* The feeling of the members upon the dissolution of the Burschenschaften is expressed in a little poem by Benzer, of Jena, the English translation of which runs as follows :

" A house we had builded,
    So stately and fair;
    There trusting to be shielded,
    In God, from storm and care.

" We lived there so gaily,
    So friendly, so free,
    It grieved the wicked daily
    Our true accord to see.

" That fair house may perish
    When greatest our need ;
    Its spirit still we cherish,
    But God's our strength indeed."

had produced a profound moral change and reformation in a large part of the academic youth, and fought against their demoralization. They banished gaming tables from their precincts, and reduced duelling to one twentieth of its former proportions. Chastity they held in high esteem, deeming it a shame to resort to licensed houses of ill-fame. Conscious of such an endeavour after inward reform, the Burschenschaft could neither aim at secrecy nor be indifferent to the favour of the authorities. The members sought by all means to secure the approbation of the governments, both by their conduct in the society and by attempts to secure direct recognition, and they had no idea that they would be considered dangerous to the state."

It could hardly have been anticipated that such a multitude of enthusiastic youths would relinquish a cherished plan at the first word from the monarchs, and as a matter of fact the more radical members maintained the societies in secret after the decree went into effect. The governments increased the evil by taking no pains to discriminate between the innocent and the guilty. The impression gained ground among the students that, notwithstanding the propriety of their conduct, no confidence was placed in them by the governments. Such conditions favoured the malcontents and led to the formation of the Tugendbund in 1822. This organization was little more than a camp for the discontented; great confusion and perplexity of ideas existed among the members in regard to the real end of the society; no one seemed to know just exactly what he wanted. It accomplished nothing, and furnished the central investigation commission at Mayence an excuse for numerous banishments and imprisonments.

The relaxation of authority in the later twenties opened the way to the formation of new Burschenschaften more closely modelled on the Corps than the earlier societies. In 1827 representatives from these societies came together and formed the second German Burschenschaft. As before, the students were divided into two parties: the Moderates, known as Arminians, who trusted to education and constitutional agitation; and the Radicals or Germans, who favoured armed insurrection. By 1830 the gulf between the two factions had grown so wide that they formally separated into two distinct organizations. In December, 1832, the Germans resolved upon a revolution to secure the liberty and unity of the fatherland. April of the following year witnessed their outbreak, which ended in complete failure. The governments again adopted a rigorous policy and suppressed the Burschenschaften in all forms, including the Arminians, who had opposed the outbreak.

The extinction of the first German Burschenschaft in 1819 was indirectly the means of bringing about the golden age of the Corps. Being aristocratic bodies of conservative tendencies, and at deadly feud with the Burschenschaften, they were encouraged by governments and court parties of the various states. Age had mellowed their old barbarous customs, and much of the grossness of the eighteenth century had worn away. Foreigners were attracted by the air of adventure and romance which belonged to the student life of this period, in which the Corps played the central rôle. An English writer thus describes it: " In the student life of Germany which is enjoyed as a brief season of youthful hilarity which in this world can come but once, a season when knowledge is not only to be gathered, but life to be enjoyed—friendships for life to be knit—love perhaps to be kindled, and the spirit of patriotism to be cherished to a degree which no after chills and oppressions of ordinary life can ever be able to extinguish—in this life there is a feeling and a sentiment to which our [English] student life is a stranger." *

The high social position of their members gave the Corps the right to consider themselves the legitimate representatives of the entire student body. At this period they were still able to hurl the terrors of their Bannstrahl, or excommunication against either students or citizens who defied them. If an innkeeper or merchant overcharged a student, a proscription would be issued against the establishment for a certain specified period, during which no student was permitted to patronize it. A student disregarding the rule, found himself placed under the ban. Guards and spies were stationed on all sides to observe infractions of the law.

The old spirit of riot and lawlessness, while to a certain extent curbed, was by no means extinct. The students of Heidelberg were in the habit of celebrating their *Kommers,* or drinking bouts, in some of the neighbouring villages. They played practical jokes on the peasants, who in return sometimes became enraged and assailed their guests in troops with heavy cudgels, and when aroused they oftentimes proved merciless antagonists, treading on and even stamping on the faces of the students who were thrown down. It was a favourite pastime of the Jena students to pursue the town watchman through the streets of the city. Sometimes they tied him to a tree, with the signboard of a neighbouring inn, representing an ox, bear, or monkey, suspended above him; on other occasions he was placed at the head of the party and compelled to march through the town until the small hours of the morning, blowing his horn, the signal of danger.

---

* Howitt, William. The Student Life of Germany, p. 9.

The drinking habits of the students were regulated by the " Bier-Komment," an elaborate drinking ritual. At the beginning of a Kommers the students sing a drinking song, " The foxes under the ban have gone," after which the crass foxes, bareheaded, must rise and drink off half a Schoppen, while the brand foxes, sitting, each drink an entire Schoppen. Any one violating the Kommers, or interrupting the proceedings, may be sentenced to drink not more than two Schoppens at one time. If a member does not drink the quantity dictated to him in five minutes the president has a right, without further proceeding, to write him down on the beer tablet as a Bierschisser. Four additional Schoppens are then added to the amount which the offender has yet to drink. The quantity of beer consumed at these festivities would seem an impossibility to the students of any other nation.

Duelling remained, as in previous generations, the pivot of student life. J. M. Hart, in his book, German Universities, describes student duelling as it existed in the early sixties at Göttingen. After explaining that student duelling is no anomaly, but, on the contrary, that the military conception of honour prevailing on the Continent makes it the only dignified and gentlemanly way of resenting an insult, Hart shows that to a large extent in the universities it had ceased to be a means of resenting insults and had become a mere pastime. " The impartial observer," he says, " must accuse the student of fighting just because he likes to fight. It is a notorious fact that nine tenths of the duels are fought without any real provocation. One student happens to bump against another in the street, or one chaffs the other too sharply. The fault of the German system is that it tolerates bloodshed, and makes student honour to a large extent conventional." With all its defects, however, he considers the German

custom of duelling more manly than the hazing prevalent in American colleges at the same period. " The
German can not play Hector one day and the meek and
lowly minded the next. By insulting in any way his
fellow, he places himself before the inexorable alter-
native, apologize or fight."

The following account of a duel by an Englishman will give the reader some idea of the sport as it is
at present conducted in Germany, and will incidentally
throw a side light on the way which the two most
marked characteristics of German student life strike a
foreigner:

" Perhaps the closeness of the room, thick with the
confined tobacco of yesterday's festivities, or the ba-
thos of students eating sausages during the encounter,
or the businesslike indifference of the waiters passing in and out, or the fumes of cigars before breakfast on a hot summer morning, or the grotesqueness
of the iron spectacles and padding, were conditions unfavourable to the heroic. At any rate, insular or not,
I must confess that when the blood began to ooze and
spurt, every other feeling gave way to an invincible
nausea and disgust: I certainly had not realized that
there could be so much bloodshed with so little damage. It is a pity that the disgusting element is so
strong, as it destroys the humour of the affair. Before
the unpleasantness began, I had great difficulty in preserving an expression of face worthy of the gravity of
the affair. I could not get rid of the impression that
the combatants were not students, but a couple of
elderly gentlemen.

" The subject of student beer drinking is not an
inviting one. Not that there is any great amount of
drunkenness, the beer is too weak for that. Quantity,
not quality, is the thing aimed at. But it is a coarse and
tedious proceeding. Its dulness is not even relieved by

3

the deviltry of a big Oxford wine.   It is worse than sinful, it is vulgar." *

The first of a new order of societies, called *Wingolf*, was instituted in 1850, at the University of Halle. While belonging to the same general type of society as the Corps and Burschenschaften, the Wingolf was composed exclusively of theological students, and therefore rejected duelling and other ruder customs.   The new society spread rapidly, and was imitated in the Catholic universities.   Since 1870, numbers of new student organizations, known as the Free Societies, of a more informal character than the old, have appeared in the German universities.   Some of them have a political end in view, like the " *Deutsche Studenten-Verein* " which represented the anti-Semitic movement in the universities; most of them, however, were for the furtherance of some particular form of culture like the Gesangvereine, or for the promotion of certain studies. The free societies must not be thought of as scientific associations; their chief end is social; the common interest forms an excuse for coming together, and insures a certain amount of congeniality.   The Free Societies differ from the older or colour-bearing group, in having a more specific purpose, and in making their fellowship less close and exclusive.

The Free Societies have by no means the prestige of the Corps and Burschenschaften, which consider themselves the true representatives of the German studenthood, notwithstanding the fact that they contain a small percentage of the students; in some universities hardly so many as one twentieth.   Of the two chief forms of colour-bearing societies, the Corps are the most aristocratic.   Their members pay great attention

---

* Baynes, A. H.   German Student Life, in Fraser's Magazine, vol. civ, pp. 638, 639 (1881).

to the externals of manners and expenditure, and hold themselves aloof from the masses of the students. Some of the Burschenschaften are simply imitations of the Corps on a little lower plane, while others preserve something of the spirit and ideals of the old Burschenschaften. All the colour-bearing societies aim at complete community of life, but are fast ceasing to be the representative student organizations of Germany.

Before attempting to characterize the German student life, we must note its relation to the social system of which it forms a part, and particularly its relation to the lower schools. In the gymnasia the youth have been watched for eight or ten years, drilled rigorously, and held in strict subordination. All forms of organized school life are denied them, including (until recently) athletic games; they are frequently overworked. When the freshman enters the university, he is for the first time completely his own master; a new life has dawned upon him. He hardly knows which way to turn his steps, every prospect seems so fair. It is no wonder that, to the German, his student days seem in a peculiar sense the springtime of life, and one is hardly surprised to hear of excesses; they are the natural reaction against his former confinement. In earlier years this feeling was heightened by the prospect which opened before the Bursch. After completing his course, he went back to live in a police State, where the government told him what to believe, and in many ways limited his freedom. Under the old *régime* in Germany the university was the one free institution in society; studenthood was the one free and glorious period of life when the man might defy the authorities and laugh at conventionality. In consequence, German student clubs have always possessed a more marked individuality than those of other nationalities; they represent to a greater extent the free play of youth.

The social life of the German student is apt to lack
that fine spirit of courtesy and respect for the conventions of society which belong to the best circles of
Oxford or Harvard.   We may quote the words of Professor Boyesen, an unprejudiced observer, on this point:
" The tone among the [German] academicians in general is rude and boisterous, their conversation is characterized by much earnestness and a conspicuous lack of
refinement.   Their jokes are ponderous and pointless,
their humour degenerates into mere grotesque drollery.
What has particularly impressed me is the absence of
that gentlemanly bearing which in an undergraduate of
Oxford or Cambridge is second nature.   The German
student is noisy and aggressive; and since the war with
France his stupendous national self-assertion and supreme contempt for all non-Teutonic nations are apt to
make him a bore or a perpetual irritation." *

On the other hand, a warmer and more cordial tone
prevails among the Germans than is found in the student societies of England or America; human relations
are beautified by it and rendered more enjoyable.   The
German student understands to perfection the art of
cultivating simple pleasure, and of extracting the greatest amount of enjoyment from the small things of life.

§ 3. STUDENT LIFE IN ENGLISH UNIVERSITIES.

BIBLIOGRAPHY.—No general treatment nor bibliography of
English student life has yet appeared.   The standard authorities for the middle ages are Rashdall, Mullinger, and Lyte ; for
the sixteenth and seventeenth centuries, Mullinger and Masson's
Milton ; for the eighteenth century, Wordsworth and Huber.
There are no general works completely covering the nineteenth
century.   Most useful to an American for the study of this
period are the volumes by his countrymen, Bristed and Everett.
Wells's Oxford and Oxford Life gives the best description of
recent conditions.   A suggestive book is Aspects of Modern

* Hjalmar Hjorth Boyesen, in The Cosmopolitan, vol. x, p. 376.

Oxford, by a Mere Don. Richard Harding Davis has written a brilliant but superficial account of undergraduate life at Oxford.

The great public schools of England have given rise to an extensive literature of student life. Selected bibliographies of value have been published by J. J. Findlay and Karl Breul. Lyte's History of Eton College should be consulted for earlier centuries. The revolution in public-school life connected with the name of Thomas Arnold can be followed in Stanley's Life of Arnold, in the volumes of Fitch and Findlay, and in Hughes's famous story Tom Brown's School Days. Edward Thring's Education and School should be read in this connection. Contemporary conditions are dealt with by Pascoe, Breul, and John Corbin's Schoolboy Life in England. Ford's Public-School Athletics, in Cookson's Essays on Secondary Education, is a paper of exceptional value. Several thoughtful articles on British athleticism have appeared in The Spectator (vols. lxvii, lxix, lxxii), in The Fortnightly Review (vol lxvii), and in The Nineteenth Century. Kipling's Stalky and Company may be read as an antidote to Tom Brown, but is said not to present the point of view of the average English boy.

The revival of learning and the Reformation influenced the English universities less than their Continental contemporaries. Notwithstanding the introduction of Greek and a few modern cosmological conceptions, Oxford and Cambridge continued strongly ecclesiastical and dialectical in their tendencies. The conservative character of the English Reformation was to a large extent responsible for this continuance of mediæval ideals in university culture. Another factor made for the same result—viz., the strength of the college system. The English college emerged from the middle ages a powerful, almost independent, self-governing corporation. Dependent directly on neither church nor state for support, handing down traditions from one generation to another, the college presented an effectual barrier to any rapid assimilation of the intellectual movements which agitated Europe.

The college exerted the same conservative influence on the student life of the times. While the asceticism of earlier centuries became somewhat relaxed by 1600, the common life within college walls enjoined by the statutes prevented the excesses which marked student life in contemporary Germany. The colleges were the chief social centres in the university, as the halls were declining in importance, and societies and clubs had not yet appeared. The only rivals of the colleges in influence were the inns of the university city. The laxity of morals and of theological opinion which prevailed at the universities was a cause of grave anxiety to the Puritan majority in Parliament during the early years of the seventeenth century. The university authorities, to disarm criticism, endeavoured to enforce a series of minute regulations, backed by numerous fines and other punishments; the undergraduates were treated like schoolboys. The students manifested their resentment at this policy, neglecting the rules, annoying their instructors, and setting the authorities at defiance. They frequently engaged in conflicts with the townsmen, and were notorious for their rudeness to strangers. Instead of adopting the modest costume enjoined by their superiors, they appeared on the streets " in hoses of unseemly greatness or disguised fashion, excessive ruffs and apparrell of velvet and silk."

The amusements of the period were rude and boisterous. Excessive eating and drinking and theological discussions of a bitter personal kind were frequent. The prevalent forms of sport were barbarous, and included bull-baiting and bear-baiting. A letter from James I forbade these diversions and games of chance within five miles of a town or university. Latin and English plays of a doubtful character formed the chief source of intellectual diversion. These productions abounded in grossness and personalities, and resulted in much ill feeling. On one occasion the prominent citizens of Cambridge were invited to a play given in their special honour. To their amazement and disgust, the drama proved to be a series of caricatures, ridiculing the prominent characters in the audience. The worst plays were written in Latin and performed in the inns of the city.

A new period in English student life begins with the last decades of the seventeenth century. The old severity of discipline and barbarism of manners disappeared; the social atmosphere of the coffee-house and the club began to be felt within college bounds. New social groups based on personal tastes arose, which were the forerunners of the existing student societies. During the eighteenth century life in the universities became more and more the imitation of high life in London. In the most fashionable circles heavy drinking was not the rule, although in some of the slow-going colleges stories were told of debauchery in even the common and combination rooms. The popular social diversions took the form either of card parties with heavy wagers, or of private theatricals. Students indulged themselves with party quarrels and disorders in the public inns. The out-of-door sports showed the same aristocratic tendency. Riding, fox-hunting, and attendance at horse races were the popular diversions. The competitive games of the present—boating, football, and cricket—were known, but little practised, and held in still less esteem by the leaders of college fashion. The students devoted their vacations to long pedestrian excursions through Scotland, Switzerland, and Germany.

The clubs, which formed so important an element in the social life of London, soon made their appearance in the universities. Of these, the political clubs were of greatest importance. As the eighteenth century was pre-eminently the age of politics and party strife in England, the universities in this mirrored the most important activity of the period. One of the first clubs, the record of which has come down to us, was the Constitution Club (1703) of Oxford, which held meetings in King's Head Tavern, on High Street. Its Whig proclivities gave great offence to the Toryism of the university. On one occasion, when the Constitutionalists were about to celebrate some party victory with a bonfire, a numerous mob seized the fagots and assaulted the room in which the club was sitting with brickbats and stones. Older yet was the True Blue Club of Cambridge, which took its colour in opposition to the orange of King William III. Its members wore a peculiar costume, and were noted throughout the university as being hard drinkers. The Tory Club of Oxford was known as the High Borlace, and gave an annual ball. Debating societies existed during this period, but, owing to their relative insignificance, the record of their proceedings is difficult to obtain. One of the best known of these was called the Speculative, in honour of the great society of Edinburgh. It met once a week in term time, and numbered among its members several men who afterward became famous. Another organization of particular interest was called the Associators, a society of university politicians, who asserted the right of appeal from the vice-chancellor's court.

More akin to the true aim of university education were the literary clubs, of which we catch glimpses from time to time. At Cambridge records remain of three such societies during the eighteenth century. One of the most famous of these, " The Old Maids," to which many celebrated *savants* belonged, met at a coffee-house after evening chapel, for the benefit of literary conversation. The Zodiak Club, which arose in 1725, was composed of twelve members, who took their names from the twelve signs. Three years later, six planets were added. The members of the club pledged themselves to recommend and elect only fellow-clubmen to all offices within their disposal. The Wranglers, of Cambridge, established the Hyson Club in 1758, while Oxford rejoiced in the possession of a Poetic Club.

Other clubs aimed simply to promote sociability. Such were the Nonsense Club, the Jelly-bag Club, the Banterers, and Free Cynics of the University of Oxford. It was a custom of the Banterers to talk at a venture; if they observed a man talking seriously, " they talked florid nonsense back and cared not what he said, which is like throwing a cushion at a man's head who pretends to be grave and wise." The Free Cynics were a philosophical club who had a series of symbolical words and grimaces unintelligible to any but of their own society. More truly representative of the age was a select social club which existed in Cambridge in 1790. The twelve members of the group appeared in coats of bright green, lined and bound with buff silk, with buttons made expressly for them upon which "Sans Souci" was elegantly engraved; the waistcoat curiously adorned with frogs was of buff material; the knee-breeches were the same colour. Once a week the members gathered in each other's rooms to play for high stakes; each month they dined together, the members bringing their friends. At the end of the year a grand anniversary was celebrated.

None of these organizations were permanent nor were they directed to the accomplishment of any important aim; they were simply groups of congenial persons who gathered together to enjoy each other's society, and at times incidentally allied themselves to a political party of some improvement scheme. They were one of the sources of amusement of a generation which loved leisure. Perhaps no other student organizations which ever existed possessed so little of the academic flavour.

This absence of the academic spirit and ideals was due to the fact that during the eighteenth century the English universities ceased to educate in any active sense of the word. The students passed their prescribed terms within college precincts, spending their time for the most part as they saw fit. A few honour men read for distinction, and all were to a certain extent influenced by literary associations and contact with learning, but there was little systematic educational training. With the nineteenth century came a greater strenuousness and sense of responsibility; college fellowships were thrown open, and the requirements for graduation made more stringent. From 1800 to 1830 a widespread internal reform gradually crept from one college to another. The ideal of university education held up by the reformers was, however, largely the result of the social and aristocratic conditions of the eighteenth century. Thus, during the present century, the aim of English university education has been in marked contrast to the German ideal prevalent on the Continent. The glory of the German university has been its thirst for truth and eager invasion of the unexplored fields of knowledge; it has aimed to produce learned *savants* and competent state officials. The English have divorced teaching from investigation; instead of specialists, they have intended to send forth " gentlemen." Says Cardinal Newman: " Liberal education makes the gentleman, the individual of cultivated intellect, delicate taste, of candid, equitable, dispassionate mind, of noble and courteous bearing in the conduct of life. University training is the great and ordinary means to great and ordinary ends; it aims at raising the intellectual tone of society, at cultivating the public mind, at purifying the national taste, at supplying true principles to popular enthusiasm and fixed aims to popular aspiration, at giving enlargement and sobriety to the ideas of the age, at facilitating the exercise of political power, and of refining the intercourse of private life." Such a conception magnifies the social function of the university; liberal culture as thus described is as much the creation of student associations and intercourse as of the mastery of definite books or sciences. The discussions of the common room and the debating club, the contests on the river, the dramatics of the university theatre, are as essential portions of training as the lectures or examinations.

The ·atmosphere of the two universities with their ancient foundations, their splendid and venerable architecture and mediæval traditions, has been favourable to the growth and realization of such an ideal of liberal culture. Matthew Arnold's characterization of Oxford represents the feelings of many observers.* Englishmen have felt that to reside in Oxford or Cambridge was in itself a liberal education. The combination of old and new, the perfection of the beauty of Nature and of art, make these university cities unsurpassed among the cities of the world. An American has described the impression which residence at Oxford left on his mind years afterward. "I have heard the Master of Balliol preach on friendship and draw delightful dreamy pictures with his perfect English and rich voice. I confess that sometimes now, around Oxford and its towers, there hangs in my mind the soft, dreamy haze which pervaded his pictures. Nowhere else has the spell of the ages so thrown the halo of romance around the flying hours."

The common life of the college is the central feature of English academic society. It enables tutor and student to come together on easy terms and facilitates intercourse between groups of friends. The presence

* Discourses in America, article Emerson.

of college fellows, men standing for the highest type of culture, gives conversation a more elevated tone than when the undergraduates are left to themselves. An American observer has said that nowhere has the art of social intercourse been carried to such perfection as in some of the Oxford colleges.

The college serves as a unit of university organization; each college has its own set of clubs, athletic, debating, literary, and social. Of these, the athletic is the most important to the average undergraduate. Collegiate good fellowship is to a considerable degree dependent on the extent to which these institutions are supported. The college clubs serve as preparatory institutions in training men for university distinctions. The comparatively large number of colleges at Oxford and Cambridge and the variety of the forms of training give almost every man an opportunity to acquit himself with some degree of credit. The college debating societies likewise perform a valuable function in training men who have neither ability nor courage to make themselves heard at the Union. Thus, a weary speech, crowded with statistics, and delivered by a hard-working scholar, will be listened to with a semblance of attention, or duly applauded at one of the college clubs; such a one would never obtain a hearing in a larger organization. Whimsical nonsense is common and forms an agreeable interlude to the more serious speeches. These small clubs are great sticklers for the forms of debate and make much of any slight infractions of its rules. The president is vigilantly watched, and if he inadvertently omits some technical formula is sure to find a vote of censure upon him immediately. Such skirmishes are always conducted with the utmost good humour.

Literary and book clubs are common, but lack the ability of the debating societies. They are also less onerous in the demands which they make on their members. These clubs derive their name from some " great one " whose personality kindles the enthusiasm of their founders, but are sometimes simply known as the college essay society. A regular meeting is held at set intervals, when each member in turn reads an essay on some literary topic which is then discussed. Although professing a literary object, they are from the necessities of the case social institutions as well.

Purely social in their aims are the wine clubs which are now something of an anachronism at the English universities. In the day of their prosperity, forty years since, they recruited their membership from the best men of the college and formed an inner society, which gave tone to the rest of the college. Now the feeling in most colleges is against them, as out of keeping with the more democratic character of modern student life. Those still in existence are, in most cases, of considerable antiquity and are fenced about with a good deal of quaint custom and a fair share of formality. Their members adorn themselves in a distinguishing coat of a particular pattern. While the novel sensations of strangeness are pleasant to a newcomer, the continued round of formalities and ill-assorted character of the members make the meetings irksome. Far different are the private " wines," which are essentially social gatherings of men who know each other well. In reality such a meeting is not a formal " wine," but a mutual smoke and talk, or perhaps a regular symposium with cards and music intermingled. In either case it contains that which is the kernel of college life—the pleasure of being together and discussing with one's friends whatever is nearest one's heart, whether athletics, literature, or social philosophy.

The numbers and leisure of an English college favour the growth of social sets or cliques, many of which become institutionalized in the clubs which have been described. The two most marked sets are the æsthetes and the athletes, between which there is much bitterness and contempt. On one occasion the athletes invaded a room belonging to one of the æsthetic set who had spoken disrespectfully of the college boat, and destroyed the fancy china and knickknacks. The bump supper, celebrating the success of the college boat, was in a former generation, one of the distinctive social events of the season. It was uproarious with speeches, hurrahing, songs, and practical jokes. In the intoxication of the moment deeds of valour were attempted which afterward removed the heroes from the scene of their prowess. Such a celebration served as an outlet for surplus energy, and resulted in much good fellowship and kindling of enthusiasm, without doing much permanent harm. Their popularity is on the wane, and in a few years they will pass away.

Mention has been made of the sporadic debating and political societies which appeared at the English universities during the eighteenth century. Early in the nineteenth century these clubs were consolidated into the Oxford and Cambridge Unions, the most famous of student debating societies. By the side of the Union strong political clubs have appeared, offering training of the same character. When these are added to the regular debating clubs of the colleges, an idea is obtained of the extent of the preparation afforded the English youth for public life.

The Cambridge Union was formed, as its name implies, by the consolidation of several small clubs in 1816; the Oxford Union resulted from a similar move in 1823. Although small, the Oxford Union included the social and intellectual *élite* of the university among its members. A few years after its birth the debates were of sufficient importance to receive adverse criticism from leading London newspapers. It early manifested great seriousness of purpose; a full set of parliamentary debates was purchased for the library, while all novels, even those of Scott and Dickens, were excluded. In 1829 the heroic age of the Union began. In the succeeding five years, such men as Gladstone, Sidney Herbert, Lord Selborne, Robert Lowe, and Dr. Tait, afterward Archbishop of Canterbury, gained the Union a position at Oxford which it has since maintained. In 1834 a writer in the Oxford University Magazine spoke of the Union in the highest terms as an instrumentality which " brings together many of the most distinguished young men of the university and exercises a great effect on the general tone of society." In this early period the Union oftentimes suffered from internal dissensions. On one memorable occasion it barely escaped dissolution; later the members were divided into two hostile factions, one of which attempted to expel the other. The debate resulted in an intense excitement, which was immortalized in an excellent mock heroic. The Union condemned the Reform Bill by a vote of eighty to fifty-four.

Charles Astor Bristed, of Yale, whose career at Cambridge fell within the early forties, left an interesting account of the Cambridge Union, of which he was a member. Compared with the average American college of the same period, interest in public speaking was weak at Cambridge. " Mere oratory is about as much valued by the English as mere scholarship with us." The debates were sometimes adjourned in half an hour for lack of speeches; the offices frequently went a begging, and at a contested election not more than three hundred and fifty votes were polled out of a possible twelve hundred. The Union was subject to brief periodic fits of excitement caused by the consideration

of some burning popular issue. While these periods of
interest were on, the society evinced its vitality by a
series of rows which usually took the form of an election contest between the reading men and the rowing
men. Owing to better organization, the reading men
or scholars most frequently won; their opponents consoled themselves by making disturbances and annoying
the assembly. The speakers of the Union were less
fluent than the ordinary American college graduate.

Personal controversies, involving bitter factional
fights within the society, and exciting election contests,
form the staple incidents recorded of the Oxford Union
during its middle period (1840–1860), the time of Lord
Robert Cecil (now Marquis of Salisbury) and Mr.
Knatchbull-Hugessen; the Conservatives were in the
ascendency and carried protection resolutions by a vote
of one hundred and two to thirty-one. Occasionally
literary and theological subjects found their way into
the Union debates. By a vote of forty-two to twenty-
one a resolution was defeated which declared " that Mr.
Thackeray's writings are not distinguished by any great
ability, and their tendency is not good." The admission
of religious papers to the library was carried by a vote
of twenty-nine to twenty-five.

At their inception the Unions were exclusively societies for intellectual training which met from time
to time in college rooms; their needs soon demanded a
library and reading room, and finally a separate building. By 1840 there was a large class of members who
joined the Union to obtain the privileges of the reading room. At the present time the Unions are the
clubs for a majority of students. It is their recreation
ground for afternoon and evening, the place where
they can write and smoke, play chess and billiards, read
books, and occasionally indulge in their taste for public speaking. A man pays rather more than three

pounds a year for three years, and during that time he has all the letters written by him in the Union stamped gratis, and the free use forever of all kinds of stationery, of about one hundred papers and periodicals and a library of twenty thousand volumes. " It is in the Union that there is to be found the true social life of Oxford, the life which really determines Oxford character " (Pemberton).

In the last sixty years the Unions have developed a style of oratory calculated to please an assemblage of young men who like to be amused, and have only a general and not always very serious interest in the questions they discuss. The audiences are the most impatient and critical that can be found; a nervous or affected speaker stands no chance before them, sentiment and rhetoric are rarely tolerated, and dulness never. The ideal union speech bristles with brilliant antithesis and epigram; the style tends to be flashy and superficial, and the matter frequently resembles newspaper leaders. The subjects which attract the audiences are those which contain dramatic possibilities, such as the painting of social evils in eloquent terms or personal issues between well-known leaders. Many of the modern debates are a mere *tour de force* between two or at the most four party giants of opposing camps. After their speeches the debate collapses from want of real interest in the subject discussed. The most popular occasions are those which give rise to personal differences culminating in repartee and sarcasm. One speaker may characterize his opponent's speech as nonsense. Threatened with fine or apology by the presiding officer, the incorrigible replies, " Sir, I beg the honourable member's pardon for insinuating that it required any ingenuity on his part to talk nonsense." More than three hundred men roar for a time at this sally; the speaker has made the hit of the evening.

4

The large political clubs, like the Palmerston and Canning, Chatham and Russell, at Oxford, are frequented by the budding politicians, and form a valuable supplement to the Unions. At their meetings excellent papers are sometimes read on topics of general interest, while their debates show a wide range of views on the political and social questions of the day. From their practice of meeting in the rooms of the different members they contribute in no small degree to an interchange of views and hospitalities between men of different colleges. Their annual dinners bring them into contact with the authorities and various political celebrities of the outside world.

The debating and political societies are recognised as important factors in the social and intellectual life of the universities. They bring the mass of the undergraduates together and give them a serious interest in the great issues of the day. They accustom their members to a wide diversity of views, and consequently make against intolerance and arrogance.

The early years of the nineteenth century witnessed a complete change in the attitude of the English student toward athletics. It is no longer the occasional student who rows or plays football or cricket when fancy dictates; now almost every undergraduate as a matter of course follows some sport. Athletics are not only the most picturesque feature of Oxford and Cambridge life, but also form the chief ties which bring men together. Chronologically, boating was developed first, followed by cricket, football, track and field athletics. The athletic movement in the university has been paralleled by an unprecedented growth in the popularity of games among the English people. In the widespread demand for strenuous exercise, the public schools seem to have taken the initiative rather than the universities: in truth, university athletics, with the exception of boating, are the outgrowth of the public schools.

Boating is by all odds the most engrossing pursuit followed by the Oxford and Cambridge undergraduate. The majority of the members in many colleges have at some period been connected with the college boat, rowing being compatible with more serious pursuits. "The river, its pleasures and duties, form a pivot around which swing, in varying but increasing force, torpids * and eights, training breakfasts and college rags, each and all embodying in their own particular way the life of the college" (J. S. G. Pemberton). It is the meeting place of all types and conditions of university people, including dons and college servants, all of whom crowd around a stretch of water not more than a mile long and five or six rods wide. Many a quiet student likewise owns his shell or canoe, and obtains the exercise necessary for health and work. On the annual races, each college is represented by a crew, and so keen is the competition that it has been said that the position of a college on the river is, in the vast majority of cases, a true index to its intellectual position in the university. During commencement, the river becomes a grand holiday scene for miles in each direction; water parties from the different colleges occur frequently. The river is instinct with the social side of Oxford life. It provides a healthy rivalry between the colleges, which does much to maintain the tone of successive generations of college men.

Cricket is second in importance to boating, both in general popularity and in the extent to which it is played. Cricket, however, can not be learned at the university, and its charms are only for those undergraduates who come from the public schools. Conse-

---

* The second-class racing boats at Oxford are called "torpids."

quently, the cricket players form a specialized class; the college, as a whole, has far less interest in its eleven than in its eight.   As an instrument of sociability cricket is inferior to boating, because it does not bring about that intimacy between leaders and the rank and file which is to be found on the river.   While boating is a bond between the different sets and types of men in a college, cricket tends to form and foster more or less exclusive sets, who hold aloof from the rest of college life.

Football as a game for university men is a recent innovation.   It was practically unknown at Oxford fifty years ago; now it is a popular pursuit during the winter months.   It is a pre-eminently democratic game, affording amusement and exercise to many who have not the time or inclination for boating.   Football excites more interest outside university precincts than any other sport except boating.   Like boating, it brings together men who come from different schools and thus tends to break down the lines of public-school caste, and enables the men from different colleges to know each other.   Next to boating it is the pursuit most representative of the modern social life of Oxford.

Field and track athletics and hunting are specialized pursuits followed by the few.   The leading lights in these amusements are generally known long before they arrive at the university, and when matriculated keep themselves apart from their fellow-collegians, forming a distinct athletic set.   The interest of each college in general athletics is confined to one or two days in the year.   These occasions are more remarkable for sociability and good feeling than for the proficiency exhibited by the majority in the sports of the day.   Hunting is, by reason of its expense, confined to the wealthy and aristocratic portion of the undergraduates, and numbers few devotees.   Walking is a mode of exercise particularly popular at Cambridge among the reading men. To cover fifteen miles in three hours is a common achievement.

The existence of separate colleges within the university greatly simplifies the problem of organization. Mention has already been made of the full set of athletic clubs maintained by each college. The athletic interests of the entire university are provided for by a number of general clubs, one for each branch of sport. The interference of academic authorities in the attempt to check abuses is unheard of, chiefly because the athletic traditions among the undergraduates is sufficiently strong to preserve a healthy athletic spirit. The greater maturity of the average English collegian is another factor which makes for clean sport.

While the percentage of undergraduates actively participating in athletics is much greater than in America, the contests lack the fierceness of energy and sense of tension which accompany similar trials of skill across the Atlantic. The English seem to play more for the love of sport and less from a desire to beat somebody than their American cousins. Controversies over details of matches and recriminations back and forth seldom occur. The athletic class is more highly differentiated from the mass of the students than in the United States, but there is an absence of professionalism in the worst sense of the term—e. g., outsiders are not hired to attend college for the only purpose of participating in athletics.

We have yet to speak of a number of miscellaneous organizations of minor significance, the most notable of which are the university social clubs, patterned after the ordinary club of London. The clubs of Oxford are the Bullingdon, Vincents, and Gridiron. Of these, the Bullingdon is the most exclusive, and was formerly the most popular, although in late years it has abdicated

the leadership in favour of Vincents. Membership in
Vincents is coveted by all the undergraduates who regard social success as an important part of their academic career. Its membership is largely made up of
successful athletes, although it usually secures the most
popular men from all the colleges regardless of muscle.
Still, in some quarters, Vincents is regarded as an athletic clique. It plays an important part in the social
life of Oxford, forming a centre where men from the
different colleges can meet and entertain their friends
with less formality than would be required in their
colleges. The Gridiron, comparatively a new club, is
a protest against the athleticism of Vincents. It has
been a moderate success, without threatening the position held by its rival.

The more important public schools are represented
by clubs of graduates at the universities. The Eton
Club of Oxford is a typical organization of this class.
All the Etonians at Oxford belong to the club, although
there is little sociability or good fellowship in its rooms.
Starched sobriety is usually in order, but the latent social force occasionally breaks through the crust and a
revival of interest takes place. The Winchester Club is
much smaller, because only a portion of the Wykemists
join it. Its small membership, however, makes it a
social body of influence.

§ 4. STUDENT LIFE AT THE ENGLISH PUBLIC SCHOOLS.

The term public school is applied to a small group of
expensive, aristocratic boarding schools of the secondary grade. These institutions are typical products of
the English national spirit; they are exclusive in character, and independent of each other and the state in
their administration. Unlike the chief secondary
schools of the Continent, each foundation possesses an

individuality of its own, and stands for a definite ideal in education. The nearest approach to the English public schools in constitution are the large academies and preparatory schools of the United States, like Phillips Andover, Lawrenceville, and Groton. These schools, however, can not for a moment be compared with their English contemporaries in influence or importance, being overshadowed by an efficient system of municipal high schools on one side and by the colleges on the other. Next to the universities among the educational institutions of England, the public schools strike their roots deepest into the past. The oldest endowment, that of Winchester, dates from 1387; Eton, the most important, from 1441. The other historic schools—Shrewsbury, Westminster, Rugby, Charterhouse, and Harrow—were the creations of the sixteenth century. A number of schools of this grade have been established in the present century, but their founders have in every instance sought to approximate the old, historic type. Thus the public school is in its essentials an organic growth of English life rather than a creation of legislators or educators.

During the seventeenth and eighteenth centuries the public schools were the seats of a hardy, independent student life. Each school had its customs and schoolboy dialects, which were handed down from one generation to another, and possessed its own particular form of football, handball (fives), or tennis, which in many cases grew out of the peculiarities of the school buildings and grounds. When the rigour of Puritanism or the indifference of the eighteenth century threatened the existence of the old English games, they found a secure home in the public schools. The games were not played by all the boys; a boy played or not, as he chose. The masters of the time deemed it beneath their dignity to devote any of their attention to such

unimportant details as schoolboy sports. Thus, at the
beginning of the present century only a few of the
Eton boys played organized games, there existing at
that time but three cricket clubs and one football club
for the entire school. The many were dependent on
bathing and boating in summer, and on books apparently for the rest of the year.

A rude form of self-government existed among the
boys. The younger were expected to fag—that is, to
render slight personal services, such as cooking and
blacking shoes for the upper boys. In most cases one
particular small boy was assigned to the service of one
particular large boy. The right of the sixth form or
highest class to discipline the smaller boys was recognised, being in fact expressly enjoined by the statutes
of Winchester. Both of these customs produced grave
abuses; the fags were bullied and tortured by a portion
of the larger boys, until the public schools were the
terror of all children of a sensitive nature. One of the
forms of torture most commonly practised was known
as giving the boys a pair of tin gloves. This process
consisted in marking the fag's hands with red-hot coals,
so that he might be hardened to holding warm dishes.
Toasting the calves of the fag's legs was another much-
practised amusement. At Eton, neglect of duty on
the part of the fags was met with brutal punishment.
For a small offence, like failing to close a shutter tight,
or leaving the seam of a sheet uppermost, a fag was
beaten with a brush on both sides of the head. An adequate idea of the atmosphere of terrorism and brutality
which was the result of such practices can only be obtained from following the career of some sensitive individual, like Shelley, who was hunted through the
streets of Eton by the fag masters.

The discipline of the masters was well calculated to
maintain such practices among the boys. It may be

described as unintelligently brutal. The rod was the universal remedy for breaches of discipline or slowness of apprehension. On one occasion, at Winchester, with one hundred and ninety-eight boys in residence, two hundred and seventy-nine cases were reported for punishment at the end of a single day. At least two of the head masters of Eton at the end of the eighteenth and opening of the nineteenth century made terrorism their avowed policy. In an emergency Dr. Keate flogged more than eighty boys in one night. Rebellions of the boys were not uncommon during this period. During Keate's administration disorder was frequent, and there is on record an insurrection during which the boys attempted to rotten-egg the head master. At Harrow the forces of disorder for a time gained the upper hand and brought the school to the verge of destruction.

Such savage rigour was unfavourable to morality as well as discipline. Drunkenness and other dissipation was rife among the sixth form or higher boys. Such a clique at Harrow organized a " Red Night-Cap Club," which took its name from a red cap emblazoned with a pot of porter, standing on two crossed pipes all in gold lace, with the exception of the froth, which was admirably imitated in silver. The older boys of Winchester were taught to live like men of the world, which, being interpreted, means that they played cards, frequented taverns, indulged in fine clothes, gave entertainments to the ladies, and indulged in dissipation generally. The younger Fox was said to have demoralized Eton by the introduction of gaming and fashionable Continental life. The sixth form at Rugby amused themselves by following the hounds, and otherwise imitating the sporting life of the surrounding gentry.

In the domain of religious training a sufficient number of the old usages enjoined by the founder were continued to irritate the boys without having any counterbalancing attempt at influence. Dr. Moberly, head master of Winchester, writes of this period as follows: "The tone of the young men at the universities, whether they came from Winchester, Eton, Rugby, or Harrow, or wherever else, was universally irreligious. A religious undergraduate was very rare and much laughed at when he appeared, and, I think I may confidently say, hardly to be found among public-school men, or, if this be too strongly said, hardly to be found except in cases where private or domestic training or good dispositions had prevailed over school habits and tendencies."

The condition of affairs above described, which existed in 1820, represented rather the indifference of the eighteenth century than the zeal and earnestness of the nineteenth; or, in other words, the public schools were fifty years behind the general movement of civilization. Their deficiencies were widely known to the thinking public and created a sentiment in favour of reform, which resulted in a number of educational experiments. The most interesting of these was the form of government inaugurated by Rowland Hill at Hazlewood School. At the beginning of the venture the constitution consisted of a number of resolutions which were afterward expanded into an elaborate and minutely detailed set of laws of more than a hundred closely printed pages. A judge, sheriff, and keeper of records were chosen by the boys, the attorney and solicitor-general by the head master. Cases were tried by jury, six boys being selected by ballot. If proved guilty, the boys were punished by being deprived of their holidays. The student government was unusually successful, saving the masters much trouble. By the ingenious device of compelling the boys to fight in secret, the custom was almost entirely done away with. The scheme received commendation from many high quarters, and was imitated in foreign countries. Its great defect lay in the fact that it produced men prematurely; its graduates were precocious imitations of maturity, or, in other words, prigs.

The reform which came in the public schools owed little to Rowland Hill, and is known through its connection with the name of Thomas Arnold, head master of Rugby from 1827 to 1843. The prevailing traits in Arnold's character were moral earnestness and vigour of mind. Himself a graduate of Winchester and Oxford, he possessed a first-hand knowledge of public-school life, and entered upon his head mastership with the definite purpose in mind of reforming the public-school system of England. While Arnold owes his fame as much to his intrinsic force of character and theological liberalism as to his educational achievements, it can not be denied that in essential particulars the public schools of England have developed along the lines which he was the first to inaugurate. In the field of school life his work was adaptive rather than creative; he reorganized and systematized the institutions which had existed previously in a loose way at the older public schools. Admiration for Arnold should not blind us to the fact that the movement he began was the next step in the march of events, and that other head masters arrived at the same conclusions independently. Nevertheless, the actual reform in the schools was the result of Arnold's work carried out by men whom he had trained, and interpreted by such books as Stanley's Life of Arnold (1844) and Hughes's Tom Brown's School Days (1856).

In brief, what were the adaptations which Arnold made in the student life of the public schools? His first move at Rugby was to reorganize the house system, which had been allowed to fall into desuetude, owing to the absence of the masters, who officiated as clergymen in neighbouring parishes. He held that each boy should have a school home and be under the direct personal supervision of one of the masters. In many of the public schools this system had prevailed for the foundation scholars (those living on the bounty of the founder), but not for the mass of students. The next step was to increase the power of the sixth form (highest class), and to make them the governing authority of the school. Here Arnold laboured to increase their sense of responsibility. He legalized the rule of the larger boys because he felt that the strongest and oldest would have their way in any event. By recognising their sway and holding them responsible, he hoped to change the character of their rule from a crude despotism with occasional spells of anarchy, to a settled constitutional government. The sixth form were in a position to be influenced by the head master; the smaller boys could only be reached through their school-fellows. As a third and final factor, Arnold was the first English educator to realize the value of athletic sports as a safety valve for the animal spirits of the boys. There is an old tradition to the effect that Arnold was the first head master in England to witness a game of football.

Such an outline gives little of the spirit of the Arnoldian reform. The changes in school government were but one step toward that self-reliance and manliness which Arnold made the keynote of school life. It does not fall within the scope of this sketch to speak of the sermons from Rugby Chapel which so powerfully affected the better element among the boys, or that strong interest in each boy's personal welfare which spared neither money nor time when there was service to be rendered. Yet the sermons and personal appeals were the forces which insured the favourable outcome of the other reforms. To ignore them would be to give a false and inadequate idea of the movement.

The reforms at Rugby were made at an opportune moment, the older schools were becoming unwieldy through size, and a new series of foundations was about to be begun. In a generation the face of public-school life was changed. The renovated system of government made away with bullying for the most part, the extraordinary growth of athletics checked the vices and dissipation of school life and turned out men of unusual physical vigour, the public schools became the seats of a deep religious life, earnestness and zeal succeeded the old indifference, and a new spirit reigned. Without describing in detail this change, the writer will pass on to an account of the present conditions of public-school life in England.

The house in the English public school, like the college in the English university, is the unit of organization. The number and influence of the houses vary in the different foundations. At Winchester there are nine houses, each containing about thirty-five boys. Since the house system has been introduced the instruction and the care of the boys have been more intimate and personal, and therefore much better than before. The presence of the wives and daughters of the masters among the boys is said to exert an elevating and refining influence, putting the gawky boys at ease in society and helping to reform the bad ones. The houses are also of advantage in giving a new boy a steady circle of acquaintances. The boys are kept much together by their meals and early hour "lock-up," while a series of roll calls prevents them from spending much time away from schools. In consequence the fellows in each house stick very close together, which leads to intense athletic rivalry between the different houses. Each house has its debating society, its football and cricket teams, and at Eton its house "four" on the river. The colleges at Eton and

Winchester contain intellectually the pick of the school, and are placed apart in a house by themselves. Rugby and Harrow, on the other hand, scatter the best scholars among the houses.

Closely connected with the house system is the government of the boys by the sixth form or highest class. At Winchester this power is lodged in the hands of eighteen prefects. Five of these have special titles, such as prefect of the hall, prefect of the chapel, and are usually chosen from the best scholars. The prefect of the hall is, as it were, prime minister of the boys; he not only has his own duties, but likewise supervision over the other prefects. He quells disturbances and acts as spokesman of the boys with the masters. The prefect is empowered to inflict bodily punishment, known as " tunding," on the lower forms in certain cases, the right of appeal to the masters always existing. The captain of the house at Eton possesses similar power, and when he is a boy of character, and has either moral or physical power, he may be said to almost control the house. When there is too much hubbub going on in the passages, or any breach of manners or lesser morals is committed, he is to a great extent considered responsible. Such matters of discipline are usually considered safe in his hands. The exercise of authority by the sixth form is generally considered a success; their commands are less resented than those of the masters, and do not provoke the instant opposition which the latter sometimes evoke. The boys themselves value their privileges very highly and resist any effort to curtail what they are pleased to consider their rights. The gain in self-respect, tact, and common sense which the sixth form gains from the exercise of these powers is by no means to be despised. Abuses of power sometimes occur, and so august an authority as the public-schools commission report that the system should be carefully watched to prevent abuses. The words of the commission are worth quoting: " It is evident that any system of this kind is exposed to some risks and open to some objections. There are objections to any delegation, express or tacit, to schoolboys, of the authority to inflict punishment on their fellows. There is a risk lest it be abused from a defect of temper or judgment; lest it make those intrusted with it imperious or tyrannical, or priggish and self-sufficient; lest boys whose character makes them illy qualified to govern others should be oppressed and discouraged by a responsibility to which they consider themselves unequal; and lest if it fall into unfit hands it should be an instrument of positive evil. There is some danger that the masters should, more than is just or right, leave the discipline of the school to take care of itself and the irregularities, the correction of which forms a part of their own duty, to be checked—perhaps ineffectually and perhaps not checked at all by the senior boys. To guard against these dangers effectually requires, we have no doubt, much judgment on the part of the head msater and no little care. . . . We are bound, at the same time, to express our belief that cases of abuse have been exceptional, and by proper precautions they may be prevented from interfering seriously with the beneficial working of the system." *

The same conservative tone pervades the report of the commission on the closely allied subject of fagging. They conclude that, " On the whole and with some exceptions, fagging, mitigated by the altered habits and manners of the ·present time, is not degrading to the juniors, makes no exorbitant demands on their time, and has no injurious effect on the character of the seniors. The relation between master and fag is generally

---

* Public School Commission Report, vol. i, pp. 42, 43 (1864).

friendly, and to a certain extent one of patronage and protection, and it sometimes gives rise to lasting intimacies." * Dr. Arnold and Edward Thring have both defended fagging on the ground that it protected the small boy from the miscellaneous tyranny of a crowd of elders. To quote from the latter: " A school with no legal form of fagging is reduced to the level of a savage tribe, and no boy can consider himself safe as long as there is a stronger arm than his own. But a legal system of fagging at once dethrones these clumsy tyrants, makes them servants instead of masters, carefully guards against promiscuous slavery, and removes the bitterness of injustice of such power as remains." †

The present tendency is to make fagging duties lighter from year to year. At Eton, three forms of fagging are in vogue—mess fagging, attention to fag master's room, and running errands. Mess fagging consists in making tea and coffee, toast, and occasionally boiling eggs or cooking, all of which seldom occupies more than three quarters of an hour. The fag caring for his master's room calls the occupant in the morning, brings him warm water, fills his bath overnight, and puts the room straight for bed. " Comehere " fags are bound to run to any member of the sixth form on hearing these words. The last one to arrive is customarily despatched on the errand.‡ A few simple duties like running errands, cooking, and washing bottles, cover the entire functions of the fag at Winchester.# In other schools the practice has almost become a thing of the past.

---

* Public School Commission Report, vol. i, p. 44 (1864).

† Thring, Edward. Education on School, p. 266. Arnold, Thomas. On the Discipline of Public Schools, reprinted in J. J. Findlay's Arnold of Rugby, p. 233.

‡ Pascoe. Everyday Life in the English Public Schools, p. 23.

Corbin, John. Schoolboy Life in England, p. 38.

To the English schoolboy athletics forms the most important element of the public-school organization, for in England the games have a recognised status with the masters. Many of the assistant masters are chosen for their prowess in athletics. A large portion of the school expenditure goes to games, and participation in them is compulsory to all those not physically disqualified. In the reminiscences of " old boys " cricket scores and close games of football seem to overtop all other sides of school life. One writer expresses the attitude of nine tenths of the public-school men when he says: " No thinking man will blame us for idolizing the athlete. The cricketer in his flannels was our hero and not the student immersed in his books. The fortune of our ancient school will stand as long as we can produce not only scholars but cricketers." *

Cricket, football, fives, and boating are the favourite forms of contest, although boating is now practically confined to Eton. Rugby and Shrewsbury are noted for their football, Harrow and Charterhouse for their cricket. Without attempting to present the details relating to the management of the games, or the struggles for supremacy between the different houses and schools, we will turn to the educational aspects of public-school athletics. What has the universal participation in games done for the English boy of the upper classes? Primarily, it has equipped him with a strong physique and excellent health. Most foreigners visiting English schools of this grade are struck with the vigorous and manly appearance of the students. This result is so obvious and generally admitted that discussion would be superfluous, although, for the benefit of the American reader, it may be said in passing that athletic contests in England are

---

* Minchin, J. G. C.   Old Harrow Days, p. 150.

5

less fierce and the training much less severe than in America.*

The spread of athletics and the better organization of games have enlisted the sympathies of the boys on the side of law. To quote from Thring again: " The internal order and discipline of every great school ought to revolve around the central principle of the perfect lawfulness of every out-of-door sport or amusement." †
To give the boys something to lose, that is the starting point in any system of student self-government. The organization of games puts a powerful weapon of control in the hands of the authorities. In another way athletics make for order by sweeping along all kinds of different temperaments and personal peculiarities on one tide of social interest.

Another valuable function of athletics in a boarding school is to fill the mind of the boy to the exclusion of more dangerous subjects. " Athletics supply an object of thought and conversation that is perfectly legitimate, perfectly wholesome, and within limits not unprofitable. Boys at school pass through a period of life during which bodies and minds are rapidly growing, interests are being developed, and prospects of new pleasures and activities are opening out. And it is much that during such a period, when dangers and perversions of energy are nigh at hand, there should be one master interest, healthy and absorbing, to dominate speech and thought." ‡ Games promote good feeling between masters and boys by giving them a common topic of conversation of a neutral nature, unconnected

---

* For a discussion of hygienic results of public-school games, the reader is referred to C. C. Cotterill's Suggested Reforms in the Public Schools, chaps. ii and viii.

† Thring, E. Education and School, p. 258.

‡ Lionel Ford. Public School Athletics, in Cookson's Essays on Secondary Education, p. 286.

with school studies or discipline. In case the masters are themselves old athletes, the two parties easily meet and fraternize on the playing fields.

To a certain extent athletics makes for character; to work for one's team rather than one's self is the first step in social education. The habituation to defeat and the hard discipline of training are alike conducive to the development of such qualities of character as good temper and self-repression. The sense of responsibility which comes from captaining a team or representing one's house or school is in itself an education; it gives a man a sense of his own real value in the community, and makes him capable of dealing with men without either timidity on the one hand or presumption on the other. While this value of athletic training has been sometimes overestimated, it should be by no means overlooked.*

The English public have fully recognised the part which out-of-door games have played in making the public-school man. Now the greatest danger seems to come from the other side, from excessive and somewhat unreasonable devotion to athletics. Not to speak of the heavy investments of capital in athletic plants and of the time given to sports far beyond the demands of hygiene, the greatest obstacle to the healthy progress in the public schools has been the growth of a spirit of athleticism. The boys leave school with more book knowledge than at any previous period, but in many cases they study perfunctorily; they possess little interest in things intellectual, whether in the form of school studies or outside hobbies. To even the larger boys, seventeen or eighteen years of age, the chief business of a public school is to play games; their culture material

---

* For a full discussion of this factor, see article entitled Psychological, Pedagogical, and Religious Aspects of Group Games, Pedagogical Seminary, March, 1899, vol. vi.

is to a great extent batting, averages, and the literature
of sport. Boys of rare mental gifts or strong characters, who do not fall in with the athletic mania, are dis-
liked by their companions and isolated, which reacts
unfavourably upon them. In short, athletics, instead
of occupying a subordinate but important place in the
life of the school, has usurped the position of first importance and forced intellectual interests into the background.

Notwithstanding its supremacy, athletics has by
no means a monopoly of attention. Societies and organizations for many purposes are found in the public
school, the most notable of which are debating societies,
literary or essay societies, natural history societies,
rifle corps, musical societies, and religious organizations. True to the political instincts of their race,
these young Englishmen concentrate their strongest
effort in discussing affairs of state. Besides the " *Pop,*"
which is the general school society, each house has a
debating club of its own, which is described as a curious
and amusing institution. " It usually consists of about
twelve members (not, as a rule, elected for any supposed talent in oratory), of whom ten are Conservatives and two Liberals. Many varieties of opinion are
represented—the Jingo and the Radical, the scornful
member and man of statistics. On the whole, these
debating societies are excellent institutions, awakening
in the boys an interest in public matters and public
questions, even if not productive of eloquence. The
meetings are generally regarded with great interest.
As an adjunct to the debating society, each house has a
good library." * At Eton these societies are conducted
by the students without interference on the part of

* Pascoe, C. Everyday Life in the English Public Schools,
p. 45.

the masters, while at Winchester the head master is always president of the Natural History and Shakespeare Societies.

The influence and character of these kinds of clubs vary in different schools. For instance, the debating clubs are more prominent at Eton than at Harrow. They play a more important part in school life than similar organizations in America, with the possible exceptions of preparatory-school fraternities and debating societies in some of the Western and Southern academies. In England these clubs have a particular value in keeping alive a variety of interests amid the flood of athleticism.* A description of the English public schools which failed to take account of their individuality and traditions would be inadequate. In this respect the public schools may be compared with American colleges. As one speaks of the Harvard, Yale, or Princeton type, so English writers refer to Etonian, Harrowian, or Rugbian character. A recent writer has characterized the output of the above schools in a manner so admirable that it seems worthy to be quoted here: " An Etonian is readily distinguished by the polish of his manner from which the crudities of boyhood have prematurely disappeared. His opinions show culture, but are apt to be narrow, and are seldom based on very solid ground. The Harrowian is more bluff and vigorous, perhaps more brutal than the Etonian. His manners lack grace, but his views are broader and his mind more virile. The Rugbian is a very distinct and not very agreeable type. He is Tom Brown pushed to a

---

* Worthy of more than a passing notice are the missions established by the public schools in the poorer parts of London and other destitute localities. Eighteen of the public schools are now thus represented. Masters say that the tone of their schools has improved since the boys have by this means been taught to sympathize with the sufferings of the poor.

morbid excess, and is marked by an arrogant contempt for the feelings and opinions of others, an unpleasant roughness of manner, and a habit of contradiction that borders on the insolent." *

The great estimation in which the public schools are held, their long traditions and list of famous graduates, appeal to the imagination and tend to fasten a pride and *esprit du corps* which has no small agency in making self-government a success. The preachers of school sermons—men like Arnold and Farrar—frequently employ this motif with great effect. The following quotation from a sermon by Canon Farrar will give some idea of the strength of this feeling. It also testifies to the manly and independent character of the men whom public-school life produces: " This school has sent forth poets of undying memory, great divines, learned scholars, governors who ruled millions of new subjects in distant provinces, eloquent orators who have held listening senates breathless at their voice, statesmen who have been the foremost to guide the destiny of civilized nations, mighty warriors who have rolled the tempestuous thunders of victory over land and sea. It is a power in English education forever. What shall be the fate of Harrow, my brothers, rests in your hands; a single generation may decide it. Our own hold on the school may be short; the average time of a boy's stay here is less than five years, but the good or harm he may do in those few years is simply incalculable. . . . Harrow boys of this generation, answer me—for I answer not the question for you either way—has the honour of Harrow risen or fallen in your hands? What has your work been? Have you strengthened a good tradition or added virulence to an evil? Supposing any one

---

* Norman Pearson, in Lippincott's Magazine, vol. xxxiii, p. 611.

of you were the last scion of an ancient and noble house, what would your feelings be if you brought on that honourable lineage a lasting, an irreparable disgrace? Yet the blot on the white scutcheon, on an illustrious line, is as nothing to any shame or disgrace brought through your weakness or wickedness upon the reputation of a noble school—a school the name of which, if you but do your duty, must and will shed more honour on the majority of you than you will ever shed on it. A pride in Harrow, if it be a manly pride, is not only pardonable but right, not only excusable but desirable. This school and not another claims your loyal allegiance; to this school and not another is your chivalrous devotion due. The public schools are among our worthiest institutions." *

In estimating the worth of student life in the public schools, one can justly say with Romanes that, if the Germans have thus far excelled in perfecting the education of work, the English have been equally pre-eminent in developing the education of play. English superiority in this field has been acknowledged by recent French and German writers of repute, and athletic movements inaugurated in both countries, based largely on English precedent. The secondary schools of America have a student life of their own which is largely an imitation of college ways and clubs. No widespread influence of English societies and games has taken place, although some few institutions, like Lawrenceville, Groton, and St. Paul's, have adopted some one feature of the English system. American observers, like President Sharpless, have spoken in high terms of the training afforded by the public schools. One American writer, Mr. John Corbin, has published a

---

* Frederic W. Farrar, in the Fall of Man and other Sermons, p. 128.

book in which the public schools are held up as models to his countrymen. He recognises that many of their most striking features, like fagging and the monitorial system, would not be tolerated in the great majority of American schools. The house system and compulsory athletics remain. These are both along the line of advance in American boarding schools, and, but for financial obstacles, would have been established. The great lesson which American education has to learn from England does not consist in the imitation of this or that particular institution, but in the realization that, in the hands of capable teachers, the schools may become an important element in character building and social education. English experience has provided us with a standard by which American student life can be measured. This is no small service.

§ 5. STUDENT LIFE IN SCOTCH UNIVERSITIES.

BIBLIOGRAPHY.—The Appendix to Volume II of Alexander Grant's The Story of the University of Edinburgh contains an account of student organizations there. Student Life at Edinburgh University, by Norman Fraser, describes the academic career of a student of pietistic tendencies. Rait's Aberdeen is useful for occasional notices. Two articles by John Nichol (Fortnightly Review, vol. xl, p. 639) and J. Leys (National Review, vol. viii, 533) discuss the general tone of Scotch student life and its relation to education. Chambers's Journal (vol. lxxi, p. 593) sums up the recent movements among Scottish students. David Masson, the biographer of Milton, has written an interesting reminiscent article in Macmillan's Magazine, vol. ii, p. 123. For additional references, see BIBLIOGRAPHY.

In 1850 the Scotch universities presented contrasts to Oxford and Cambridge in their constitution, their studies, in the constituency to which they appealed, and in the spirit which animated them. The English universities were the most conservative in Europe; the culture of a gentleman rather than professional efficiency was their aim. They were the exclusive possession of the upper classes, attracting to their halls a smaller proportion of the population than the universities of any other European country. The four universities of Scotland, on the other hand, were relatively the most popular institutions of higher learning in Europe; their strongest departments were professional, and their methods represented the strongest utilitarian tendencies. They were called the great public schools for a majority of the middle classes of the country, and it was said that nine tenths of the most successful Scotchmen who worked in any degree with their heads had passed at least a session or two at one or other of the universities. From their poverty, and the lack of regular preparation on the part of their students, they were not able to compete with Germany in specialty and thoroughness, or with Oxford and Cambridge in regard to the scholarly finish of the work done.

Poverty has always been the lot of the great majority of Scottish students. Legends float down from bygone generations of students who walked from a distant region of the country barefoot in order to save their only pair of shoes, and with all their wardrobe contained in a small knapsack which they carried on their backs. In term time they existed on hard cheese, which they had brought from home, and a little oatmeal. At the University of Edinburgh there were men who worked at bookbinding or printing, made pills and potions in druggists' shops, acted as copying clerks in lawyers' offices, or even engaged actively in the carpenter trade while carrying on studies at the university. In fact, the greater part of the student body were recruited from the labouring and lower and middle classes. Such men could not but be noted for the strenuousness of their labours, the eagerness of their efforts, and the keenness of competition, which, together with the unhygienic conditions of their work, often resulted in tragedies. Some necessarily fell back disheartened, and perhaps soured with disappointment; a large number are permanently weakened in health, and many never emerge from the conflict. To quote the eloquent words of a Scottish writer, " There is not a churchyard on Scottish soil which is not the resting place of some bright-eyed youth who paid for his ambition with his life, who has been vanquished in the fight, and crept wearily home to die." (J. Leys, in National Review.)

Such an atmosphere of struggle and intensity was unfavourable to the development of healthy student life. There could be none of that exuberance of spirit which accompanies all the manifestations of the play instinct. The lack of collegiate life, except at St. Andrew's, accentuated the evil. The Scotch students were not a body of young men associated together for any object, but a number of isolated youths, each living his own life in his own way, scattered up and down a great city, and brought together two or three hours a day for the purpose of instruction. Two or three youths of similar tastes might form a group which resulted in lifelong friendships; but the fact that the students had nothing in common but their studies prevented any fellowship on a large scale. The Puritanical distrust of the world, fostered by Scotch theology, tended to degrade student life in the public estimation, or, to be more accurate, prevented the need of a student life from being felt. There was nothing in the life of a majority of Scottish students to answer to the influences which at Eton and Oxford moulded the character and manners of an Englishman, and in many quarters there was opposition to the introduction of any such instrumentalities. Competent judges estimated that there was less student life in the Scottish universities than in the higher institutions of either England, Germany, or America.

Critics of Scottish education realized the need and pointed out the fact that the national character was weak in the very points which an active student life would tend to remedy. The Scotch type abounds in fire and strength, has almost an infinite capacity to work, and an almost superhuman desire to succeed and command. The Scotchman's hunger to push and get the better are often liable to culminate in displays of envy, hatred, and uncharitableness. The master defects of his mind are a want of grace, flexibility, and repose, and the magnanimous qualities which make the gentleman at ease. It was a matter of regret to many that the university system encouraged mere activity and emulation, and did so little to refine, moderate, and humanize those who came under its influences.

In the northern universities of this period muscular training was neglected. Cricket and boating clubs did not exist, curling and golf were confined to a comparatively small portion of the country. Walking for walking's sake led to nothing, and obviously served no practical purposes. The picturesque country in the neighbourhood of the universities, abounding in romantic associations, had no charms for the hardworking students. Football had been left behind at the grammar school with marbles and other childish things.

The only physical recreation which the students permitted themselves were town and gown rows and rectorial elections. The snow riots in Edinburgh between the students and the lower class of the citizens first began to be noteworthy in 1831, the date of the great riot, when the police, instead of maintaining order, joined the rabble against the undergraduates. Formidable snow riots took place again in 1848 and 1854, while the last affair of importance occurred as recently as 1861. The rectorial election takes place every three years, and at one time was the excuse for a carnival of misrule. The contest was fought out along purely party lines, and in the campaign, speeches were not the only weapons employed. For a week before the election the quadrangle was turned into a battle ground by the opposing parties, who were armed with flour of various colours, pea-shooters, dried flatfish, and similar weapons. Both town and gown rows and rectorial elections, valuable as they were in generating bonds of union between the students, were too occasional in character to materially alter the state of isolation before described.

The important social institution for the minority of the students were the debating societies. At Edinburgh the first of these organizations to be founded was the famous Speculative Society in 1764, which soon assumed and steadily maintained a brilliant reputation as a school of debate for future lawyers, divines, and statesmen. This society possessed its own hall and library. In the most brilliant period of its existence it numbered among its members Walter Scott, Lord Jeffreys, and Henry Brougham. The Theological Society was founded in 1776, the Royal Medical Society in 1778, and the Dialectic Society in 1787. Later additions to the group were the Scots Law Society in 1815, the Diagnostic Society in 1816, and the Philomathic Society in 1858. The circle of questions discussed in these societies was much wider than in English and American debating clubs. Political issues have not assumed such importance, and more attention has been given to ethical and psychological problems. Earnestness and fire, often to the extent of bitter personalities, marked the discussions of the debating society during this period. The debate often became a fierce give-

and-take fight, in which the president's office was no sinecure.

Scotch writers have rated high the social influence of these early debating clubs. Says Professor Masson (Macmillan's Magazine, vol. xi): Nowhere in the university was the crossing of influences from the different faculties and professors, and the importations at the same time of independent influences, more observable than in the debating societies. The very great importance of debating societies as the nonofficial part of the apparatus of the university deserves to be noted. . . . To this day I have known nothing of the sort better on the whole, and it remains a question to me whether the excitement and mutual invigoration afforded by them were not that agency in the university life of Edinburgh which gave zest and unity to the rest."

Student journalism at the University of Edinburgh began in 1823. The University Journal and Critical Review, instituted at this time, was a solid little production, full of justly critical remarks on the various deficiencies of the constitution. It continued through twelve monthly numbers. Another magazine of the same scope was published in 1831. Of greater interest to the historian are the humorous sheets which enlivened university circles at various intervals. In 1824 appeared the Lapsus Linguæ or College Tatler, a biweekly *brochure* of four pages, which contained much ephemeral cleverness and aired many university grievances. Its personalities were so pointed and its caricatures so coarse that it was threatened with actions for libel. In the year 1832 no less than three of these comic journals—the Nimmo or Almas Tawse, the Anti-Nimmo, and the University John the Giant Killer—began publication. The most famous of these light publications was the Magna (1834), a weekly sheet. Twelve numbers appeared. The editorial board formed the

Magna Club, which afterward gave itself the formidable name *Oineromathic*. It is worth noting that this club developed many of the characteristics of an American fraternity. The members wore a red ribbon across the breast, terminating in a silver triangle which bore the Greek words **ΟΙΝΟΣ ΕΡΩΣ ΜΑΘΗΣΙΣ**. Many men who afterward became famous joined the order. The club aimed to promote truth, philanthropy, and good fellowship. It was afterward called the Universal Brotherhood of the Friends of Truth.

During the last fifty years (1850–1900) forces have been at work which have essentially modified the character of Scottish student life. The general athletic movement of Great Britain and the influence of the English universities have been two powerful factors in producing the change. To-day athletics play a large and influential part in the life of the Scottish student, although as a rule less time and money are spent on amusements than is the case with their brethren of the south. The universities take part in all the games of the country and maintain a keen rivalry among themselves. Their contests, however, are by no means as famous as those between Oxford and Cambridge. An athlete of parts is sure to win for himself a favourable share of attention at any Scottish university. The students of the University of Edinburgh maintain the Rifle Company's Shooting Club, a boat club, a golf club, and a general athletic club for gymnastics, football, tennis, and cycling.

More direct efforts to promote sociability have taken two forms. In 1876 the Students' Club was founded at Edinburgh for the purpose of creating a common life which was lacking under the system of separate lodgings. This club rents a building of its own, and is a club in the usual sense of the term. It is conducted on a simple and frugal plan, merely supplying a place for

common meals and for reading newspapers and periodicals. University Hall, established largely through the
energy of Patrick Geddes, aims to create the common
life of an English college, and is conducted on co-
operative principles. The Hall consists of five or six
boarding houses, clustered in the most historic and picturesque portion of the old town. The idea of common
life takes root slowly among the Scotch, and University
Hall even now contains less than one hundred students.

A new departure of great interest to an American
observer is the Representative Councils which have
been created in the Scotch universities within the last
few years. The Representative Council is selected by
the whole body of the students annually, and is intended
as a means of communication between its constituency
and the governing body of the university. The members are afforded an opportunity to exercise themselves
in debate and to play at the work which they may be
called upon to do later. The Representative Councils
have not effected that change in academic life which
was at first hoped from them.

English influence has been nowhere stronger than
in the remodelling of the debating societies which now
tend to combine the rôle of the club with their former
functions. All the old societies of Edinburgh still exist,
and are graded in order of importance by age. The
Speculative has an entrance fee of five guineas, which
limits its membership to young advocates; the Dialectic and Diagnostic are the general debating societies
for senior students, and the Philomathic is given over
to freshmen. The literary and debating societies associate themselves together in the form of a federation.
The office of president of the associated societies is
an honorary one and held by some distinguished man,
who usually delivers an address. One of the happi-
est speeches of the Earl of Rosebery was delivered in

this capacity. The Union or associated debates are open to all members of the university, and are justly popular affairs; even a professor in evening dress occasionally condescends to defend the constitution of the country against the young lions of radicalism.

The tendency to multiply organizations, so noticeable in England and America, is not absent from Scotland. In addition to the societies we have described, the Scottish universities contain professional, musical, and philanthropic organizations. The list of professional societies at Edinburgh is much briefer than a similar list at Harvard or Pennsylvania. To the Medical, Scots Law, and Philosophical Societies, dating from an earlier period, Edinburgh has more recently added an Agricultural Discussion Society, a Chemical Society, and a Natural History Society. The marked ethical character of Scottish culture is reflected in the strength of the moral and religious associations. There are two Christian Associations in Edinburgh, a Missionary Association, and a Total Abstinence Society.

Many of the recent tendencies in Scotch student life seem to parallel those in the United States; the late growth of athletics, the general interest in debating, the attention to student self-government—all these point to a similarity of problems. As far as can be ascertained, the growth of these problems in each country has been quite independent of the other. It is to be hoped, however, that the results of Scotch student experience will before long be placed before the American reader much more in detail.

CHAPTER II.

PREVIOUS to the American Revolution, nine colleges of high learning were founded in the English colonies of North America. Of these, only three—Harvard, William and Mary, and Yale—dated their existence from a period previous to the middle of the eighteenth century; the six late foundations—Dartmouth, Brown, Kings (now Columbia), Rutgers, Pennsylvania, and Princeton—with the exception of the last of the series, had no opportunity to develop an independent student life. Our study must in consequence be limited to the records of three or four colleges, which records have been by no means thoroughly explored and exploited by the special students of the subject.

The colonial colleges were established by graduates of the English universities who intended to reproduce the conditions of Oxford and Cambridge. To a considerable extent they succeeded. From their English models, Harvard and Yale inherited a strong ecclesiastical bias, a curriculum tinged with scholasticism and a system of almost monastic common life and discipline. But the conditions of life in a new country made any duplication of or even approach to the English university system an impossibility. The Oxford or Cambridge college was a unit in a larger whole, the university; Harvard, Yale, and William and Mary were isolated institutions. The English college was the product of centuries of growth; it was largely governed by tradition, and frequently possessed great wealth. The colonial colleges were poor and in close dependence on the community; the Church controlled them and the State supported them. Their intellectual environment possessed few of the resources of an older country and limited the range of their activity. The colonists were involved in a hand-to-hand contest with Nature which absorbed their energies. Europe was far away, and communication with the other colonial centres dangerous and uncertain; men were self-centred, their horizon was narrow; fighting Indians and planning settlements left no leisure for the free play of speculation. But for the dominant theological interests there would have been no colleges until the middle of the eighteenth century. Under existing conditions practical interests necessarily predominated; the colleges were little more than schools for training clergymen. The disinterested love of learning, the atmosphere of criticism and discussion which were not wholly absent from Oxford and Cambridge in the most degenerate decades of the eighteenth century, could not be found at Harvard or Yale until nearly the end of the period.

Our first glimpses into the social life of the students discover a dreary round of fast days, early chapels, severe punishments, and bad board; the students seem to be mere boys and are treated as such. As the eighteenth century advances the signs of restlessness begin to make their appearance, and gradually a change in morals and manners takes place. Profane cursing and swearing, the frequenting of taverns and alehouses, the custom of keeping wine, beer, and distilled liquors in college rooms, all increased, to the sorrow of the governing authorities. Tutors were insulted and unlawful combinations against the college government were frequent. Laws were made, penalties inflicted, and re-

monstrances repeated without eradicating these evils or
even materially diminishing them.*

Student excesses culminated during Commencement
week. In 1693 the Harvard authorities warned the
students against the dangers of an oversupply of plum
cake. Nearly thirty years later (1722) a law was
passed to the effect that no plum cake, roasted, boiled,
or baked meats or pies should be made by any " com-
mencer." Distilled liquors were likewise forbidden.
During the eighteenth century Commencement became
more and more a public occasion; it was flocked to by
graduates and visitors from every section of the colony.
A procession of official worthies from Boston, headed by
the royal governor of the province, lent pomp and dignity to the affair. At no other time was such an assemblage of wealth, dignity, and beauty brought together.
There was great difficulty in maintaining order, and dis-
graceful scenes sometimes occurred on the Common.†

The first form of student association to come into
being was the class which was for many years the accepted unit of college life before it possessed any formal
organization. Being for many years an almost uncon-
scious product of surrounding influences, few records
of its early history remain. The early laws of Harvard
(1647) recognise the class, not as a social organization,
but as a scholastic division for teaching purposes.‡

---

* Quincy, J. History of Harvard University, vol. ii, p. 90.

† Accounts of Commencement will be found in the following
monographs : Northrop, Cyrus. Commencement (at Yale), Yale
Book, vol. i, p. 366. Quincy, Edmund. Commencement Day (at
Harvard), Harvard Book, vol. ii, p. 147. Todd, Henry Alfred.
Commencement Day (at Princeton), Princeton Book, p. 169.

‡ For those unfamiliar with American college usage it may
be well to state that the class consists of all those students who,
in the natural course of events, will graduate in a given year.
The class is known by the year of its graduation, as, for instance,

The employment of the word in these two diverse signi-
fications has led to much confusion. It is evident that
the social organization was an outgrowth of the scholastic division, but even the approximate date of its appearance can not be given. We know that by 1725 at
Harvard, and 1745 at Yale, the members of classes were
ranked according to the social position of their fathers,
a usage which points to the existence of the class as a
recognised student institution.* Class day was not included in the programme of Commencement week at
Harvard until 1760. Previous to this date the seniors
met informally and chose one of the members to
bid farewell to the college and faculty in a valedictory
address. The early class-day programmes consisted of a
" Latin oration sandwiched in between two prayers." †
The list of class orators did not begin until 1776, the
poets not until 1786. It is probable that the class as
a social unit existed as early as the beginning of the
eighteenth century.

The distinction between men of different years was
made at the English universities; ‡ the terms freshman
and sophister (sophomore) were in use there, but the
tutorial system of instruction, and the existence of a
large number of colleges which served as social units,
prevented these distinctions from assuming importance.
The class association was the product of the conditions

the class of 1895 which would enter college in 1891. Each year
of the college course has its name, the first being known as the
Freshman, the second as the Sophomore, the third as the Junior,
and the fourth as the Senior. For many years during the early
period every student necessarily belonged to some class.

* F. B. Dexter. On Some Social Distinctions at Harvard and
Yale before the Revolution, in the Proceedings of the American
Antiquarian Society, Worcester, 1894.

† James Russell Lowell. Class Day, Harvard Book, vol. ii.

‡ Masson, David. Life of Milton, vol. i.

of early colonial life. The most important factors in
its development in the order of their importance were
(1) the recitation method of instruction, (2) the freshman laws, (3) the system of common life, and (4) the
gulf between professor and student.

It was evidently the design of the founders of Harvard to reproduce the form of instruction of a Cambridge college. In many respects such a duplication
was impossible. The poverty of the colonists reacted
on the methods employed in teaching. The resources
for the establishment of fellowships and tutorships of
the English type were wanting; the names persisted,
but the institutions perished. Instead of personal tutors and university lectureships, economy dictated the
formation of a uniform course of study which in turn
led to the adoption of the recitation method of instruction, which was the prime factor in developing the class
as a social institution. The men of the same year re-
cited together during their entire residence of four
years, which naturally gave rise to a strong tie of association.

The so-called " Freshman Laws " were another
strong force in producing class feeling. By this unique
code the first-year students were consigned to a form
of servitude similar to the fagging of the English
public schools. The sophomores tutored the freshmen
and instructed them in the manners of the college.
The freshmen were to run errands for all the upper
classes, and, in some instances, particular freshmen
were assigned to college dignitaries. We find references to president's freshmen and tutor's freshmen.
In connection with their employment, a curious hierarchy of privilege developed itself. A tutor could take
a freshman from a fellow, a fellow's rights were superior to those of a senior sophister, a senior sophister's to a junior sophister's, and a junior sophister's to

a sophomore's.   The freshmen had collective duties, one of which was to supply the upper classes with balls and bats on the playing field.*

A rigid ceremonial of the Spanish-Bourbon type was instituted.   The freshmen must take off their hats on the approach of an instructor or upper classman; they must also pause on the approach of one of their superiors.   The laws interdicted all impertinence on the part of the novice.   He was not allowed to rap on the doors of the upper classmen or to play with them. He belonged to a separate and inferior caste.

The Freshman Laws were in force in a number of colleges until the opening years of the nineteenth century.   While Princeton led the way in their abolition by a resolution of the faculty in 1767,† they remained fixed at Dartmouth ‡ until 1797, and at Yale and Middlebury until 1804.   Harvard # abolished the code previous to the Revolution, but so strong was the outcry against this curtailment of privilege that the laws were again established.‖   Their significance in the evo-

---

* The Freshman Laws of Harvard are published in an appendix to Josiah Quincy's History of Harvard University, vol. ii, p. 541, and in B. H. Hall's A Collection of College Words and Customs, pp. 213, 223.   An excellent abridgment is found in B. C. Steiner's History of Higher Education in Connecticut, p. 111.

† McClean, J.   History of the College of New Jersey, vol. i, p. 298.

‡ Hall, B. H.   A Collection of College Words and Customs, p. 225.

Quincy, J.   The History of Harvard University, vol. ii.

‖ Anomalous as these rules, sanctioned by the highest governing body, appear to us, they were entirely in accord with the educational traditions of that age.   Indeed, we find similar codes in the institutions of continental Europe, dating in their origin from the middle ages.   As we have already seen (Chapter I), the worst excesses of pennalism in the German universities were occasioned by regulations almost identical in theory with those

lution of the class system was twofold. As we have already indicated, they fostered a strong class feeling by segregating the freshmen at the outset of their career. Scarcely less important was the degeneration of the tutoring and instructing of freshmen into rough horseplay, and finally into the hazing and rushing of the modern period. The Freshman Laws contained in germ all the abuse to which first-year men have since been subjected.

A third influence were the common meals and dormitory life which belonged to all the colleges of the eighteenth century. The common life was jointly the product of English precedent and the necessities of a new settlement where dwelling houses were at a premium. Just what part this factor played in the formation of the class is now difficult to determine. It made some strong form of association inevitable, without determining to any considerable extent what that form should be.*

The conditions of discipline, particularly the relation between professor and student, likewise made for some strong form of association. Indeed, it is with considerable difficulty that the college graduate of to-day comprehends the relations between the two elements in the eighteenth-century college. Like its English prototype, the colonial college was pervaded with a strong ecclesiastical flavour. Many of its regulations were those of a theological seminary. Prayers were read twice each day, usually at unreasonable hours.

---

we have just described. Relics of similar customs have survived in the English colleges until the last generation. The *ateliers* of Paris have to-day their rough ordeal for the newcomer, although it apparently rests on a recent tradition.

* For an account of the part played by the Commons, see Butler, Daniel. Commons (at Yale), Yale Book, vol. i, p. 297. Hall, B. H. Commons (at Harvard), Harvard Book, vol. ii, p. 75.

As a literary exercise, the students were compelled to summarize the previous Sunday's sermon. Much of the time during the senior year was expended on large quartos treating of divinity. Blasphemy and the diffusion of irreligion were the most heinous of crimes. The professors' chairs were usually filled by clergymen, and the presidents were uniformly ecclesiastics. The factional contests over the management of the colleges were nearly always founded on theological differences. New colleges were established for the same reason. Yale was a protest against the doctrinal laxity of Harvard, Dartmouth an embodiment of evangelical distrust of Yale formalism, Brown represented the Baptists, Kings (Columbia) the Episcopalians, Princeton the Presbyterians.

As a result of this predominant ecclesiastical bias one would expect a certain austerity and rigour of discipline. The long list of regulations and penalties which one discovers far surpasses expectation in this respect. Rules dealing with every possible variation of conduct were drawn up, with lists of fines attached. The Harvard laws enumerated eighty-three separate offences.* Most amusements were forbidden. The students could not hunt or go sailing without permission, at New Haven. Theatrical performances, billiards, cards, and dice were on the black list. A student might not lie down on his own bed in daytime nor spend his own money without first securing the consent of the authorities. He was strictly prohibited from leaving his own room except at certain specified hours, and was never permitted to attend elections or mingle with the citizens. The teaching force of the

---

* Josiah Quincy. History of Harvard University, vol. i, p. 515; the appendix contains a reprint of the Harvard laws. A digest of the Yale code is given in B. C. Steiner's History of Education in Connecticut.

college did police and detective service in discovering and punishing all violations of this code.

During the later colonial period the class bond was a close one.   Class activity showed itself in annual football games and wrestling matches, and occasionally in rebellions against the college government.   There was as yet no thought of formal organization, although the institution of class-day orators opened the way for the election of temporary officials.

The debating society,* both within and without academic precincts, was largely an outgrowth of that great enlightening movement of the eighteenth century, known in Germany as the *Aufklärung*.   The marked characteristics of the Aufklärung was its tendency to submit all problems to the test of reason.   The world and its inhabitants were to be judged from the standpoint of pure intellect.   Knowledge and discussion were exalted above the will and the feelings.†   Such a creed could not but stimulate popular discussion, for it was directed not to select groups of specialists, but to the drawing-rooms and average common sense.   In its home the Aufklärung led to the formation of numerous acad-

---

* Unlike the class association, which is national in its origin, the debating society has a racial basis.   If a distinction is made between the debating society and clubs, having in view some definite policy of revolutionary propaganda, we find that the former class is largely confined to peoples of an Anglo-Saxon origin.   They are a testimonial to the strength of representative government and parliamentary discussion, and indicate the dominant interest in politics which has characterized the English race for the last three centuries.   The debating society also indicates the nature of the Anglo-Saxon political interest, which has been concentrated less on international complications and military achievement and more on the adjustment of the relations between the individual and society.

† For a characterization of the Aufklärung, see H. A. Taine, Ancient Régime, Book III ; John Morley, Voltaire.

emies which discussed all subjects, from scientific agriculture to thè existence of a God. In England it strengthened the various royal societies, re-enforced the club movement, and later originated different schemes for diffusing knowledge among the masses. The soil of America was prepared for the new stimulus. The conditions of frontier life favouring versatility and individual initiative and capacity and the strength of local institutions, both political and ecclesiastical, all aided the rapid growth of free discussion. During the latter half of the Puritan period we find self-improvement societies * which soon expanded along general culture lines. These organizations, however, were local and scattered, of necessity, because of the physical conditions of settlement. It remained for the first half of the nineteenth century to organize these isolated attempts in the Lyceum movement.

The universities could not long escape the contagion of the new ideas. At Oxford and Cambridge, debating clubs, the forerunners of the modern unions, were being slowly evolved from associations purely social in character.† The Speculative Society of the University of Edinburgh, renowned for its great names, dates from 1764, while the Historical Society of Dublin was an earlier growth.‡ Thus far no evidence has come to light bearing on the relations between these societies and the early organizations of Yale, Princeton, and Harvard. They are simply mentioned here as one of the phenomena of the eighteenth century.

In addition to the general movement of the Aufklärung, which in itself was probably sufficient to account

---

* Thorpe, F. N. Benjamin Franklin and the University of Pennsylvania, p. 20.

† See Chapter I for an account of these societies.

‡ Stubbs, J. W. History of the University of Dublin from its Foundation to the Beginning of the Nineteenth Century.

for the existence of the American debating societies, there are other conditions which strengthened the initial impulse and to a certain extent determined the direction which it should take.

The first and most important factor in the environment was the political activity of the colonists. Together with religion, politics formed the chief culture interest of the people. The debates in the assemblies, the contests with the royal governors, the large degree of authority accorded the localities, all these tended to foster a lively interest in public affairs—an interest not confined to a capital or to a single class in society, but equally diffused throughout the community. The churches, both established and dissenting, were an additional source of culture to the people. The meagreness of the press, the cost of books, the absence of theatres and other facilities for amusement, gave the platform and pulpit a culture significance which they have since lost with the increasing complexity of civilization.

The dominance of the speech and the sermon was recognised by the educational institutions. Syllogistic disputes, one of the common modes of instruction during the middle ages, still survived in the colleges of the eighteenth century. The curricula and Commencement programmes of that period present a strange and almost grotesque jumble of the mediæval and modern, of Puritan theology and French rationalism. At the same Commencement disputes of the old type, as " *Materia cogitare non potest*," are found side by side with debates on the " Expediency of the Americans in their Present State becoming an Independent State," and orations " Concerning oratorical Art and Benevolence." *

---

* From a newspaper account of a Commencement, transcribed in Tolman. W. H., History of Higher Education in Rhode Island. p. 102.

Systematic instruction in both syllogistic and forensic disputation was offered in the colleges. By the Yale curriculum of 1755 syllogistic disputations fell to all. Seven years later it is recorded that the two upper classes disputed syllogistically Mondays, and on Tuesdays spoke forensically upon the issue involved in the problem " Whether Adam knew that eternal damnation would be his doom if he did eat the forbidden fruit." *

At Princeton, the authorities arranged a systematic course. Preparatory instruction was given to the three lower classes, who practised declamations of their own composing. The seniors, who received the largest share of attention, appeared in a series of disputations on natural and revealed religion which were delivered on Sunday " before a promiscuous assembly." This practice was intended to habituate them to face an audience, and was also found conducive to religious ends. Secular oratory was represented by a monthly oration of their own composing, which was critically examined by a member of the faculty in regard to spelling, punctuation, and the use of figures of speech.†

With such an interest in public speaking, debating societies could not be long appearing. The date of the formation of the first society, and even the names of the early clubs can not be given because of the disappearance of the records. This omission is not a matter of high importance because we possess full accounts of their proceedings shortly after they became prominent. A much more serious gap in our knowledge, as we have already indicated, is the inability to ascertain their relations to similar organizations in Great Britain.

The earliest society, the record of which has been

---

* Steiner, B. C.   History of Education in Connecticut, p. 112.

† McClean, J.   History of the College of New Jersey, vol. i, p. 267.

preserved, was the Crotonian Society of Yale, which had a brief existence and made way for Linonia, the oldest permanent society, and the Brothers in Unity (1768).* Contemporaneous with Crotonia and Linonia at Yale, were the Plain-Dealing and Well-Meaning Clubs of Princeton. A fierce rivalry, involving the interchange of scurrilous pamphlets, led to their suppression by the faculty. A year after this action, were founded the American Whig and Cliosophic Societies, the most venerable and powerful of college debating clubs in America, and the only organizations of this early period which still survive in their original capacity.†

During the middle decades of the eighteenth century the Harvard faculty took particular pains to improve the public speaking of the students, a move which led to the foundation of speaking clubs. The Calabogus Club was organized as early as 1758; the Whitefield Club in 1759. We are left to conjecture the programmes of these early societies. The Institute, of 1770, the most famous of the debating clubs of Harvard, was founded by John Phillips, John Warren, and other members of the class of 1771. In 1773 the Mercurian, another important speaking club, united with the Institute, and gave it a position of primacy. Among the subjects for orations during the pre-Revolutionary period we note " The Odiousness of Envy " and " The Pernicious Habit of drinking Tea." ‡

* Coes, E. B. The Literary Societies (of Yale), Yale Book, vol. i, p. 307.

† Cameron, H. C. The American Whig Society, Princeton Book, p. 184. Jacobus, M. W. The Cliosophic Society, Princeton Book, p. 201. These two sketches are condensed and popularized by G. R. Wallace in his Princeton Sketches, p. 54.

‡ Thayer, W. R. History of Harvard University, p. 77, in Hurd's History of Middlesex County, vol. i. Peabody, F. G. The Institute of 1770, in Harvard Book, vol. ii, p. 341.

The literary exercises of these early societies covered a wide range of territory, and lacked the dominant political bias of the post-Revolutionary period. Theological issues, mathematical problems, and even acrostics and puzzles found a place. Some of the typical questions for discussion were the following: To extract the square root of $\frac{16}{99}$.—Why is the weather coldest when the sun is nearest us?—Can finite Nature commit infinite sin?—Is God the author of sin?—Does the soul always think?—Was the flood universal? Ought the slave trade to be abolished?—Is a tax on hogs politic? *

No small portion of energy was expended on dramatic entertainments, which often incurred the suspicion of the faculty. These plays were usually light in character and along the lines of the modern farce. The exhibitions were popular and the prominent college characters took part in them. Nathan Hale, of Revolutionary fame, and James Hillhouse, played in a performance called " The Beaux' Stratagems." On another occasion a musical dialogue was sung by two prominent members of the college in the parts of Damon and Clara.†

---

* Coes, E. B. The Literary Societies of Yale, Yale Book, vol. i, p. 311.

† Idem., p. 312.

CHAPTER III.

STUDENT LIFE IN AMERICA DURING THE REVOLUTIONARY PERIOD, 1775–1840.

§ 1. THE CLASS IN THE REVOLUTIONARY PERIOD.

OWING to the lack of authorities, no attempt was made in the preceding chapter to describe in detail the activities of the class during the colonial period. It is probable that much which we are about to describe concerning its activities during the Revolutionary period applies to the earlier conditions as well.

As we have before indicated, the old theory of discipline, by which the college faculty was entitled to exercise a parental supervision over the students, had a determining effect on the direction which the activity of that organization took in its after-career. The professors and tutors were not only instructors, but also policemen and night watchmen. They were in duty bound to capture and punish all rebels against the severe college discipline of the time. This led to most unfortunate results.

One writer testifies that no small proportion of the breaches of the peace had for their sole object the drawing out of this somewhat grotesque posse, whose manœuvres around a bonfire were wont to elicit shouts of laughter and applause of the authors, whom they strove in vain to discover.* The college buildings of

---

* A. P. Peabody, in Harvard Register, February, 1880.

that period, unlike the quadrangles of the English universities, were not designed with a view to discipline, and their open and isolated position made the detection of disorder difficult.* The immediate control of the dormitories was in the hands of the tutors, who were oftentimes overcome with the dignity of their station but inexperienced in dealing with men.† Ineffectual as this supervision was from a disciplinary standpoint, it promoted friction between teacher and student, and prevented the professors from exercising the influence due their station.‡

As a result of the system outlined above, the students considered the faculty their natural enemies. There existed between the two parties little kindly intercourse, and that little was in secret. If a student went unsummoned to a teacher's room, it was nearly always by night. A class looked with contempt on any of its members who should enter a recitation room before the ringing of the bell, or remain after the close of a recitation to ask a question.⁎ So strong was this feeling of antagonism to the faculty, that the students who obeyed the regulations and attempted to be on friendly terms with their instructors were given opprobrious nicknames, the most common of which were Blues, Blue Skins, and Blue Lights.‖ At Harvard they were known as Fishers and Piscatorians. A man was accused of " fishing " often on the slightest pretext. Any stu-

---

* Wayland, F. Thoughts on the Present Collegiate System.

† Reminiscences of Scenes and Characters in College, by a Graduate of Yale, Class of 1821, p. 133.

‡ Quincy, J. P. Coercion in the Later Stages of Education, Old and New, vol. viii, p. 47.

⁎ Peabody, A. P., in Harvard Register, February, 1880, quoted in Bush, p. 190.

‖ Hall, B. H. College Words and Customs, pp. 30, 31. Cutting, George A. Student Life at Amherst, p. 132.

dent who showed lively interest in his studies, or was unusually courteous to his instructors, or who refused to join in some general disorder, was open to suspicion. To furnish the faculty with information concerning any prank or violation of the statutes was the most heinous crime a collegian could commit, and the bare suspicion of it subjected a man to social ostracism.* A member of the faculty who attempted to be on friendly terms with the students was likely to discover that his kindly efforts were misconstrued, and that he was being regarded with special fear as a spy.†

The factors which we have enumerated—viz., the recitation method of instruction, the Freshman Laws, the college dormitory, and the antagonism between faculty and students—produced a vigorous common life and *esprit du corps* early in academic history. By the beginning of the eighteenth century the class was recognised as a fully developed social institution. It was without formal constitution, and its only officials, with one or two exceptions, were the officers chosen just before graduation to officiate at the class exercises. The place and functions of the class in student life remained approximately the same during the purely college period of American superior instruction—that is, from the eighteenth century to 1870, when the university idea began to be influential. Without further introduction of a historical nature, we shall attempt to describe the different activities in which it played a part.

First in importance come the relations of the classes with each other. From the middle ages to the modern art school it has been customary to subject the new student to some form of initiation. The tendency was

---

* Peabody, A. P. Harvard Reminiscences, p. 188.
† Ibid., p. 137.

7

embodied in the old Freshman Laws, and their disuse opened the way for numerous perversions. We shall describe these perversions under the general term of " hazing," making our usage of the term clear as we proceed. Hazing may be defined as the process of persecution to which the freshmen are subjected by the sophomores. Hazing shades off by slight degrees to the mere practical joke. During the first month at college the freshman found himself the victim of numerous annoying customs. He was jeered at as he went by on his way to recitations, and returned to find his lamp wicks removed, and his bed and belongings piled in the centre of the campus.* His property was at the mercy of the upper classmen. The more valuable possessions were usually surreptitiously returned after a season, but his catalogue and umbrella, his pipes and tobacco, neckties and towels, remained in other hands.† His room was liable to invasion at all hours, and his person and belongings formed the means of amusing his tormentors.

Such annoyances as these formed the prelude of more elaborate customs, one of the most common of which was known as " smoking out." A band of sophomores seizing a room, would close the windows, cover up the keyhole, and endeavour to sicken their victim by the density of the tobacco smoke. While waiting for the process to be effectual, the freshman would be compelled to scan Euclid or a Greek grammar, make speeches, sing songs, dance, recite the alphabet backward, or perform any other nonsensical action that the ingenuity of his persecutors could suggest.‡ If he proved obstinate or unwilling, the sophomores would throw a blanket over his head and blow tobacco smoke

---

* Cutting, G. A. Student Life at Amherst, p. 123.

† Bagg, L. H. Four Years at Yale, by a Graduate of '69, p. 252.

‡ Ibid., p. 250.

up under it until he was either stifled or sick. At the University of Vermont a pumpkin was taken, a portion of the top cut away, and the interior filled with fine-cut tobacco. It was then placed on the freshman's table and fire blown into it. After the fire died away and the room was filled with smoke, the sophomores put the freshman to bed, with the pumpkin for a nightcap.*

Another custom, essentially different, was observed at the University of Virginia, and known as " initiation." The freshmen were prepared for societies which had no existence by a peculiar process. The newcomers were compelled to give a written list, tested under oath of the entire number of their shirts and other necessary articles of wardrobe. This list they were to commit to memory and pass an examination upon, which was usually accomplished with due satisfaction. Then the freshmen are remanded to their rooms, where they are kept awake by a hideous discord of horns, tin pans, and horse fiddles, made under their windows. About two hours before dawn they are taken out one by one. Each freshman is taken in tow by a group of upper classmen, led around through the dark, and finally left in a lecture room, where he is told to ring for whatever he wants, either hot biscuits or coffee, but forbidden to leave the room without an express order from the faculty. His stay is proportioned to his knowledge of the world.†

" Tutoring freshmen " at Yale, a somewhat similar performance, had for its basis a burlesque on the old custom of " instructing freshmen." Great pomp and solemnity were observed on this occasion. The sophomore who acted as chairman wore a powdered wig of venerable aspect, and his desk rested on a pile of huge Hebrew folios. After the freshmen have been duly impressed by

* Hall, B. H. College Words and Customs, p. 435.
† Ibid., p. 265.

the affected seriousness of the scene, the chairman in eloquent and pathetic language describes the temptations of a great city and the thorns and dangers to which a novice is exposed, and the vortex of ruin into which, if he walks unwarily, the newcomer will be plunged. Then, reversing the picture, the orator fires the youthful ambition with glowing descriptions of the honours which await the successful, and opens to eager view the dazzling prospect of college fame.*

" Salting the freshmen," at Dartmouth, consisted in placing salt and water on their seats in chapel. These elements were symbolical of cleanliness, preservation, and health. Custom at Bowdoin substituted molasses for the salt and water.†

While the tricks and customs enumerated above were commonly spoken of in a loose way as hazing, they must not be confounded with hazing proper, which was a much more serious and cold-blooded affair. Some individual among the freshmen, odious to the sophomores, either from conceit, strength, or obstinacy, was singled out by a self-appointed committee, waited upon, gagged, blindfolded, and rendered helpless. He was then hurried away to some desolate locality, where various indignities were practised upon him. His hair was commonly cut off and his body branded with indelible ink or smeared with paint. At Harvard he was sometimes placed in a barrel in the river Charles. In colleges not so conveniently situated to streams, the vicitim was put under a pump for a considerable period. In cases of extreme hazing unmentionable indignities were perpetrated.‡ From the necessities of the case such deeds

---

* Hall, B. H.   College Words and Customs, p. 468.

† Ibid., p. 399.

‡ McCosh.   Discipline in American Colleges, North American Review, vol. cxxvi, p. 439.

were performed at night. When the process was completed, the freshman was left half clothed with a gag in his mouth, and his hands bound behind him, or else would be dropped in a cemetery where he would be compelled to wait until morning, when the gates opened.

To the credit of American studenthood be it said that on an average not more than two or three such affairs occurred each year in a typical college, and in these cases the students who suffered brought the punishment on themselves in a majority of cases by some foolhardy boast or deed. On the other side, the number of sophomores who engaged in hazing of the type described above was never very large—probably not more than a dozen in a class of seventy-five or eighty. The majority, however, made only a passive opposition to the practice. The evil doers did not suffer in the estimation of their classmates, but on the other hand were often elected to the highest offices. The hazing was not always done by a self-constituted committee. Occasionally a secret tribunal, descending from class to class, added the terrors of mystery to those of violence. Yale possessed such an institution, which was known as the Court of the Areopagus. It published a list of officers abounding in strange names and titles. The decrees of the court were executed by two judices, three accusators, four lictors, and four carnifices. They assumed names formed by odd-looking combinations of letters, like Nchokotsa, Mochoasele, Kantankruss, or Phreshietaugh. The list was printed in heavy black type, and surrounded by mourning rules.*

The governing boards of the various colleges tried to extirpate hazing, but without success. Public senti-

---

* Bagg, L. H. Four Years at Yale, by a Graduate of '69, pp. 308, 309.

ment among the students condemned the man who gave information to the faculty, and there was no other means of obtaining information. The students defended hazing on the ground that it was the only available method of disciplining conceited freshmen. The real reason for its maintenance lay rather in the conservatism and reverence for tradition which marks the earliest period of youth. That freshmen had always been hazed seemed sufficient cause why hazing should be continued. The desire to have smart stories to tell to classmates and in public had a marked influence in perpetuating the custom.*

The " rush " differed from " hazing " in being a free and open fight, in which the two sides were almost equally matched. It took place on leaving prayers at chapel where the freshmen came out first and the higher classes in the rear crowded them, pushing and " rushing " them until a fight arose. Sometimes it also occurred in other places. From this primitive free fight was developed in time an organized formal conflict or match game, taking place on an open field under fixed conditions, and resulting from a challenge sent from one side to the other.† The rush had been preceded by the wrestling matches which occurred between college classes during the eighteenth century. At Harvard it was the sophomores who challenged the freshmen. If the second-year men were defeated, the juniors threw down the gauntlet, and, in case of their failure, the seniors. The class of 1796 at Harvard abolished this custom.‡ The football game, annually played between the freshmen and sophomores, resem-

---

* Edward Hitchcock. Reminiscences of Amherst College, p. 335.

† Jordan, D. S. College Discipline, North American Review, vol. clxv, p. 403.

‡ Hall, B. H. College Words and Customs, p. 498.

bled a rush much more than the modern game of that name.

The majority of the rushes of the period belonged to the casual rough-and-tumble category. An excellent description of one of these encounters is contained in Cutting's Student Life at Amherst,* the main features of which will be here given. This rush was caused by a misunderstanding concerning the ownership of a squirt gun which the class of 1861 proposed to bury. The burial itself was intended to symbolize amity and friendship, as the class in question had decided to discontinue hazing. The juniors, from whom the sophomores had stolen the squirt gun, tried to recover it while the sophomores were at dinner. The juniors broke in the panels of the door and cut through the plastering of the room which contained the prize, but were held at bay by a few guards with pistols. The sophomores, hearing the noise, attempted to rescue their imperilled guards by ascending the stairs. The juniors forthwith chopped away the stairs and armed themselves with the timbers. A series of hot hand-to-hand encounters ensued, in which the sophomores were victorious. They steadily fought their way up the stairs, wrested the clubs away from their antagonists, and dragged them by their legs downstairs. At the moment of success the president of the college interfered. Many sore heads and bruised limbs resulted from this fray. In the annals of every American college there are to be found records of numerous fights, very similar in general features to the foregoing.

The regularly organized rush was not without its representatives during this period, particularly in the larger colleges. In the freshman-sophomore rush at Yale each party formed a solid mass with its heaviest

---

* Cutting, G. A. Student Life at Amherst College, p. 131.

men in front. When the formation was completed the mass rushed toward its opponents and endeavoured to push them out of the building, or sweep them from the walks and street, to go through them, break up their ranks and disorganize them generally. The rush itself presents a scene of a seething, struggling mass of men, shoving, crushing, trampling one another, snatching caps, tearing clothes, and fighting for dear life to work their way through the opposing mass with some show of unbroken ranks. After the first onset the parties draw off and go through the process again. The contest usually results in a draw. The " banger rush," at the same institution, was a more satisfactory affair. The freshmen provide themselves with three or four strong canes known as bangers, which they place in the hands of their strongest members; the entire class surrounds the champions in a close, compact mass, which the sophomores must penetrate and wrest the clubs away.[*]

The University of Pennsylvania developed a unique form of rushing, known as the " bowl fight." The sophomores are given a certain number of minutes to place in a great wooden bowl, which they have prepared for the occasion, the lowest honour-man in the freshman class. Should the freshmen succeed in holding their bowlman from the hands of the sophomores until time is called, they then struggle to break the bowl. The bowl fight took place in the public street, and the police and " muckers," as the residents of West Philadelphia were called, participated in the fray. The conflict is described as a wild scene.[†]

---

[*] Bagg, L. H. Four Years at Yale, by a Graduate of '69, pp. 256, 257.

[†] Levin, J. S. Undergraduate Life in Thorpe's Benjamin Franklin and the University of Pennsylvania, p. 408.

The students of Princeton have likewise shown considerable originality in devising modes of rivalry. At the beginning of a term it is customary for the lower classes to placard the town with posters taunting their rivals and challenging them to fight. Some of these proclamations are large enough to be seen at a distance of five miles. The opposition must tear the posters down, and numerous rushes result. The men are sometimes impelled against each other with such force that the front ranks are actually lifted in the air by the shock. The " cane spree " is another Princeton institution. The freshmen appear in front of the post office with canes, which the sophomores " grab." A series of contests are then arranged for, the juniors acting as seconds for the freshmen, and the seniors acting in the same capacity for the sophomores. The seconds arrange conflicts between men of equal strength and weight. The men are sometimes coached for weeks. On the first moonlight night in September or early October the groups come together for a series of encounters. Statistics of the canes captured are collated. If the freshmen win, they are allowed to carry canes.*

As to the general utility and results of hazing and rushing, the opinion of the outside public and the student public differed materially. To the student the danger attendant upon interclass rivalry only added spice and zest to college life. It was the common hardships and persecutions of the freshman year which knit the members together in the common bond of fellowship, and gave that air of adventure and risk which made the college something more sacred than merely an institution for instruction. In the memoirs and reminiscences of college life no element is more emphasized than the

---

* Alexander. Undergraduate Life at Princeton, Scribner's Magazine, vol. xxi, p. 663.

charm which this rough apprenticeship lent to undergraduate life. The ordinary citizen saw the problem in
an altogether different light. Usages so rough that
they would not for a moment be tolerated elsewhere
continued to flourish in institutions which were expected to send forth the intellectual leaders of the
next generation. It was claimed that hazing and rushing brutalized the students. Dark stories of wrecked
careers and ruined constitutions found their way into
print. While there was undoubtedly much of exaggeration in this view, there were certainly many facts which
supported it. Hazing undoubtedly terrorized and made
miserable the lives of the more timid freshmen. It is
difficult now from the evidence at hand to estimate just
how much physical injury was wrought by these customs, because it was to the interest of all parties concerned in such affairs to keep the evidence below the
surface. If we take the stories of undergraduate life
which have come down to us as the criterion, the damage
must have been considerable. The writer, however, has
been able to collect only a few authentic cases of serious
injury. Hitchcock * and Peabody,† in their reminiscences, both refer to cases of fatal illness occasioned by
hazing.*

By no means all the surplus combative energy of
the undergraduate was devoted to internal contests.
The governing boards of the colleges were often a target
for student opposition. The rigid discipline of the
period and the antagonism between faculty and students
have been previously referred to, but the active reaction
of the students has yet to be treated of. In the follow-

* Hitchcock, Edward. Reminiscences of Amherst College,
p. 334.

† Peabody, A. P. Harvard Reminiscences, p. 32.

‡ For record of a tragic case, see Powell, L. P., History of
Education in Delaware, p. 118.

ing paragraphs an endeavour will be made to present the most important conditions.

It must not be forgotten that the national manners of a half century ago were essentially those of a frontier people—rude, boisterous, and over-assertive; yet we hardly expect to find that, at Harvard, outrages involving not only a large destruction of property, but even peril to life—as, for instance, the blowing up of public buildings with inhabited rooms—occurred every year.* The undergraduates of Yale celebrated Christmas by smashing the windows of the college buildings and barring the doors so fast that the professors were compelled to smash them in with an axe. Incidentally the lamps were filled with water, the president's house painted red, white, and blue, and a cow placed on the top floor of the dormitory.† Whether at home or among the Northern colleges, the Southern students possessed the greatest aptitude for violence and the most daring in carrying their plans into execution. The chief staple of college annals in the Southern colleges was furnished by the incidents of innumerable petty outrages on the part of the students which the faculty attempted (usually without result) to punish. The historian of Delaware College records numerous expulsions for such offences as overturning stoves, breaking windows, thievery, drunkenness, and personal assault on members of the faculty.‡ The students of South Carolina College seem to have indulged in violence more systematically than their contemporaries. At night it was a common occurrence for the students to disguise themselves, paint their faces black, and ride across the college yard

---

* Peabody, A. P. Harvard Reminiscences, p. 45.

† Steiner, B. C. History of Education in Connecticut, pp. 163, 164.

‡ Powell, L. P. History of Education in Delaware, pp. 96, 97.

shouting and sounding horns. To get drunk and dis-
tribute free whisky at the well on the college campus
and go roaming around breaking windows and stoning
professors' houses seem to have been quite common oc-
currences. The professors were sometimes called liars
to their faces.*

It is not with this general violence that we are
mainly concerned at the present juncture, but with the
rebellions which occurred from time to time against the
regulations of the faculty. These rebellions were not
usually accompanied by acts of violence, but took more
the form of strikes or boycotts. One of the most common grievances on the part of the students was in the
quality and quantity of food served in the college commons. We have reliable authority that the rations were
unusually bad. One graduate considered the board furnished at Yale as absolutely destructive of health. The
ordinary breakfast consisted of a dish known as " slum,"
which was composed of the remains of yesterday's boiled
salt beef and potatoes, hashed up and fried in a frying
pan.†

Another frequent cause of dissension was in the distribution of Commencement honours. It is difficult for
a modern student to realize the value attached to a part
fifty years ago. In many ways it was considered the
test of a man's success in his college career. It was
no pleasant occasion when the disappointed student saw
flowers showered upon his successful rival, while he was
compelled to take his diploma in silence. Since the appointments depended on the individual judgment of the
professors, the cry of injustice could always be raised.
The spirit of rebellion is therefore rife in college about

* Meriwether, Colyer. History of Education in South
Carolina.

† Reminiscences of Scenes and Characters in College, by a
Graduate of Yale, Class of 1821, p. 117.

Commencement time, so that if any event should turn up they could form a nucleus of opposition, rebellious feeling could easily crystallize about it.*

Any sudden change in the curriculum or methods of instruction might be the occasion of a revolt. The students were obstinately opposed to an innovation which might signify increased study. In 1790 a public examination was instituted at Harvard. The students evinced great discontent, because it was not with this understanding that they entered college. They considered the new regulations as an *ex post facto* law. By various moves they endeavoured to prevent the examination, even to the extent of actual violence. It was seven years before the difficulty was satisfactorily disposed of.†

We have the notices of rebellions in the different colonial colleges, going as far back as 1750. Harvard was early subject to these disturbances. The rebellion of 1766 was of such dimensions that it interrupted the regular work of the college for more than a month. It arose because of dissatisfaction with the commons. Another outbreak took place in 1768, and led to the expulsion of numerous students.‡ The most famous uprising of the Harvard undergraduates occurred in 1807. The exercises of the college were brought to a standstill. As in most controversies of the sort, the students were nominally beaten, and their leaders rusticated. Often, however, the revolts were indirectly effectual in procuring the desired result. No less a person than Dr. Channing, the great leader of American Unitarianism, was expelled from college for participation in this revolt. The rebellion of 1807 gave rise to an extensive

---

* Hitchcock, E. Reminiscences of Amherst College, p. 331.
† Hall, B. H. College Words and Customs, p. 181.
‡ Bush, H. G. Higher Education in Massachusetts, p. 59.

literature of a humorous character. One of the most famous products was a mock-heroic entitled The Rebelliad or Rebellion Poem,* an epic written in five cantos, by Samuel Alden and Charles Stetson, which throws valuable light on some of the customs of the times. Another prolonged rebellion at Harvard took place in 1834, during which property was destroyed.†

The freshmen and sophomores of Yale rebelled in 1819 because of the quality of the commons, and in 1828 there was a more extensive uprising, known as " The Bread and Butter Rebellion." The students struck, and were consequently expelled, but readmitted to college upon apologizing. The year 1830 marks the outbreak of Yale's most formidable insurrection. This was the Conic Section's Rebellion, and was caused by a change in the method of teaching mathematics. The students refused to demonstrate theorems from the blackboard, preferring their text-books instead. The faculty declined to accede to their petition for change, and a large portion of the class refused to recite. Others signed a paper indorsing the position of the malcontents, and prayed the faculty to punish all equally. This suggestion the faculty promptly acted on, expelling forty-one students by a single resolution. The rebels were refused admission elsewhere and were compelled to come to terms. The outcome of this controversy put an end to rebellions at Yale.‡

In the colleges of the Middle and Southern States the rebellions were more riotous and violent in charac-

---

* Copy in Boston Public Library. Another interesting publication of an anonymous nature was published under the title Don Quixote at College, or the History of the Valiant Adventures lately achieved by the Students of Harvard University, Boston, 1807.

† Peabody, A. P. Harvard Reminiscences, p. 84.

‡ Steiner, B. C. History of Education in Connecticut, p. 163.

ter. At Princeton there were six formidable disturbances during the first three decades of the present century. In 1806 half the students were expelled, and the
college dealt a blow which impaired its usefulness for
years. On one occasion the rioters gained full possession of the college buildings and defied the authorities.* At South Carolina College the commons were a
source of endless boycotts and rebellions by the students. At one time all the students but twenty-eight
were suspended for refusing to inform on one of their
number. Again, sixty were suspended; while, at one
session, seventy-seven refused to return because the
petition on their favourite grievance, eating, had not
been granted.† The University of Alabama presents
much the same record. In 1837 the entire senior class
was dismissed. Eight years later, all the students were
expelled because they refused to swear to their inno-
cence in a certain affair and thereby implicate the guilty
parties. Another attempt was made to enforce this ex-
culpation law in 1847. Faculty action was met with an
organized rebellion, which left but one senior and two
freshmen in attendance at recitations.‡

While, in some instances, the entire student body
participated in the rebellion, the decision was made
separately by each class in its own meeting. Many of
the revolts were confined to one or two classes. It was
the class spirit of cohesion which made organized strikes
and boycotts possible. The faculty realized that the
class organization furnished the support to outbreaks,
and its attitude toward the class was bitterly hostile.

---

* Maclean, J. History of the College of New Jersey, vol. ii,
pps. 72, 154, 167, 168, 253, 268.

† Meriwether, Colyer. History of Education in South Carolina, p. 157.

‡ Clark, W. G. History of Education in Alabama, pp. 43,
59, 65.

The laws of Harvard prohibited class meetings unless the call was signed by three responsible students and countersigned by the president. The three students were held responsible for all violations of the college statutes. Union College considered all class meetings held without license as unlawful combinations, and punished them as such.* Similar rules existed in the other American colleges; at Yale any form of class organization was absolutely prohibited.

To the college president a class meeting seemed capable of infinite folly. It was, to a certain extent, a mock caucus controlled by the fermenting element of the class. The more judicious members stayed away and attended to their private affairs.† "Under class pressure or class vote, students will sign a petition or incur an expense they do not believe in, or cut a recitation they desire to attend, and be forced into relations and conditions they condemn. The boldness of the ill-disposed and reckless is not met with an equal counter-courage and decision of the good." ‡ If the notion comes to prevail that the class can have any influence whatever in shaping faculty action, bad results are almost certain to follow. These utterances of contemporary college presidents express in a modified form the ideas which dominated faculty action in the last generation.

Town and gown rows deserve attention in the discussion of the sphere of the class in student life. Such conflicts between the students and the outside public were by no means as important or numerous in American seats of learning as in the mediæval or modern Eng-

* Hall, B. H. College Words and Customs, p. 78.

† C. K. Adams. Discipline in American Colleges, North American Review, vol. cxlix, p. 17.

‡ Bartlett, S. C. College Disturbances, Forum, vol. iv, p. 428.

lish universities. The antagonism has always existed, and left evidences of its presence in various small customs. It is rather in the old-time academies that we must look for the town and gown spirit in its most marked manifestations. Most American colleges were situated in towns too small to threaten the supremacy of the students. Serious and well-developed contests of this character are found only where a strong alien element existed in the town itself. Thus, the Yager fights at Bowdoin were almost entirely with the lumbermen in the spring of the year.* At New Haven the sailors were commonly the aggressive element. Here the conflicts between the townsmen and students were unusually frequent and severe, which led to the growth of a peculiar institution, " The Bully Club." In the early fights with the sailors a huge club was captured. Each year this club was bestowed on the strongest man in the senior class, who henceforth acted as class president, and led the students in conflicts with the town. In addition to the major bully, or president, there was also a minor bully, usually a small man, who acted as vice-president. This curious institution came to an end in a fight at a Commencement procession in 1840, caused by the appearance of two leaders, one claiming the old name of bully, the other rejoicing in the more refined title of marshal.† During the existence of the Bully Club, at least one pitched fight a year took place between the classmen and the " townies." For the most threatening exhibition, we must pass to a later period. In the great riot of the townsmen in 1854 the students were compelled to force their way through a hostile mob. A student stabbed one of the rioters, which so angered the townsmen that they tried to batter down

---

* Hall, B. H.   College Words and Customs, p. 504.
† Bagg, Lyman H.   The Bully Club, Yale Book, vol. ii, p. 460.
8

the college buildings with an old cannon. The police succeeded in spiking this and in dispersing the mob before any serious damage was done.*

Another evidence of the dominancy of the class as a social unit is seen in the number of customs and ceremonials which clustered about it. While chiefly humorous in character, these customs were not without their effect in giving undergraduate life a certain unique charm and individuality. Many of them dealt with the relationship between the classes. For instance, freshmen were everywhere debarred from carrying canes and wearing beaver hats. A curious tradition at Yale prevented them from sitting on the college fence with the upper classmen until after they had beaten the Harvard freshmen at baseball.† The seniors alone might relax themselves by spinning tops, playing marbles, rolling hoops, or indulging in an exciting game of " nigger-baby."

In a number of institutions the close of the freshman year of apprenticeship was celebrated in an appropriate manner. The chapel bell was rung from midnight until the rope was worn out. This signified that the freshmen had lost their rust. The upper classes were diverted by a display of fireworks and enlivened by a serenade of discordant sounds made to issue from tin kettledrums, horse fiddles, trumpets, and horns. At the beginning of their college career at Hamilton the freshmen were invested with the insignia of their responsibility. The sophomores present a heavy cudgel, six feet long, of black walnut, and bound with brass; inscribed on a silver plate are the words " Freshman Club." The club becomes the property of the one who can hold it out at arm's length the longest time, who

---

* Steiner, B. C.   History of Education in Connecticut, p. 201.
† Ibid.

henceforth acts as a leader. The freshmen form a procession and try the virtues of the club on the chapel door.*

The personal peculiarities of the members were made the occasion of curious class customs. At Harvard the laziest man in the class received a leather medal from his classmates, while the ugliest man was consoled with a jackknife. At the University of Indiana it was the greatest liar who received the jackknife.† Another Harvard custom gave the best mathematician in a class a large slate, which on leaving college was presented to the best mathematician in the class below, who in his turn passed it on to the next class. The class of 1848 at Amherst presented one of its members who had been newly married with a crib, a family Bible, and a copy of Mrs. Ellis's Treatise on Domestic Economy. Another Amherst class gave its smallest member a new beaver hat and arranged an elaborate presentation ceremony.‡ It was quite a common custom for the senior class to set aside a certain sum of money for the first legitimate child born to any member after graduation. The money was expended for a silver cup, which was presented to the child at one of the annual class dinners. In one instance a baby jumper was voted to the second member of the class thus favoured.#

A strong tendency toward burlesque is observable in many student customs. One of the most widespread forms has been that of mock programmes known as rakes and bogies. The bogie was usually a caricature of some programme of an entertainment by another class. They were always satirical, touching upon the personal

* Hall, B. H.   College Words and Customs, p. 399.
† Ibid., p. 267.
‡ Cutting, George A.   Student Life at Amherst, p. 121.
# Hall, B. H.   College Words and Customs, p. 68.

foibles of the opposition; usually they were scurrilous
and abusive, and often vulgar and obscene. The college authorities universally forbade the publication of
bogies, and so they were distributed and printed in
secret. The detective efficiency of a college faculty was
always measured by its skill in discovering the authors.
When detected, the guilty parties were at once expelled.*

A more healthful form of amusement was found in
burlesque entertainments, which the lower classes organized in derision of the solemn ceremonial of junior
exhibitions and Commencement week. Like the mock
programmes, the mock entertainments dealt exclusively
in satire of a personal character. The humour was usually broad, with an inclination to coarseness. A med-
dlesome person would be assigned an oration on " The
Busybody "; a poor punster would speak on " Diseased
Razors." Two persons not noted for personal cleanliness would discuss the differences between original and
alluvial soils. A dabbler in natural history would read
an essay on " The Humbug." Three persons, one very
tall, one very broad, and the third very fat, would hold
a conference on length, breadth, and thickness.† The
presentation of the Wooden Spoon at Yale was the most
celebrated of the mock ceremonials. A wooden spoon
was given the man who took lowest place on the regular
junior programme. The exhibition at one time was
given in secret, and students disguised as Indians excluded the faculty and general public. The poorest
scholar in the class was chosen master of ceremonies.
The witty and clever members burlesque the usual ora-

---

* Alexander, Undergraduate Life at Princeton, Scribner's
Magazine, vol. xxi, p. 678 ; Start, A. B., History of Tufts College, p. 45 ; Cutting, G. A., Student Life at Amherst, p. 131.

† Hall, B. H. College Words and Customs, p. 325.

tions, dissertations, and disputes, and keep the audience in a perpetual roar of laughter. The presentation of an expensive and elaborately carved wooden spoon to the hero of the occasion, forms the culminating point in the entertainment.*

The Navy Club at Harvard deserves the credit of being the most original invention of this description yet recorded. It was designed to furnish consolation to those who had received no Commencement parts, and the men most in disfavour with the faculty received the highest appointments. The student who had been expelled from college the greatest number of times became Lord High Admiral. The rear admiral was the laziest man in the class. The most profane member was chosen chaplain, and the most obscene, boatswain. The club commonly procured a large schooner, which was anchored in the Charles River. The Lord High Admiral occupied the quarter-deck and ruled with despotic authority. He could commonly be seen reclining on a couch attended by two subordinates, who made his slumbers pleasant by guarding his sacred person from the mosquitoes. The operations of the Navy Club closed with an excursion down Boston Harbour. The vessel was well stocked with certain kinds of provisions, which, when afforded assistance from the stores of Old Ocean, formed the requisites of a grand clambake on the shores of Cape Cod. The return to Cambridge was marked by no little noise, disorder, and dissipation.†

The burning of a text-book at the close of the term's study was another widespread ceremony. The usual mock programme of sermons, poems, and orations opened the celebration. Then a large coffin was placed before the altar, within which lay the veritable Euclid,

---

* Hall, B. H. College Words and Customs, p. 495.
† Ibid., p. 331.

arranged in a becoming winding sheet, the body being composed of combustibles, and thoroughly saturated with turpentine. After midnight, the company leave the hall, form an orderly array, bearing the coffin in their midst. Those who composed the procession were arrayed in disguises to avoid detection, and bore a full complement of brilliant torches. The skeleton himself, bearing a torch, might be seen dancing in the midst, to the great amusement of the spectators. The concluding exercises were a mile away. These consisted in walking over the coffin, thus surmounting the difficulties of the author, boring a hole through the copy of Euclid with a hot iron, so that the class might see through it, and finally burning it upon a funeral pyre to throw light upon it. At Trinity College, Conic Sections was substituted; at Hamilton College, Convivium; and at the University of the City of New York, Zumpt's Latin Grammar.*

It must not be thought that all the class ceremonials and occasions were of this burlesque character. Not to speak of junior exhibitions, the Commencement itself partook largely of the nature of a class celebration. The old-time Commencement Day was a great public holiday. In colonial days the governors and legislators attended with a great retinue from a distance. In popularity it equalled the county fair and Western camp meeting. At Cambridge the Common was covered with drinking - stands, dancing - booths, and mountebank shows during Commencement week. To the senior class the occasion seemed an important crisis in their careers. It was Commencement Day that determined the success or failure of a college career. In the college stories of the time the hard-working hero, who has shunned the temptations of college life, delivers

---

* Hall, B. H. College Words and Customs, p. 44.

the valedictory, honoured by the world and envied by his companions. He receives showers of bouquets from the galleries, and eventually wins the heroine; while his rival, the villain, curses his own laziness and neglect. The importance of Commencement was so great because it was the single social event of the college year.

Commencement week always began with the baccalaureate sermon delivered in the college chapel, where sage words of advice were heard by the class, sobered by the thought of going to battle with the world. With the exercises of Commencement Day the class as an organization had little to do, their energy finding free play in class day. After the formal programme, with its odes and speeches of a somewhat stereotyped order was completed, and the class history, abounding in sly allusions and good-natured characterizations, had been read, the class was free to indulge in the original features of the day. There was a great variety of these. A common form of memorial consisted in planting a class tree. At Yale long clay pipes were smoked, which were afterward presented to their lady friends.* At Amherst the class made the round of recitation rooms, stopping in each to caricature the peculiarities of its owner. Afterward the faculty were serenaded. The class held its last meeting in the banquet hall at midnight. At this time were divulged the tender secrets of the heart until then unknown, and here, too, past estrangements were forgotten, and the members pledged each other to eternal friendship.†

Before completing our picture of the class at this period mention must be made of the numerous societies

---

* Steiner, B. C. History of Education in Connecticut,. p. 198.
† Cutting, George A. Student Life at Amherst. Also Levin, J S. University Undergraduate Life in F. N. Thorpe's Benjamin Franklin and the University of Pennsylvania, pp. 408, 409.

founded on the class as a basis : at first, merely an informal group of friends of the same year; after a time, a society would be organized, having for its principle some whim or fantastical notion. Such clubs would naturally cease to exist after the graduation of the class. Information concerning organizations of this class is somewhat scanty, but we have been able to collect notices of a number of typical societies. Such, for instance, were the Philopogonia and Mu Kappa Sigma of Amherst. Philopogonia * was formed by an agreement of the class of 1852 to abstain from shaving for an entire term. The razors of the members were sealed up, deposited under lock and key, and a committee of vigilance appointed to see that no one broke the rule. At the end of the term a grand supper was held. The member having the longest beard delivered an oration, and the man having the next longest a poem.†

The Mu Kappa Sigma Society appeared in 1857. Its meetings came on Saturady night, after which some act of rowdyism was perpetrated. The notice of meetings was adorned with a woodcut from a comic almanac or illustrated newspaper, representing scenes of dissipation and violence. The notice likewise contained two or three lines of cipher indicating to the initiated the special objct of the meeting. The students at large taxed their ingenuity with fruitless endeavours to decipher these cabalistic signs. It was later discovered that the entire affair was simply a burlesque on secret societies; the signs were meaningless. The plan originated in a meeting of a few friends every Saturday night, held to make molasses candy. It was known as the Molasses Candy Society.

Another group of friends fitted up an underground

---

* Philo-pogon, or love-beard.
† Cutting, G. A.   Student Life at Amherst, p. 125.

apartment with culinary features which were said to be
quite complete. The entrance was concealed by a trapdoor, and so secret were its proceedings that for years
their midnight banquets escaped the notice of vigilant
officials. The room was at last discovered as a consequence of the trapdoor being accidentally left open.
The wine kegs, chicken bones, and bottles found among
the *débris* told wonderful tales. The society was called,
by its initials, the H. E. O. T. T., which being interpreted would read, " Ho, Every One That Thirsteth." *
An organization of a more serious purport was the
Τι κρι, inaugurated in 1834, by the members of the class
of 1837. It aimed at social, literary, and religious
improvement, but was secret in all its proceedings.
Some one of the members must be absent from each
meeting. The members present were then compelled to
state every fault of the absent member, social, literary,
and moral. These criticisms were soon afterward presented in writing to the absent member, who at the next
meeting must make his defence, if he had any, to the
charges—then he might join in the benevolent attempt
to criticise his now absent successor.†

It must be confessed that predatory clubs outnum-
bered the more innocent forms of association. The
" Ranters " of Bethany College, Virginia, were a typical
predatory band. They committed all sorts of rascality
and mischievousness, both on their fellow-students and
on the neighbouring inhabitants. The company was
commanded by one selected from the party called Grand
Ranter, whose orders must be obeyed, under the penalty
of expulsion of the person offending. Among the tricks
commonly indulged in were those of robbing hen and
turkey roosts, and feasting on the fruits of their labour;

---

* Cutting, G. A.   Student Life at Amherst, p. 124.
† Ibid., p. 65.

of stealing from the neighbours their horses to enjoy the pleasure of midnight rides.   If detected, or betrayed to the faculty, they revenge themselves by shaving the manes and tails of the favourite horse belonging to the person informing.*   Similar bands were known as "Moonlight Rangers" at Jefferson College, Pennsylvania, and as "Annarugians" at Centre Callege, Kentucky.†

The Pandowdy Band of Bowdoin was a company of students who devoted themselves to serenading unpopular members of the faculty.   "It had no regular time and place of meeting, and the number of performers varied from half a dozen or less to fifty.   The instruments are commonly horns, drums, tin kettles, tongs, shovels, triangles, pumpkin vines, etc.   It is regarded on all hands as an unequivocal expression of the feelings of the students.   It corresponds to Calliathump of Yale, and horn-blowing at Princeton." ‡

The activity of the class did not cease with graduations ; reunions were held at yearly intervals.   Most important were the triennial and decennial celebrations.   These meetings were a much more vital bond of union with the college than the Alumni Association, or local College Club.   There is no more pathetic and yet inspiring sight in American college life than the return of a few bent men to their Alma Mater on the fiftieth anniversary of their graduation.   The class secretary kept a record of the doings of the members, and from time to time issued a volume containing an account of the latest reunion, with songs and speeches. The most useful portion of the work is the biographical record of the different members, stating their professions, publications, degrees and offices, the time and

---

* Hall, B. H.   College Words and Customs, p. 385.
† Ibid., pp. 10, 326.   ‡ Ibid., p. 342.

place of their marriage, and the names of their children.* Some of the older colleges have hundreds of volumes of these records—a striking testimonial to the hold which the old class organization maintained of its members.

From a pedagogical standpoint no discussion of the class can be adequate which fails to emphasize the closeness of the bond which knit the members together. When young men are perforce treading side by side the same paths, working out together the same difficulties, playing the same games in the same hours, there inevitably grows up an intimacy not readily possible under other circumstances. The conditions favoured the creation of an *esprit du corps* seldom equalled. The applause won by the leading members was regarded by peculiar complacency by each member as belonging to the common fund of class credit. After graduation, the glory won by the great men of the class gave a certain prestige to the class itself. Men speak with pride of belonging to the class of 1837 at Yale, or the class of 1877 at Harvard.† Each class had its individuality, and was thought by its members to be the one class in college. This collective pride and feeling of achievement was in itself a good.

But the class *esprit du corps* performed another service; it furnished an energetic unit for the formation and diffusion of public opinion. We have the word of President Porter, of Yale, that the class system was essential to an efficient college life. " I indeed do not see how an American college without fixed classes could have an efficient common life. In the American col-

---

* Bagg, L. H. Four Years at Yale, by a Graduate of '69, p. 540.

† Reminiscences of Scenes and Characters in College, by a Graduate of 1821, p. 194.

lege the class is the charmed circle, within which the individual contracts most of his friendships and finds his fondest and most cherished association. The sentiment of his class is that which influences him most efficiently, and is to him often the only atmosphere of his social life." * There was a general impression that a strong class feeling produced a strong college feeling, and created a habit of loyalty which stuck to a man.†

The enforced intimacy of the four years' class association resulted in the cultivation of a certain practical judgment of men. In the old days about three fifths of the talk of the undergraduates was about one another. It began when the sub-freshmen met to be examined for admission, and continued until graduation. The amount of attention which men paid to one another, and the time devoted to estimating one another's social, moral, and intellectual qualities, and discussing details of conduct, were extraordinary. It can not be said that every man in the class knew every other man, but the apparatus for bringing men of the same class together was efficient, and it usually did happen that by the end of the freshman year nearly every man believed he knew, or knew about, every man in his class whose acquaintance it seemed likely to be worth his while to make. Men were misjudged, misunderstood, overestimated, and underestimated, but acquaintance was very general and constantly ripening, and estimates were in a constant state of revision and reconstruction.‡

Such relations were favourable to the formation of warm friendships. As the colleges have grown larger,

---

* Porter, N. The American College and the American Public, pp. 191, 192.

† Wallace, G. R. Princeton Sketches, p. 187.

‡ Martin, E. S. Undergraduate Life at Harvard, Scribner's Magazine, vol. xxi, p. 535.

and the pursuits of the students more various, the opportunities have become rarer for that close intercourse in which are formed those intimate personal ties for which maturer life affords no equivalent.*

The four years of the old college life produced a striking and unusually happy effect on the students themselves. At the end of four years they have been a good deal modified, externally and internally, and for the better, by contact with each other. The rude have become more gentle, the effeminate more manly, the timid more free and unembarrassed, and the conceited more modest. And this effect is greater and happier in proportion as a class is more numerous and gathered from a wider range of country.

§ 2. THE DEBATING SOCIETY IN THE REVOLUTIONARY PERIOD.

It was the wave of political interest produced by the Revolution which made the debating society for fifty years the strongest force in American student life. Few periods in history show such an exclusive absorption in politics and such a high level of political intelligence. Politics was the chief culture interest of the people, and absorbed nearly all the ability of the country. This political fervour, combined with an exuberant Americanism, had its absurd side in the excessive sensibility to foreign criticism, and in the prevalence of high-sounding phrases and bombast; † but below the surface there existed a firm faith in democracy as a social force, and in the world-mission of America which has since passed away.

---

* Story, Moorfield. Harvard in the Sixties, p. 8.

† See the volumes of Captain Basil Hall and Mrs. Trollope for a description of this side of American life.

An ideal of such universality and definiteness was not slow in affecting the youth of the country; and with the coming of peace and the establishment of new colleges, one notes in all sections of the country the rise of strong debating clubs. Such were the Athenæan and Pincinian Societies of Bowdoin; the Social Friends and United Fraternity of Dartmouth; the Athenian and Alexandrian Societies at Amherst; the Philogian and Philotechnian Societies at Williams; the United Brothers and Philermenians at Brown; the Philorhetoreans and Peithologians of Wesleyan; the Philolexian and Peithologian of Columbia; the Zelosophic and Philomathean of Pennsylvania; the Washington and Jefferson of the University of Virginia; and the Dialectic and Philanthropic of the University of North Carolina. To these must be added the three (formerly two) societies of Yale, the one at Harvard, and the two Halls of Princeton, which were mentioned in an earlier chapter. It is worthy of note that with two exceptions (Yale and Harvard) just two prominent societies were found in each college, which is a strong testimonial to the strength of the competitive principle.

The mere annals of any of these organizations are devoid of general interest or significance, and consist of the records of election contests, petty rivalry, and the monotonous succession of useful but commonplace exercises. Consequently, in the following pages we shall aim only to present the salient features during the period of greatest prosperity, which is, roughly speaking, from 1790 to 1840. The different phases of society activity will be treated in the following order: internal management, literary exercises, general influence, decline, and value as a means of culture.

The structure of the clubs was simple and needs little explanation. There always existed a written constitution or fundamental law. The constitutions of different societies scattered throughout the country were similar. The officers provided for were those common to the average voluntary society: president, vice-president, treasurer, secretary, and vice-secretary, besides librarian, scribe, senior critic, and junior critic. At Yale provision was made for professors, chosen from the members who were to deliver one lecture a term on such subjects as history, composition, oratory, natural philosophy, mathematics, and geography. In regard to the division of labour, the debating society was a worthy rival of the early town meeting. At one election of Linonia (Yale), forty-seven different officials were chosen.*

The majority of the positions were sinecures, mere harmless attempts to satisfy the officeholding instinct. The society presidency, however, was an important college honour and eagerly competed for. At Amherst the elections were as hotly contested as those of the State and national governments. All the arts of the politician were brought into play,† including, on some occasions, wine and brandy.‡ According to Bristed,# the elections gave rise to an intriguing factious spirit unworthy of the generous instincts of youth. Such elections were considered an admirable preparation for practical politics.

Another important element was the rivalry between the two societies which divided student interest. They competed in the selection of members, in the size of their libraries, and in the distribution of college honours. The feeling was usually one of bitter antagonism

---

* Yale Book, vol. ii, p. 317.

† Hitchcock, Edward. Reminiscences of Amherst College, p. 326.

‡ Durfee, C. A. History of Williams College, p. 167.

Bristed, C. A. Five Years at an English University, last chapter.

and jealousy. Attempts made at Amherst and else-where to combine the work of the two societies into a harmonious whole uniformly failed. When only one society had been formed, it invariably split into two rival factions as soon as numbers permitted.

The bitterest hostility occurred at the beginning of the year in the struggle for new men. At Yale a sys-tematic campaign was undertaken. Runners were sent to the preparatory schools to pledge the sub-freshmen; committees of students haunted the trains, the New Haven depot, and the hotels, in search of new students. The campaign culminated in the "statement of facts," a public meeting in which the orators from each society extolled the virtues and eulogized the departed heroes of their own organization while pouring contempt and ridicule on their opponents.* At Amherst, on such occasions, the whole college became the scene of exas-perated strife. Study was encroached upon and per-sonal hostilities excited which did not die away with the occasion.† The historians of Williams, Dartmouth,‡ and Bowdoin give similar testimony. In some colleges the faculty interfered and apportioned new men to the societies by some impartial method of allotment. Even this could not put a stop to intrigue and faction fights. To fully appreciate the bitterness and prejudice to

---

* Bagg, L. H.   Four Years at Yale, by a Graduate of '69, p. 194.

† Hitchcock, Edward.   Reminiscences of Amherst College, p. 326.

‡ "The records of the societies contain accounts of con-spiracies and attempts to destroy the societies, accompanied by reports of committees treating the subject with the dignity of a danger to the State.   One of these conspiracies terminated in the destruction of nearly all the records of the Social Friends, and almost caused the dissolution of that society."   Smith, H. P. History of Dartmouth College, p. 86.

which the system of rival debating societies gives rise, one must visit the small denominational colleges of the far West, where the system survives in much of its original strength.*

The regular programme consisted of prepared orations, debates, declamations, and critical papers treating of literature and science. Extemporaneous speaking was the most common, but the literary dissertations or essays received most attention, and were often spoken of as being of unusual merit. To check carelessness, committees were appointed to judge of the quality of the declamations offered. Loose work was rejected, while unusual finish of speech was rewarded with honourable mention.† The proceedings were conducted with decorum, and points of order settled with rigid regard to precedent. At the regular sessions of the clubs the speeches were elevated in tone and marked by a dignity of manner.

The societies felt themselves in nowise bound by the limitations of their constitutional programmes. Extras of various sorts relieved the tedium of political discussion; this was particularly true of the period of decline, when for the first time a conscious effort was made to attract the public. A common amusement took the form of an anonymous box containing jokes, gibes, criticism, sallies of wit, and caricatures. The farce still remained an occasional resource. At times the members impeached the president with much ceremony and mock dignity, or resolved the society into a senate, a congress of the nations, or a court for the trial of a breach of promise suit.‡ In addition to these, various expedients existed in the form of vacation diaries, soliloquies, odes, panegyrics, hyperboles, and se-

---

* Cutting, George A. Student Life at Amherst College, p. 24.
† Ibid., p. 18.   ‡ Ibid., pp. 22, 28, 48.

9

lect anecdotes and pithy sayings of literary characters. In the best days of the literary societies these variations were of rare occurrence and minor consequence; their importance belongs to the period of struggling decline.

Occasionally the anonymous box or pithy sayings of literary characters appeared in journalistic form. In many cases college papers trace their origin to this source. So strong were the societies that they sometimes took upon themselves the responsibilities of publication. At Columbia, the Peithologian Society issued the " Recreations " ; its rival, the Philolexian, the " Observer." * The societies of Wesleyan and the University of North Carolina likewise issued papers.

Another form of society activity was the society libraries, which were frequently valuable supplements of the regular college library, which was likely to be weighed down with theological and Latin tomes, the modern shelves being but scantily filled. This deficiency was supplied by the society library which furnished the students with their current reading matter. Into the building up of libraries, the principle of rivalry largely entered; notwithstanding the poverty of the times, subscriptions of fifty, twenty, and ten dollars were not uncommon. The poorer students solicited books among their friends. Public sentiment was such that students often contributed beyond their means. The books chosen were usually of a miscellaneous character, although, with the exception of Yale, there is little evidence that any large proportion of the funds was expended on fiction. By the end of the period under discussion the two Bowdoin societies had each

---

* Bradley, W. A.   Undergraduate Publications at Columbia, Columbia University Quarterly, vol. i, p. 358.

collected from five to six thousand volumes; the societies of Williams had collectively ten thousand volumes;
those of Brown, three thousand volumes each; and the
Columbia societies a thousand volumes of recent literature which the college library did not contain. Owing
to the change in values, the increase of wealth, and the
decreased cost of producing books, these figures should
be multiplied by five to indicate the real significance of
the effort in modern terms.*

Such was the college debating society of the first
decades of the century, vigorous in its expressions and
antagonisms, covering a wide circle of interests, sufficiently powerful to assume the responsibility of college
enterprises and to supplement the resources of the curriculum; it filled a much larger place in student life
than its successor of to-day. To complete the sketch
there remains to be added an account of its social side
and of its position in the college world of which it
formed a part.

The debating society was intimately connected with
the ceremonial events of the college year. The society
anniversaries at Commencement brought the alumni
back to the old halls and the scenes of their early tri-
umphs. Distinguished clergymen and statesmen delivered charges to the undergraduates in the elevated
but pompous diction of the period. The society members who belonged to the graduating class were attired

---

* For accounts of the various society libraries, see Cleaveland
and Packard, History of Bowdoin College, p. 28 ; Durfee, C. A.,
History of Williams College, p. 81 : Cutting, G. R., Student
Life at Amherst, p. 20 ; Tolman, W. H., History of Higher
Education in Rhode Island, p. 198 ; Smith, B. P., History of
Dartmouth College, p. 141 ; Reminiscences of Scenes and Char-
acters in College, by a Graduate of Yale, Class of 1821, p. 111 :
Brodt, P. E., Debating Societies at Columbia, Columbia Uni-
versity Quarterly, vol. i, p. 50.

in a special paraphernalia and decked out in colours and medals for the occasion.*

In other ways the debating society performed important social functions. It appealed to many of the same interests which the fraternity afterward utilized. While secrecy of meetings was a recognised principle with all the early literary societies, this feature was a distinctly minor one. The same may be said of initiation ceremonies; they were merely incidental and without special significance. Many of the societies adopted badges, colours, and mottoes. At Amherst the badge of the Alexandrian Society was a section of blue ribbon on which was stamped an engraving of rolls of parchment, as seen in ancient Alexandria, underneath which was placed an appropriate inscription.† The rival Athenian Society adopted white ribbons with different symbols and inscriptions. The motto of the Dialectics of North Carolina was, "Love of virtue and science"; that of the Philanthropics, " Virtue, liberty, and science." ‡ Great care was lavished on the society halls; expensive furnishings were purchased, and the walls covered with the portraits of distinguished alumni. Each succeeding class as it graduated added to the resources of the society. The comfortable, almost luxurious, appearance of the debating halls presented a marked contrast to the bare and bleak class rooms by which they were surrounded.

The early debating society was one of the great interests of the student world; its meetings were eagerly anticipated, and its exercises considered to be of much

---

* Cleaveland and Packard. History of Bowdoin College, p. 99.

† Cutting, G. R., Student Life at Amherst, p. 41; Schelling, Felix E., Organizations within the University, in F. N. Thorpe's Benjamin Franklin and the University of Pennsylvania, p. 414.

‡ Smith, C. L. History of Education in North Carolina, pp. 92, 93, 108.

greater importance than the regular recitations * of the college, a belief strengthened by the sympathetic attitude of the faculty. We have the testimony of a hostile critic that the champions of the debating hall were held in greater esteem by their fellow-students than the men who gained the traditional college honours for proficiency in their studies.† The athlete had not yet arisen as a college hero, so the orator and writer represented the ideals of the academic youth. The debating society was strong in the affections of its alumni; distinguished statesmen affirmed its value (W. M. Evarts, George William Curtis), and urged its adoption on the students of a new generation.

Such a condition of affairs was not destined to endure; a new organization, appealing more directly to the interests and sentiments of youth, entered the field, and the debating society lost ground before it. The fraternity struck the older association at its weakest point. About 1830, the debating societies, through increase of numbers, began to be unwieldy, and in consequence a victim to factional contests. In some colleges cliques for controlling elections in the literary societies had crystallized into formal clubs before the appearance of the fraternities.‡ The fraternity greatly hastened this tendency to dissolution; the debating society became the arena in which rival fraternities or secret and non-secret societies fought for the supremacy. The literary exercises were neglected, while rival factions struggled for the offices, as college honours; the new organizations became the centre of interest, while the

---

* Cutting, G. R., Student Life at Amherst, p. 23; Cleaveland and Packard, History of Bowdoin College, p. 98; Smith, C. L., History of Education in North Carolina, p. 92.

† Bristed, C. A. Five Years at an English University, p. 463.

‡ Hall, B. H. A Collection of College Words and Customs, p. 454.

old traditional societies slowly died. The process did not take place in all the colleges at the same time; indeed, as we shall see later, there are portions of the country in which the antagonism never became so fierce. The conflict in the Eastern colleges began as early as 1840, and by 1870 the old societies had become merely a tradition. Such is the cause assigned by the standard Eastern historians for the downfall of the debating society. Yale, Bowdoin, Trinity, Amherst, Dartmouth, and Tufts all tell the same story; occasional testimony from the South and West confirms it.*

But such an explanation fails to account for all the phenomena. How did it come about that in the colleges of the middle West the fraternity and debating society exist side by side in the same institution? To answer this question we must penetrate beneath the mere surface events, and describe the new social movement of which the fraternity was merely representative. Its rise marks a new turn in American life. The free democracy of frontier gives way to complexity, social classes, and divisions. A leisured class is evolved, indifferent to politics, but sensitive to higher refinement. This differentiation extends to the colleges. Men no longer have all tastes in common. One man devotes himself to music, another to boating, and a third to German novels. The content of instruction becomes richer with each decade. The student body in time becomes too large for the old institutions, the class and

---

* Cleaveland and Packard, History of Bowdoin College, p. 28; Steiner, B. C., History of Higher Education in Connecticut, p. 243; Smith, B. P., History of Dartmouth College, p. 182; Cutting, G. R., Student Life at Amherst, p. 29: Tyler, W. S., History of Amherst College, p. 316; Start, A. B.. History of Tufts College, p. 68; Merriam, L. S., History of Higher Education in Tennessee, p. 169; Parker, L. F., Higher Education in Iowa, p. 152.

the debating society, which are based on a free common life. Most important of all these factors, the athlete arises in the land. The student hero is no longer the writer of adolescent verse, or the president of the debating society, but the captain of the team—a man of much muscle, and perhaps little intellectual achievement.*

This change occurred only in the older and wealthier sections of the country, particularly in the section dominated by large manufacturing and commercial interests—in other words, in New England and the central States. In this territory we find the old debating society virtually extinct; the forms of voluntary forensic training which exist are embodied in organizations of a new type, which recognise debating as a specialty rather than as a general interest. But in the Mississippi Valley, which is predominantly agricultural and the home of a thrifty, ambitious middle class which determines the type of culture, the differentiation has not proceeded so far as in the East. The colleges are smaller, more limited in their curriculum, more local in their horizon. In consequence, we still find the old debating society existing in the West, sometimes as powerful now as in the early days of the century, more often as a strong although not a predominant factor in student life. Not infrequently it exists side by side with the fraternity without hostility. When an institution expands from a local college to a national seat of learning, the debating interests are usually weakened by the change.

In estimating the value of the training offered by the debating society, we will first sum up some of the critical

---

* This standpoint is also taken by Mr. P. E. Brodt in his Debating Societies at Columbia, Columbia University Quarterly, vol. i, p. 50.

discussions which appeared in this period.   Archbishop
Whately,* in an address before the students of Dublin
University, attacked the debating societies because they
encouraged precocity, loose thinking, and conceit among
their members.   Some of his objections are sound, from
a logical rather than a pedagogical standpoint; for instance, he argues that young men are too immature to
discuss problems which perplex the ablest statesmen,
forgetful of the fact that young men must some time
begin to discuss public affairs if the line of able statesmen is to continue.   His second point—that debating
encourages miscellaneous reading at the cost of orderly
mental development—has lost some of its force in these
days when the doctrine of interest plays such a part in
education.   Whately also claimed (1) that a debating
society gave a man a careless faculty of pouring forth
illy digested thoughts in well-turned phrases, or, in
other words, that it produced lazy thinkers; and (2) that
it caused premature readiness of speech rather than a
well-balanced mind.

Our next critic, Charles Astor Bristed, devotes the
closing chapter of his book (Five Years in an English
University) to a criticism of the methods of forensic
training current in his day at Yale.   He first notices
the lack of adequate criticism in the operations of the
literary societies.   " There are gathered together from
thirty to one hundred young fellows whose capacity to
criticise is not equal to their disposition, and whose disposition is modified by their interest." †   They are in
such a position that one can not utter his opinion without incurring the suspicion of jealousy.   The consequence is, that the loudest and most showy efforts are

---

* Dangers of Debating Societies to Young Men.   Bentley's
Miscellany, vol. xix, p. 615.

† Five Years in an English University, p. 467.

most applauded. Bristed has here hit upon the most fundamental weakness of the debating society and the one most emphasized by modern teachers of forensics.

The predominant interest in oratory at an early age defeats its own end. The ambitious student begins at the wrong end; he acquires manner before matter, and a style in advance of his thought. "Even here he does not study the best models and confine himself to them, and swallows a great deal of second- and third-hand matter. He acquires a childish fondness for metaphors more or less mixed, and for all sorts of figures, as if they were the sole test and standard of excellence in composition. In short, he aims at fine writing, and sits down not to express his ideas on a subject, but to write a piece. His untimely doctrines do not fructify. His graces and ornaments of trope and metaphor, like the flowers which a child sticks in the ground to make a garden, grow faded and lose vitality for the want of nutriment and root. He wrote fluently at eighteen. At twenty-six he writes a trifle more fluently but in no respect better." *

But the effects of this fundamental superficiality do not end with style; they extend to thought as well. "When a youth acquires the talking facility and propensity without a proper training and knowledge to support it, when most of his authorities are third or fourth hand, hearsay, or the last newspaper article or the confused recollection of what was first imperfectly read, it follows inevitably that he must make many mistakes which his verbal dexterity will be brought into requisition to protect. And from this combination of inaccuracy of detail with facility of expression results one of our greatest national faults—a tendency to defend rather than prevent mistakes.† Frequent debating en-

---

* Five Years in an English University, p. 468.   † Ibid., p. 471.

courages a sophistic habit most dangerous for a young man to acquire, since it puts him in an unfortunate frame of mind, for the reception of knowledge and truth —victory, not truth, to effect a presumption rather than to secure the acquisition of knowledge—is the end of debate. The benefit proposed, sometimes without an attempt to disguise it to the pupil, was that he should be able to humbug the people and get on in the world (that is the plain Saxon of it), which he was to accomplish by always being ready to talk about anything, and never be at a loss for a plausible argument." This practice leads to a great waste of time in Congress and other public bodies.

Bristed is not alone in his severe judgment of the American debating society during this early period. Francis A. Walker speaks in more sweeping and less specific language. He refers to the desire for grandiloquent, oratorical display as the curse not only of the college but of the public life of the times.* A Yale graduate of 1821, in a book of college reminiscences, supplies a number of sketches and anecdotes which sustain and supplement the statements of Bristed and Walker.†

---

* " But, however the type of college hero might vary, speech-making, debating, and fine writing were the be-all and end-all of college training, as in the world outside college, speech-making, debating, or fine writing were the sole recognised signs of greatness. Statesmanship itself was perverted to seek occasions for oratorical displays. Men of business, men of affairs, men of prudence, moderation, and reliability were crowded out of our legislative halls by shrill-voiced declaimers who could catch the ear of a nation given over to the lust of words." Walker considered the decline of the debating society a healthy sign in American life. Francis A. Walker, College Athletics, Harvard Graduate Magazine. vol. ii, p. 3.

† Reminiscences of Scenes and Characters in College, by a Graduate of Yale, Class of 1821, p. 111.

It must be taken into consideration, however, that the weakness of the instructing force and the limited character of the course of study left the students to their own resources. And if their standards of excellence were low, it was chiefly because their life reflected all too faithfully the ideals of the outside world. The dialectical and rhetorical excesses of this period have their distinct warning: they emphasize the old and trite truth that matter is more than form, and facts are more important than style. However, this truth is not likely to be forgotten by the present generation of students. The manifold and highly specialized courses of instruction with a scientific literature in the social sciences leave little room for the loose thinking of sixty years since.

The first and most obvious function of the debating society, and the function most universally recognised, was that of furnishing an opportunity to master the mechanics of speech.* There is a certain readiness and fluency, the capacity to put a point on short notice which most men only acquire with continuous practice; to learn to speak well one must speak often. The debating society also gives the student his first rough introduction to parliamentary law. While both these opportunities may perhaps be supplied by a course in forensics, the sense of freedom and individual initiative is absent to such an extent that the training on these points is greatly inferior. The debating society possesses another advantage in the comparative ease with which it reaches large numbers of men. In many cases

---

* For a study of the pedagogy of the debating society see articles on Discussion Classes in Chambers's Edinburgh Journal, vol. ix, p. 107; and McElligott, James N., Debating Societies as a Means of Intellectual Discipline, Barnard's American Journal of Education, vol. i.

it is not so well calculated to produce a few brilliant speakers or parliamentarians as to send forth a large number of men who have attained to a fair standard of excellence. It need not be argued that in a democracy such a consideration is of great weight.

However, to the mind of the writer, it would seem that the chief function of these societies is not so much to master the mechanical conditions of public speech as to create and strengthen a permanent interest in public affairs. If we agree with the recent utterances of a prominent professor of pedagogy and say that the object of education is the creation of permanent interests, then the debating society is one of the most important of our educational institutions. The discussions usually do not furnish new and accurate data for judgments, but they produce personal reactions in other men; they stimulate their members to think on a wide circle of interests which otherwise would hardly receive serious attention. A foundation is laid which gradually collects around itself the accretions of miscellaneous reading and chance discussion, until a broad intelligence finally results. Not only is such an interest on the part of a large portion of the citizens essential to the creation of that public opinion, which in America, at least, is essential to the proper management of public affairs, but it has an individual function as well. A man who daily follows the turns of European diplomacy, the careers of statesmen, or the advance of Western civilization in the Orient, has a culture resource which elevates and expands his personality and raises him above the narrowing influences of neighbourhood and vocation.

An admirable expression of this idea is contained in a quotation from the London Spectator, which we give in full: " There is a stimulation which comes from the discussion of great questions. There is an intellectual vivifying, and broadening, and clearing which comes from the influence of mind over mind which few things effect as well as a good discussion. Debating societies for young men are not, properly speaking, schools for loquacity at all. There is an age—the university age —when adequate speech on the various ends and motives of life become something altogether beyond mere speech, the natural work, the appropriate action, the characteristic tendency of the mind, and when there is every reason for aiding the expressive crystallization of thought and feeling; an age when theoretical discussions ought to be, if they are not, the very means of life and growth, when it is as silly to call such discussions mere talk as it is later to call a cabinet council such. This is not talk; it is the preparation for action, it is the springing up and organization of the intellectual energy, it is intellectual volition. Without the mere talk of young men's theoretical discussions, the collision of taste with taste, of intellect with intellect, of conscience with conscience, of spirit with spirit, the characters of the best men of the nation would hardly come to birth at all." *

On a lower plane the debating society furnishes a field for the study of the individual in relation to group action. It reproduces to a certain extent the tendencies and reactions of Congress or Parliament. From participation in these play activities the student learns the turns, tricks, artifices, and humours of public bodies.

In the old literary societies there was a certain breadth and *esprit de corps* which made them a strong bond between the student and the college, besides furnishing an opportunity for the student to develop in many directions, which is not possible to-day. The close contact of man with man which characterized

---

* Taken as quoted by E. E. Aikens, The Secret-Society System, p. 44. Reference not verified.

them gave rise to those close friendships which are justly prized as one of the best products of American college life. Indeed, the question may be fairly put: Whether the old open organizations, like the class and debating society, were not better calculated to develop enduring feelings of comradeship than the modern system of fraternities and special clubs? *

To sum up briefly the pedagogy of the debating society. We may conclude that its chief function is to prepare students for public life. This aim it accomplishes by giving them mechanical dexterity of speech, by deepening their interest in social and political problems, and by anticipating the rules and conditions of parliamentary bodies. While we have noticed that excessive devotion to debating without proper standards leads to certain grave evils, it is likewise evident that the character of the instruction given in our larger colleges is at the present time a sufficient safeguard against these abuses.

§ 3. Miscellaneous Societies in the Revolutionary Period.

a. Fraternities. — The Phi Beta Kappa, the first Greek-letter society in America, was organized Decem-

---

* Mr. Philip E. Brodt, of Columbia, speaks of their many-sidedness in the following words: "As one traces this development of the all-inclusive society into the club which trains men in speaking alone, he recognises how many organizations now provide the facilities which a single organization used to give, he must feel how much we have lost by this minute division of interests. It was a wholesome, democratic life when a single society had in it enough to bring together men of every taste and class; and there was in such a life a breadth of opportunity for a student to develop in more directions than one, which is hardly possible to-day." Debating Societies at Columbia, in Columbia University Quarterly, vol. i, p. 52.

ber 5, 1776, at the College of William and Mary, by five students. The choice of a Greek name seems to have been purely accidental. The meetings of the society seem to have possessed the same general character which belongs to the fraternity meetings of to-day. The aim of the organization was social with some incidental literary training; non-collegians were occasionally admitted to membership. Charters were granted to a number of local lodges in Virginia, but they were never heard of afterward. Because of the exigencies of warfare, the parent society ceased to exist in January, 1781.*

Mr. Elisha Parmele, a graduate of Harvard, and formerly a student of Yale, received grants of two charters for the Northern extension of the order in 1779. In 1780 the Alpha of Connecticut was formed, and in 1782 the Alpha of Massachusetts. In the various Northern colleges the fraternity took upon itself different forms of activity. The society at Yale made efforts to keep up a literary communication with Harvard, but failed. Its real life was confined to the local membership. Attempts were made to found a periodical and establish a fund for indigent students; these efforts were also doomed to failure. The Yale chapter was in reality a select debating society with initiation suppers where " the juice of Bacchus flowed." Regarded with great jealousy by outsiders, its records were twice stolen during its early history. The annals of the Phi Beta Kappa are famous for a long series of orations and poems. The anti-Masonic excitement in 1830 caused the abandonment of the secret features of the order at both Yale and Harvard.†

---

* Baird, W. R. American College Fraternities, third edition, pp. 275, 276.

† Yale Book, vol. i, pp. 325-327.

At Bowdoin the Phi Beta Kappa (1824) became a form of learned academy, no undergraduates being admitted. Papers and subjects for investigation were assigned to members of the college and other learned men. This scheme in time fell into disuse and an address and a poem were substituted.* Since 1830 the membership in the Phi Beta Kappa has been almost exclusively an honorary distinction granted to the best scholars of the senior class. At Amherst, for instance, all those who at the end of the junior year had an average of more than eighty-five were at first chosen. Afterward the faculty nominated that fifth of the junior class whose standing was the highest.† The first imitation of the Phi Beta Kappa was a senior society at Yale, the Chi Delta Theta, founded in 1821. If we can judge from the branch at Amherst, it was a select literary society. The exercises consisted of translations in prose and verse from the classical authors, dissertations on literary subjects, and criticisms of ancient and modern books of note. At the conclusion of the programme the college Professor of Literature criticised the proceedings. At one time several successive meetings were devoted to the study of Shakespeare.‡

The Phi Beta Kappa and Chi Delta Theta must be considered preparatory to the modern fraternity movement which may be said to date its origin from the organization of the Kappa Alpha Society at Union College in 1825. It was in its external features an imitation of the Phi Beta Kappa, but the tie between its members was a much closer one.

The leading Greek-letter societies were formed as follows: The Delta Phi Sigma at Union (1827), the

---

* Cleaveland and Packard. History of Bowdoin College, p. 29.
† Cutting, G. A. Student Life at Amherst College, p. 52.
‡ Ibid., p. 50.

Alpha Delta Phi at Hamilton (1832), the Psi Upsilon at Union (1833), Chi Psi at Union (1841), Delta Kappa Epsilon at Yale (1844), Zeta Psi at New York University (1844).* The same period witnessed the rise of a large number of local societies at different institutions, particularly at Trinity College and Wesleyan University. The latter boasts three prominent societies during this period: the Tuo Philosophers, afterward known as the Thecanians; the Mystical Seven (1837); and the Phi Nu Theta, known as the Eclectic.†

b. *Athletics.*—During the Revolutionary era some attention was given to athletic sports and gymnastics from time to time in spurts, but no formal organization was provided for. Athletics was regarded as a waste of time by the faculty, and the athlete was not respected by the student. Occasionally the students of Harvard and Yale kicked a football about on the Common or in the street, and a yearly game took place between the sophomores and freshmen, which partook largely of the nature of a modern rush.‡

Dr. Follen was the first to introduce systematic gymnastics. He equipped an old room in one of the buildings at Harvard with masts, parallel bars, and the usual variety of apparatus for athletic training. Under his direction, the students were taught to run with a minimum of fatigue, their bodies thrown slightly forward, arms akimbo, and breathing through the nose. He led the entire body of students from the Delta to the top of a hill in the neighbouring town of Somerville.# In September, 1826, the Yale corporation appropriated

---

* Baird, W. R. American College Fraternities, third edition, p. 6.

† Steiner, B. C. History of Education in Connecticut, p. 279.

‡ Hall, B. H. A Collection of College Words and Customs, p. 207.

Peabody, A. P. Harvard Reminiscences, p. 120.

10

three hundred dollars for the cleaning and preparation of the grounds for a gymnasium and "the erection of apparatus for gymnastic exercises with a view to the promotion of the health of the students." This gymnasium was not under cover.* From Bristed we learn that athletics was greatly neglected at Yale during this period, and that the exercise was too slight and irregular to be of service to the students.†

Among the Princeton students shinny, which was known as hawkey and hurley, was as great a favourite with the students as football in the other colleges. The players were equipped with a stick five feet long, two and a half inches in diameter, and curved at one end. A grand contest took place annually between the juniors and sophomores in this game.‡ The undergraduates of Amherst devoted considerable attention to football in the early days, but, as the century advanced, baseball, cricket, wicket, pitching of loggerheads and quoits and round-ball gained in popularity. In 1826 a gymnastic society was formed, the chief object of which was the erection and support of apparatus for gymnastic exercise in a certain grove. The faculty forbade the establishment of bowling alleys because they would be noisy, and, although innocent, might be perverted. Occasional addresses were given before the society on physical culture.# At Bowdoin football and baseball in their simpler forms were occasionally indulged in, but boating was unknown. Tramping down the river to a certain consecrated rock, and swimming, were the most popular amusements.||

---

  * Yale Book, vol. ii, p. 458.
  † Bristed, C. A. Five Years at an English University.
  ‡ Hall, B. H. A Collection of College Words and Customs, p. 423.
  # Cutting, George R. Student Life at Amherst College, pp. 111, 112.
  | Cleaveland and Packard. History of Bowdoin College. p. 96.

The attitude of the governing power toward student athletics is well expressed in a resolution passed by the Princeton faculty on November 26, 1787: "It appearing that a play at present much practised by the small boys among the students, and by the grammar scholars, with balls and sticks" (shinny), "in the back campus of the college, is in itself low and unbecoming gentlemen and scholars, and is attended with great danger to the health by sudden and alternate heats and colds:

"As it tends, by accidents almost unavoidable in that play, to disfiguring and maiming those who had engaged in it, for whose health and safety as well as improvement in study as far as depends upon our exertion we are accountable to their parents and likely to be severely blamed by them, and inasmuch as there are many amusements both more honourable and more useful in which they are indulged—therefore the faculty think it incumbent upon them to prohibit students and grammar scholars from using the game aforesaid." *

Francis A. Walker has described the attitude of the students of the time toward athletics: "There was more than indifference, there was contempt for physical prowess. A man known to be especially gifted in this way was thereby disparaged in public estimation; if he was known to make much of it, he was more likely to be despised. It was taken for granted that he could not be good for much else. Brains and brawn were supposed to be developed in inverse ratio; strength was closely akin to brutality." † With the exception of the two gymnastic clubs already alluded to, there were no athletic organizations during this period, unless the famous Bully Club be placed in this category.

---

* Quoted by G. R. Wallace. Princeton Sketches, p. 77.

† See article College Athletics, in Harvard Graduate Magazine, vol. ii, p. 3.

c. Self-governing Institutions.—The application of
the principles of the Declaration of Independence to
the government and discipline of students was an idea
which could not but occur to a generation so thoroughly saturated with the formulas of democracy as
the Americans of the period from 1780 to 1840. A
limited scheme of self-government was among the principles which Jefferson laid down for the University
of Virginia. A board of six censors was named by
the faculty from among the most discreet students,
" whose duty it shall be, sitting as a court of inquiry, to
examine the facts of offences, propose minor punishments which they· think proportioned to the offence,
and make a report to the professors, who may commute
the offence." After one year's trial the scheme was not
re-enacted. To the average educator of the times such
a plan seemed fanciful and impracticable.* However,
the University of Virginia did away with the usual system of espionage and recognised the student's responsibility as a man. There were no exasperating rules; a
student must respect the rights of others; in every respect he possessed all the liberty which he would have
had in New York city.†

At Trinity College, Hartford, Connecticut, a mock
court known as the Grand Tribunal was established; it
consisted of the junior and senior classes, and had for
its special object the regulation and discipline of sophomores. The Grand High Chancellor presided at all
business meetings, assisted by judges, advocates, sheriffs,
and aids. No sophomore could be tried who had three
votes in his favour, which made trials somewhat infre-

---

* A Hostile Account of the Virginia Plan is found in an article
entitled College Instruction and Discipline, American Quarterly
Review, vol. ix, p. 294.

† Stevens, W. L. Self-Government in Colleges, Popular Science
Monthly, vol. xix, p. 697.

quent. Rarely more than one took place in a year, while sometimes two years elapsed without a session of the court. When the selection of the offending sophomore had been made, he was arrested some time during the day of the evening on which his trial took place. The court provided him with one advocate, while he had the privilege of choosing another. These trials were often scenes of considerable wit and eloquence. The faculty of the college acted as police to keep out sophomores who would be likely to create a disturbance.*

At Amherst a similar institution was known as the House of Students. One of its objects was to enact such laws in addition to the statutes of the college as the good of the community would seem to require. Closely associated with the House of Students was a Court of Justice which the students instituted, and which met after the rhetorical exercises. Duly organized with judge and officers, it tried petty cases in the college, and its decisions were much respected by both faculty and students. It is said that Professor Jacob Abbott had something to do with the establishment of the court. Before it were brought cases of alleged injuries to college buildings, instances of discourtesy and indecorum, outrages, encroachments on the rights of the students, etc. Sometimes petty cases of college discipline were yielded to the court by the faculty. Fines were imposed on those found guilty. The judicial branch was much more successful than the legislative, and continued in operation for a longer period. The proceedings in both were conducted according to the forms of law, with judge, associate judges, jury, counsel, witnesses, etc. The shrewd cross-questioning of the witnesses and the charges of the judge were not soon

---

* Hall, B. H. A Collection of College Words and Customs, p. 239.

forgotten by the participants in the trials. Their influence was salutary, and much amusement was afforded to spectators of the proceedings.

The burlesque element enters largely into some of the student courts established during this period, as, for instance, that at Union College, New York. In this institution buildings were divided into sections, a section comprising about fifteen rooms. Within each section was established a court composed of a judge, an advocate. and a secretary, who were chosen by the students resident therein, and held their offices during one college term. Each section court claimed the power to summon for trial any inhabitant within the bounds of its jurisdiction who might be charged with improper conduct. The accused might either defend himself or select some person to plead for him. Such residents of the section as cared to do so acted as jurors. The prisoner, if found guilty, was sentenced at the discretion of the court, generally to treat the company to some specified drink or dainty. These courts often afforded occasions for much fun, and sometimes called out real wit and eloquence.*

Early in the century rowdyism became such a nuisance at Yale that certain individuals belonging to the freshman and sophomore classes constituted themselves a vigilance committee or voluntary police force, which patrolled the college in the dark and reported such as they detected or suspected. The innocent were as likely to be laid hold of as others. The majority of the classes were opposed to this club law and haphazard mode of dealing with offences in the dark, and it soon passed away.†

---

* Hall, B. H. A Collection of College Words and Customs, p. 407.

† Reminiscences of Scenes and Characters in College, by a Graduate of Yale, Class of 1821, pp. 131, 132.

None of the experiments in self-government which we have enumerated and described influenced the college discipline permanently or played an important part in the student life. Where their origin can be traced we find that they were the result of the influence of some one individual indoctrinated with democratic ideas. The relations between faculty and students were such that there was neither trust on one side nor confidence on the other. The ages of the students, varying from fourteen to thirty, and the *in loco parentis* theory of discipline, cut the ground from under any self-governing experiment.

d. Journalism.—To the historian of student life college journalism has a peculiar value; the spirit of youth, elsewhere limited and checked by the actual environment, finds here its fullest and freest expression. The sentimentality, the contentiousness and fickleness, the yearning for the vague and unknowable, a strong sense of humour as well as a marked tendency to imitation, are all exhibited in their bare simplicity in student publications, especially those of the earlier period, before the modern critical spirit was abroad; they are a rich storehouse of material for the student of the adolescent mind. These publications are perhaps not less valuable to the student of literature, for in its enthusiastic admiration youth catches the dominant note of the age more clearly than the mature mind of critic or writer, and consequently reflects more faithfully the attitude of the general reading public. In this section, however, we are interested in college journalism more from the standpoint of pedagogy. The question we shall endeavour to answer is, " What part has college journalism played in the education of the American student? "

The earliest student papers were either the product of a few private individuals working usually in secret, or were published in the interests of a debating society.

One of the regular numbers of the old debating society programme consisted of the reading of a journalistic production, largely humorous and partly critical in character; a custom still continued in many high schools. When the first of these written papers was published it is impossible to say, although we have definite record of such publication in the first decade of the present century. The Literary Tablet of Dartmouth appeared in 1803, the Literary Cabinet of Yale in 1806; neither of these journals nor their successors * for more than twenty years lasted beyond their first few numbers. In a majority of cases both financial support and permanent organization were lacking. At Yale there were seven unsuccessful experiments before the foundation of the first permanent venture, The Yale Literary Magazine, in 1837. A brief *résumé* of conditions at Amherst will give the reader some idea of the character of college journalism during this period.

The Sprite, a magazine of thirty-two pages, made its appearance in 1831; it was edited by a number of individuals who styled themselves the Elves of Gunnistan. The contents of this periodical presented little variety, and consisted of tales of a romantic and fanciful nature, together with essays, poems, and humorous sketches. The publication of The Sprite ceased with six monthly numbers, owing to the lack of financial support and the want of harmony among the editors. The next year produced a similar periodical, The Shrine, issued by one member of the junior class. The personal enthusiasm of its contributors made this venture a success, and it attained to the long life of two years. The Guest appeared in 1833, published by a secret literary club, but soon expired. The first publication on a per-

---

* Smith, B. P. History of Dartmouth College, p. 163; College Journalism, Yale Book, vol. i., p. 338.

manent bias, The Horæ Collegianæ, issued by the senior class, came out in 1837, and lived for three years. It was said to be the best representative of magazine literature which the college ever had. Eight years after its demise The Indicator (1848) entered the field. It likewise had an existence of three years, and owed its death to the profundity of its articles which were unsuited to a student periodical. It was succeeded by The Experiment, which was written, edited, and printed by one student, who hoped thereby to pay the expenses of his education. This ambitious youth died on the appearance of the fifth number of The Experiment. Finally, in 1858, a permanent magazine, The Amherst Collegiate, was established.*

Of the two types of college journal, the light ephemeral paper and the heavy literary magazine, the former is by all odds the most interesting as a portrayal of student life. One of the most interesting of these productions was the Students' Companion of Yale, edited by the Knights of the Round Table, the membership of which consisted of Arthur Fitzeddyn, the narrator; Roland Hopeden, the novelist; Launcelot Grammont, the reflector; Jeffrey McGrawler Blackwood, the critic; Francis Haller, the philosopher; Thomas Blondel, the troubadour; Raphael Werner, the delineator; Sir Tristam Trapp, the politician; and Harry Tudor, the recorder. While these mythical personages were all caricatures of actual individuals, the paper was written by one man, David Francis Bacon, of the class of 1831.† The sale of this periodical was good because of its mysterious origin. Many of these publications were abusive and scurrilous, like The Little Gentleman and Grid-

---

* Cutting, George R. Student Life at Amherst College, pp. 66–70.

† Yale Book, vol. i, p. 347.

iron of Yale; others more kindly humorous, like The Mummy Monster and The Boule Dogue of the University of Pennsylvania.*

The monthly literary magazine, on the other hand, is conspicuous for its dignity and heaviness of manner. " It must be strictly literary in character; propriety and taste forbid that it should intermingle with the facts and feelings of the world at large. Discarding politics, business, and polemics, it must be sustained as a thing of letters and taste." † Its prose articles were written in a ponderous style of the Johnsonese order, which tended toward bombast, personified the virtues, and feared to call a spade a spade. The subjects for the leading articles were general and elevating to a degree rather amusing to a modern reader. Imagine a modern junior trying his hand on " Classical Learning," " National Defence," " The Possibility of the Return of the Dark Ages," " Mathematical Learning," and " Sociability and Ceremony." In the treatment of these topics the standpoint is that of the orator and statesman rather than the man of letters or the scientist. The ideas of the author were merely the common-sense reaction of a man of ordinary intelligence clothed in vague and high-sounding language. Most of these productions were also remarkable for their exuberant patriotism. Besides the leading articles, these magazines published philosophic sketches and verse. The philosophic sketches are much after the manner of Rasselas and discourse of the vanities of life under such titles as, " On Emily," " Money," " Environment," " Love, Courtship,

---

* Schelling, Felix E. Organizations within the University, in F. N. Thorpe's Benjamin Franklin and the University of Pennsylvania, p. 415.

† Reminiscences of Scenes and Characters in College, by a Graduate of Yale, Class of 1821, p. 81.

and Marriage." The verse is bad, consisting of heavy Latin odes and clumsy translations of Horace. Occasionally, on the last page, there appear a few items concerning the college world, but a modern reader can not but be struck with the total lack of the picturesque and the local. Most of the articles might have been written at Calcutta for anything that the reader perceives to the contrary. The general impression which perusal leaves on the mind is that of a compromise between Johnson's Tatler and the early numbers of the Edinburgh Review.

The first periodical of this type which has come down to us is The Harvard Lyceum (1810–'11). The editors announced that the subject of American literature would receive particular attention both in regard to its comparative and its absolute state, and the causes which placed it in its present condition. To this end forensic discussions, the solutions of curious and interesting mathematical problems, studies in natural history and the classics, and essays of moral and religious import are all solicited. The editors throw incidental light on their political views by remarking that science and literature seem to be all that is old-fashioned and good that we have left: "They have flourished even from the manure of the French guillotine." A mock heroic in ten books, describing a journey along the coast of the Northern States, was the special feature of The Lyceum, which was otherwise marked by a general spirit of heaviness.

The romantic note predominates in the first number of The Yale Literary Magazine, published in 1837; the influence of Scott and Byron is seen on every page. The titles of some of the leading stories run as follows: "Love's Difficulty," a dramatic sketch; "The Trial of Love," "A Fragment of an Unfinished Tragedy," "The Skeleton of Tooloola," and "The Fatal Oath, a Fragment of an Unpublished Drama." The general articles are represented by such subjects as " Destiny," " The Pleasures of the Imagination," " Ancient and Modern Republics." The political articles are more to the point than in The Lyceum, and references to student life are more numerous, although even here they form a small part of the magazine. The early volumes of The Yale Literary Magazine are fair imitations of the periodical literature of the times.

To edit or contribute to the college magazine was one of the common avenues to college fame or notoriety. The writer stood on a pedestal just a step lower down in the scale than the orator. A literary editorship was one of the coveted class honours at Yale. Some of the more conservative critics like Bristed and the graduate of 1821 might question the value of so much practice in fine writing, or carp at the waste of time, but to the undergraduate world such editorial experience, together with oratory, seemed the most useful feature of education. Not the lack of enthusiasm but the small size of the colleges and the poverty of many students were responsible for the failure of so many journalistic enterprises. The list of college editors during this and the following period (1800–'70) includes the names of Edward Everett, William M. Evarts, Andrew D. White, D. C. Gilman, and Phillips Brooks.

Previous to this section we have treated of the important and typical associations, those which are in a peculiar sense characteristic of student life. In addition to these there has been a number of student clubs of minor importance and connected by closer bonds to the outside world. Such are the religious, philanthropic, political, musical, professional, and industrial associations. While they are of minor importance, their frequency and persistence forbid their total exclusion.

e. Religious Societies.—The most important societies

of this class are the religious circles which were formed in American colleges in the first decades of the nineteenth century. Previously the atmosphere of the college had been so predominantly ecclesiastical and theological that there was no room for voluntary associations. Their rise was due to the spread of what may be called the emotional type of religious experience which resulted from the evangelical movement of Whitefield and Wesley. The formal legalistic conceptions of the early Puritans found expression in long and frequent public services rather than in private gatherings for the comparison of emotional experiences. In a majority of instances " the societies of inquiry or praying circles " were the direct results of revivals. Another operating cause was the prevalence of sceptical views among the students, due largely to French Revolutionary influence.

The governing body of the college was, with the exception of one or two institutions like South Carolina College, distinctively Christian and denominational, but the students frequently went to the other extreme. Princeton is now the stronghold of orthodoxy, but of the Princeton students of that period we are told by Mr. Wallace that " French scepticism was carefully cherished by the young men as the badge of polite learning and freedom. The gay and reckless spirit which accompanied this philosophy of life was not wanting. It was necessary to ride hard, drink deep, and fear nothing. At one time there were only twelve students at Princeton who acknowledged their adherence to the old faith, and even so late as 1841 the little band of Christians were dubbed *religiosi.*" * At Washington College, Pennsylvania, students of a religious character were called monkeys and lapears.† The tendency was by

---

* Wallace, G. R. Princeton Sketches, p. 78.
† Hall, B. H. A Collection of College Words and Customs.

no means confined to these two colleges, and was strongest in those institutions where the Southern element was particularly numerous. At no time in American history has the line been so closely drawn between the Church and the world.

On December 11, 1802, the Saturday Evening Religious Society in Harvard College was organized for the express purpose of promoting the growth of practical and experimental religion. It was founded largely through the efforts of Eliphalet Pearson, Professor of Hebrew and Oriental Languages at Harvard, and afterward one of the founders of Andover Seminary and a leader of the Evangelical and Orthodox wing of Congregationalism. The society was formed for the express purpose of arresting " the decay of religion within our walls." In 1819 a second association was formed, known as the Wednesday Evening Society. In 1821 the two united under the name of The Society of Christian Brethren in Harvard University. Only those were admitted who believed in the doctrines of depravity and regeneration, in the existence of three persons, Father, Son, and Holy Ghost, the atonement, and the mediation of Christ; and could also furnish to themselves and others satisfactory evidence of a saving change of heart. Each member signed this confession. One important element in the work of the Christian Brethren was a valuable library.*

Religion was at a very low ebb in Princeton circles at the opening of the second war with England (1813). In this year four students began a prayer meeting, and succeeded in inaugurating a revival in college in which forty or fifty students were converted. The Philadelphian Society, the direct outcome of this movement, was

---

* Cooke, Joseph Pratt. The Christian Brethren, in Harvard Book, vol. ii.

formed in 1825. Confined to professors of religion, the society exerted influence abroad by the distribution of tracts on the first Sabbath of each month. The subject of missions was also to be brought before the society monthly, followed by a collection. Among the early rules of the society was the following: " The members shall hold themselves bound in honour to make no unnecessary disclosures of any rules or transactions of the fraternity." For some time the society met with considerable opposition, even from religious students, on the ground that it was a secret organization. In 1826 secrecy was somewhat relaxed, and prayer meetings were held on Sunday morning, open to all the students. A Thursday evening lecture was instituted, which was addressed by members of the faculty and by the resident clergymen. In 1855 a valuable library was destroyed.*

The Theological Society of Amherst was formally organized in 1821; its name was afterward changed to the Society of Inquiry. The members met informally on Sabbath evenings, in a quiet way consulted with each other, compared data which they had acquired, communicated intelligence, and spent a few moments in prayer. Members were few, and the influence exerted by the society was chiefly felt by its own members and was never great. Its object has been to form a bond of union and sympathy between Christian men in college, and in this it succeeded. The society corresponded with similar organizations in other colleges and with missionaries in the field. Its museum of curiosities in time grew to be quite extensive, consisting of idols, implements of various kinds, costumes, and a multiplicity of other things illustrating the religious beliefs, and the arts and customs of foreign lands. The

---

* Duffield, John Thomas. The Philadelphian Society, Princeton Book.

society possessed a theological library of two hundred and fifty volumes, and its tables were covered with a liberal supply of religious papers.*

At Williams the Theological Society dated from the first year of the century. By its side existed a missionary organization, the Mills Society of Inquiry (1820), the members of which were considered pledged for missionary work. Both these societies were the results of revivals. The Missionary Lyceum of Wesleyan was not organized until 1834. The Theological Society of Bowdoin was in existence in 1812; its object was more moral than theological. It owned a valuable library, which was lost in the great conflagration of 1821. By its side existed The Praying Circle, a distinctly religious organization. The great revival of 1821 of Brown University resulted in the formation of the religious society which held meetings in the college chapel. Six years later the Society for Missionary Inquiry appeared in the field, which aimed to supply its members with information respecting the moral and religious condition of the world. A Moral Society which existed at Yale in the twenties was a rather lifeless affair, although its debates were said to be interesting, and access to its library a privilege.†

Closely allied to the Missionary Society in aim was an occasional organization intended for some benevolent or philanthropic purpose. In 1815 there was instituted at Bowdoin a benevolent society made up of undergraduates, graduates, and friends of the college,

---

* Cutting, George R. Student Life at Amherst, p. 60.

† Durfee, C., History of Williams College, p. 117; Steiner, B. C., History of Education in Connecticut, p. 279; Cleaveland and Packard, History of Bowdoin College, p. 29; Tolman, W. H., History of Higher Education in Rhode Island, p. 197; Reminiscences of Scenes and Characters in College, by a Graduate of Yale, Class of 1821, p. 107.

which aimed to loan money to needy students. On the evening before Commencement a public address was delivered before the society in church, after which a contribution was taken for its benefit. "The liberally minded made it an object to be present for the advantage of this contribution." It aided a number of students, and perished after a useful existence of twelve years.*

During the same period an amusing experiment in the way of a Plain Dress or Lycurgan Society was tried at Yale. At the outset the society simply aimed to encourage plainness of apparel and simplicity of life and manners in opposition to luxury and effeminacy. The members interested in the cause were to exert an influence by setting a good example. In time the society was induced to adopt a distinctive dress, a sort of rustic cousin to the ordinary garb of the Quakers. The costume was so unbecoming to men of large and awkward frames that it caused the downfall of the entire enterprise. The Lycurgan Society checked extravagance for a time and was imitated in other colleges.†

The Anti-Venenean Society of Amherst found a common bond of unity for its members in the forswearing of ardent spirits, wine, opium, and tobacco, as articles of luxury and diet. This organization was first formed in 1830, and included one hundred and eighteen out of the two hundred and eight students in college at the time of its foundation, and for a number of years afterward included about three fourths of the membership of each class. The society was something of the nature of a pious fiction, as no meetings were ever

---

* Cleaveland and Packard. History of Bowdoin College, p. 29.

† Reminiscences of Scenes and Characters in College, by a Graduate of Yale in 1821, p. 127.

held, although the members were awarded elegant diplomas at the end of their college course.*

f. Political Clubs.—The political parties of this period had not yet developed that complex network of machinery for carrying elections which is now one of the marked features of contemporary campaigns, so no attempt was made by the politician to organize the students. The latter were so representative of the community at large that their political opinions coincided with those of the parties from which they came. The few societies of a political character which existed at this period were half philanthropic in their aims and exercised almost no influence. At Amherst, where the most complete inventory and history of student organizations have been made, we find records of a Colonization Society (1828), which aimed to support a colony of negroes in Liberia; an Antislavery Society, which existed for three years (1832–'35), until it was suppressed by the faculty, and a Peace Society (1838), before which addresses were occasionally delivered. Colonization societies, and occasionally an antislavery society, which inevitably caused trouble, existed elsewhere.† In general it may be worth noting that, as in other English-speaking lands, the students, instead of being a revolutionary and disturbing element, like those in Continental Europe, were inclined to be more conservative politically than the average citizen.

g. Military Organizations. — The first military organization at Harvard was the Martimercurian Band, which existed in 1793, but how long before and after this date I have not been able to discover. The Harvard Washington Corps was the outcome of the military enthusiasm enkindled by the approach of the War

---

* Cutting, George R. Student Life at Amherst, p. 55.
† Ibid., p. 94.

of 1812, and lasted twenty-two years. Membership was confined to the senior and junior classes, the juniors serving as privates and the seniors as officers. At first its organization was that of an ordinary militia company, but it afterward became a battalion. In accuracy and variety of military movements the corps excelled every militia company in the neighborhood of Boston, and received the commendation of trained soldiers. The company was allowed two grand parades a year; after some experience, visits to Boston were prohibited. The chief offices were much sought for by the leading members of the class, the captaincy being the chief honour of the year. The military office brought with it a strong sense of dignity, and the men committed no offences when trusted in their military capacities. Still, it was thought by the college authorities to be favourable to dissipation, which, together with lack of interest, led to its death in 1833.* A similar organization existed at Trinity College, Hartford.

h. Musical Societies.—The first musical organization concerning which we have a record was The Singing Club of Harvard College, which was formed in 1786 and continued to 1803. Its programme was largely devoted to psalmody, with some slight attention to instrumental music. The Pierian Sodality, which still continues, was founded in 1808; its social features were more strongly marked than the musical. The Sodality was divided into two parts; one section specialized on light sentimental music for serenades, and the other part prepared for college exhibition. A preparatory club, known as the Arionic, was instituted for novices, from which promotions were made to the Sodality. Low as was the standard of

---

* Lothrop, S. K. Harvard Washington Corps, in Harvard Book, vol. ii.

the Sodality, it was often on the point of perishing for lack of members; at one time only six in a class of seventy played sufficiently well to secure membership. The Harvard Musical Association grew out of the Pierian Sodality, but afterward confined itself to graduates.*

At Yale a musical society existed in the year 1812, but the particulars of its activity at that early period have not come down to us. Some time after its formation it assumed the name Beethoven, and furnished music at prayers and Sunday exercises. It was frequently known as the College Choir. The orchestral portion consisted of flutes, tenor violins, violoncello and double bass, " a most sonorous ophicleide," a big drum, with numerous guitars and Brazilian mandolins. The Beethoven Society likewise indulged in numerous serenades.† The Pæan Band of Amherst, organized in 1824, was a regularly constituted society with by-laws and officers. The instruments were furnished by contributions from the students and faculty, in return for which the band furnished music gratuitously on Commencement Day and on other state occasions. The graduating class supplied a jug of port wine for the refreshment of the weary musicians on Commencement. Contemporary with the band there existed the Lutheran Society (1822), the special function of which was to provide sacred music for Commencement. The Beethoven Society of Amherst employed outside musical teachers and endeavoured to cultivate the musical talent of the students.‡ Similar societies existed at Bowdoin * and elsewhere.

---

* Dwight, J. S. The Pierian Sodality, Harvard Book, vol. ii, p. 363.

† Stoeckel, G. J. Music and Musical Societies, Yale Book, vol. ii, p. 482.

‡ Cutting, G. R. Student Life at Amherst, pp. 89–91.

Cleaveland and Packard. History of Bowdoin College, p. 30.

i. Scientific Clubs.—The Harvard Natural History Society came into existence May 4, 1837; all members of the junior and senior classes who were interested in natural history belonged to it. The scientific interest of the members centred in the collection and mounting of specimens, ornithology, entomology, and botany were the favourite branches. Cambridge was at this period an excellent collecting ground, although members were by no means dependent on their own collections. The society met in the members' rooms every other week to listen to lectures delivered on some subject of interest. These lectures were simple talks which made the centre of discussion, although the chief interest lay in comparing notes on collections.*

A club of like purpose, organized at Amherst in 1822, was known as the Linnæan Society. Botany, geology, and mineralogy were the favourite subjects. Papers bearing on various scientific topics were presented at the meetings. Much time was also spent at these gatherings in analyzing specimens which the members had found in the Connecticut Valley. On one occasion the club offered a prize of scientific books to that member who should collect the finest herbarium. Interest waned and the society died out, only to be resurrected in 1831, as the Society of Natural History. The new association was a select body, open only to eight members from each of the three higher classes; the qualifications were " a good moral character, a respectable standing in one's class, and a distinguished reputation as a naturalist." Afterward a law went into force that one sixth of each class should be elected to membership. The society adopted a splendid badge in the form of a gold key of hexahedral form, with " N. L. D., 1831," on one

---

* Hale, Edward Everett. The Harvard Natural History Society, Harvard Book, vol. ii, p. 387.

side, and a small scroll containing an engraving of the word " Nature " and the owner's name on the other. The proceedings of the society were secret, and consisted, as before, of dissertations, analyses, and general information on natural history. A library and cabinet were established, the scientific periodicals of the day were subscribed for, and correspondence maintained with missionaries in foreign countries and with distinguished naturalists. Upon graduation it was customary for each member of the society to add a book to the library. Among the famous members of the society was Henry Ward Beecher, who made phrenology the centre of his interest. The club lived not quite twenty years, and died in 1848 because of the increased facilities for scientific instruction in the college.* The Society of Natural History at Williams College sent out a scientific expedition which made large collections in Nova Scotia.† At Bowdoin two short-lived scientific organizations, The Caluvian and Alpha Phi, collected cabinets of minerals and a few paintings, which on their demise were turned over to the college. ‡

Another form of professional activity was found in the medical colleges where clubs arose for the purpose of supplementing the regular courses and of preparing the students for examination by quizzes. The Medical Institute of the University of Pennsylvania was chartered in 1817, and has had a continuous existence since.⁑

---

* Cutting, George R.   Student Life at Amherst, pp. 57, 58.
† Durfee, C.   History of Williams College, p. 218.
‡ Cleaveland and Packard.   History of Bowdoin College, p. 28.
⁑ Schelling, Felix E.   Organizations within the University, in F. N. Thorpe's Benjamin Franklin and the University of Pennsylvania, p. 412.

CHAPTER IV.

§§ 1 AND 2. THE FRATERNITY AND ATHLETIC CLUB DURING THE TRANSITION PERIOD.

THE fraternity was the representative growth of the transition period from 1840 to 1870. We have described in preceding sections the origin and growth of the secret-society idea. In this chapter we will pass over rapidly the detailed history of the separate societies, which is of no particular interest to the general reader, and which Baird has already described in a manner that leaves nothing to be desired, but will lay chief stress on the controversial aspects of the new order of societies, in addition to describing the peculiar systems of secret societies which grew up at Harvard and Yale.

Harvard has developed a society system of its own, making sociability and congeniality the basis of membership, founded largely though not exclusively on a class basis; these organizations have been of slow growth. Of these clubs there are three classes: the sophomore societies, the senior societies, and general societies.

The Institute of 1770, the older sophomore society, was originally a debating club of the seniors, organized by the class of 1771. In 1825 two rivals of the same

167

aims coalesced, making it the only society in the field for many years. At first a senior society, it became a junior, then a sophomore organization. While its social duties encroached on its original functions, still, at the end of the period under discussion it preserved to a certain extent its character as a debating society; because of this fact it can hardly be considered a typical Harvard organization. In the late sixties its programme was described as follows: " The entertainment was of a literary character, consisting of debates not always too eloquent or brilliant; a lecture, usually a fair sophomore production; and a paper made up of original contributions which perhaps compared favourably with similar efforts at young ladies' seminaries. It was not so much the entertainment that was enjoyed by the young fellows as the meeting together and getting acquainted, the freedom of the hour, and the sense of proprietorship." Its meetings were the only opportunity afforded the class to form an estimate of the talents of the different men until the senior societies were reached.*

A rival organization with similar ends was organized in 1886, known as the Everett Athenæum, which made a specialty of music and theatricals.

The senior societies are much more noteworthy. The oldest of these is The Famous Hasty Pudding Club, founded in 1795, " to cherish the feelings of friendship and patriotism." The name of the club was derived from that clause in the constitution which provides that " two members in alphabetical order shall provide a pot of hasty pudding for every meeting." After a brief and unsuccessful experience as a debating society, the custom of mock trials was introduced, which lasted until 1847–'48. Next in order came the presentation of regular plays, which began with Bombastes

---

* Tripp. Student Life at Harvard, p. 288.

Furioso, in 1845. Since that date the production of two or three lighter plays each year has represented the literary side of the club's activity. In 1834 the club became a secret organization in reality, and an elaborate and amusing initiation ceremony was arranged. Each year's membership chose their successors.*

The O. K. Society arose from an opposition to the Greek fraternity system at Harvard in the year 1858. The membership was confined to sixteen men of the senior class. The society has never, with one exceptional period, occupied rooms of its own, but has met at the rooms of its different members in rotation. Declamation and the reading of original papers formed the staple programme of the early exercises, great attention being given to elocution and oratory. For a number of years theatricals played an ever-increasing part in the exercises until 1870, when they were entirely excluded by a new constitution.

At one time the O. K. endeavoured to play a part in class politics, to the great detriment of the order, which finally decided not to interfere in the elections. At this period, the late sixties, there was an intense rivalry between the O. K. and the Hasty Pudding. The initiation ceremonies of this organization, which we include below, are an interesting specimen of undergraduate rhetoric.†

---

* See Introduction to the Eleventh Catalogue of the Officers and Members of the Hasty Pudding Club in Harvard College, pp. 5, 6.

† On the entrance of the neophyte the President inquires, " Whence and what are ye, execrable shape ?

Verily I bring unto thee the elect, the chosen one, arrayed in clean garments, to await thy bidding.

President.—Has he performed his duty ?

Messenger.—Since set of sun, his labour knew no pause nor intermission.

President.—'Tis well. Let him be seated. Time will tell.

Pi Eta, founded in 1866, was not permanently sanctioned by the faculty until 1869. Its success was due to the increasing size of the class, which made a second society a necessity. It early secured permanent quarters which were elaborately fitted up. The Signet, the last prominent senior society, was founded in 1870, at the very end of the period. It was small in size and devoted to literary work of a high character. Theatrical performances were excluded.*

The Porcellian Club, the first distinctly Harvard

But first our Grand Astrologer must read the meaning mystic of the starry hosts. Strangers attend.

Grand Astrologer.—Brothers, since the red sun dipped in the glowing west his fiery disk, spangling the azure vault in quick succession as darkness spread her veil, I've watched revolving planets, fixed stars, and blushing Luna spring forth to life and light.

Impending evil then methought, to my prophetic eye, glared down from out the starry constellations; Mars glowed with fiery rage, and Sirius went barking through the sky with angry bloodshot eye that told of torrid equatorial heat. E'en Venus's smile was sickly, and great Jupiter looked glum and ominous of dangers dire and pestilence and woes unutterable.

A comet, too, there was dragging behind infinity of tail, which swept in hyperbolic curve along, swifter than forked lightning, as though it would annihilate the sun in greedy ruin. The air is heavy with a coming woe. The laboring stars are pregnant with a meaning, strange, mystic, weird, that puzzles e'en a prophetic eye to pierce.

President.—Some dire calamity, methinks, impends above the neophytic heads. But hark! The High Pontiff draws nigh."

The High Pontiff proceeds, in even more direful language induced by his inspection of the unlucky omens contained in the entrails of a dorbug, till the trembling neophyte is reduced to a proper frame of mind; when he is subjected to a searching interrogation and allowed to read his initiation work. Harvard Book, vol. ii, p. 400.

* See Signet Society, in Harvard Book, vol. ii, p. 414.

society to include members of all classes, was formed in 1791. At that time a number of intimate friends were in the habit of meeting in each other's rooms on alternate Friday nights for social intercourse; the exercises terminated with a supper. The association was known as The Argonauts; but one evening a young pig was roasted whole, and so successful was the occasion that the club was afterward known as The Pig Club. It early aspired to an exclusive social position and assumed the title of Gentlemen's Club, which it soon altered to Porcellian. The club consisted of sixteen members. Its founders aimed to establish the society " on some of the strongest principles of our nature; upon sociability, brotherly affection, and generosity; and upon those qualities of liberality and courtesy and that spirit of a true gentleman which are best expressed in the Greek motto of the society." The business affairs of the club are managed by three trustees, all of them graduates, who hold in trust all the property of the club, including library, pictures, and furniture. Small as the membership has been, the roll of graduates shows many of the most famous of the sons of Harvard, including Wendell Phillips, Channing, Story, Everett, Prescott, Adams, Palfrey, Charles Sumner, Oliver Wendell Holmes, James Russell Lowell, and John Lothrop Motley.

The A. D., another purely social institution, was organized in 1826 as an honorary chapter of the Alpha Delta Phi; as its active organization was prohibited by the Harvard faculty, it became in 1838 the honorary Yale chapter. Eight years later it received official recognition from the college authorities because of the excellence of its literary work. The anti-fraternity movement of 1859 resulted in a gradual change. It ceased to be a chapter of a secret fraternity and became a club of the usual Harvard type.

The Yale system of secret societies is much more strongly organized and much more extensive in its operation than that of Harvard. During this period a rigid class basis was maintained throughout, each year of the course having its distinctive societies. Without detailing the growth of the system, which discovers a mere tissue of petty jealousies, we will endeavour to describe the Yale system as it existed at the end of the period (1870).

The freshman societies at this time were the Kappa Sigma Epsilon, representing careless literary excellence; the Delta Kappa, standing for good fellowship and sociability; and the Gamma Nu, an open society of hard-working scholarship. Practically all the members of the freshman class belong to these clubs. A systematic campaign was waged for months in advance at all the important fitting schools. Many men are pledged long before they reach New Haven, and a keen struggle ensues for the possession of the men from a distance. The trains are infested with representatives of the various societies, who jump upon the platform of the moving cars, fight the brakemen, incommode the travellers, and defy the police, in the desire to offer the advantage of the best freshman society to the incoming student.

A week after the opening of the term, when all the men are pledged, comes the initiation. Each freshman is taken in hand by a particular sophomore, who at the appropriate moment guides him to a building from which the sounds of pandemonium are issuing. " A red devil in the passageway, assisted by a living skeleton redolent of phosphorus, quickly blindfolds him, and he is hurried upward. When he has reached an elevation apparently of several hundred feet, a new element in the continual din assures him that at last he is in the inquisitorial hall. But just as he begins to reply to the last nonsensical question put by an attendant fiend, some one jostles against him, and down, down, down he falls, until he strikes a blanket held in readiness for him. Then he flies up into the air again amid admiring shouts of ' Go it, Freshie! ' ' Well done, Sub! ' ' Shake him up! ' until a new candidate demands the attention of the tossers. Then he is officiously told to rest himself in a chair, the seat of which lets him down into a pail of water, though a large sponge probably saves him from actual wetting; his head and hands are thrust through a pillory, and he is reviled in that awkward position; he is rolled in an exaggerated squirrel wheel, a noose is thrown around his neck, and he is dragged beneath the guillotine, when the bandage is pulled from his eyes and he glares upon the glittering knife of block-tin which falls within a foot of his throat and can not possibly go farther. Being thus executed, he is thrust into a coffin, which is hammered upon with such energy that he is at length recalled to life, pulled out again, and made to wear his coat with the inside outward. This is a sign that the initiation is over." *

The exercises of these societies were of a literary character, consisting of debates, declarations, and orations. Select reading, essays, and society papers which were the miscellaneous productions of regularly chosen editors, were sometimes read. In conclusion, a criticism of the proceedings is offered. Occasionally a prize debate varies the regular order of proceedings. Each freshman society likewise possesses its song book, which it pretends to conceal. At times the success of members of the society in some collegiate contest is celebrated by a " peanut bum." A sack containing a bushel or two of peanuts is emptied upon the floor and an indiscriminate scramble is made for them by the

---

* Bagg. Four Years at Yale, p. 64.

upper-class guests and their entertainers; cigars are distributed, and in some cases lemonade; nothing stronger
is found in the freshman halls. At first a freshman
prides himself on his society and its secrets, but gradually his interest lessens, and by the third term the
society work is badly demoralized by the upper-class
elections.

The sophomore societies, two in number, Phi Theta
Psi and Delta Beta Xi, were much more select in character, containing less than half of an average class. The
members of these societies, turning their backs on the
heavy literary performances of their freshman days, go
to the other extreme and do little in the way of work
or improvement.

The halls of the societies are club rooms where
the sophomores drop in on Friday nights to play
cards, smoke clay pipes, and sip ale with one another.
During this year the loud-mouthed sporting element is
likely to be in the ascendency while the substantial men
remain in the background.

While these societies do not actually encourage dissipation, they can fairly be charged with being frivolous and purposeless in character. The members of a
sophomore society look back on their connection with
it as a joke, and to solicit money from them for it would
be a hopeless task.

Through the three junior societies—the Psi Upsilon,
Alpha Delta Phi, and Delta Kappa Epsilon—Yale is
connected with the regular fraternity system of the
country. Owing to the fact that the Yale societies are
for the junior year only, the tie between their members
is looser than in other colleges. The Yale chapters are
also less careful in preserving the secrets of the orders.
The literary exercises of the junior society are more
varied than those of previous years, and combine features from each of them. The regular programme is

less formal than that of the freshman society, and there is less prominence to the social features than in the sophomore societies. There are music and dancing as well as singing, and of course smoking and card-playing and occasional suppers. Much care was given to the composition of society songs, which were frequently sung in public. The senior societies were closely connected with college politics, most of the important honour positions being filled in the junior year. These organizations inspire more affection in their members than the clubs of the two previous years; their members frequently give large sums of money for the erection of costly halls. This feeling extends still more strongly to the graduates.

The senior societies of Yale—the Skull and Bones, and Scroll and Keys—were perhaps the most unique student institutions in the country. They were absolutely secret, their members never mentioning the society names in the presence of outsiders, nor do they in any way refer to rival societies. Pledges and electioneering are avoided. In theory the membership is made up of the best men of the year, fifteen in each society, who must be noted either for scholarship, literary ability, athletic prowess, good fellowship, or great wealth. The mystic symbols, badges, and numbers are particularly prominent, and are carried into the most ordinary details of society life. For instance, the official notes of the Skull and Bones are written to old members upon " black-bordered paper of the catalogue size, with or without the society head at the top. Society communications sent through the mails are often inclosed in black-edged envelopes, bearing at the end a printed request to the postmaster to return them to the society post-office box if not delivered within a certain time. They are sealed with a skull and bones, and the letters S. C. B. impressed upon black wax."

Each senior society possesses a hall of peculiar structure. The Skull and Bones Chapter House has been described as a " grim-looking, windowless, tomb-like structure of brown sandstone, rectangular in shape, showing a front of about thirty-five and a length of forty-four feet, and it is at a guess thirty-five feet high. The entrance in front is guarded by a pair of massive iron doors a dozen feet high, finished off in panels and of a dark-green colour, while heavy clasps of brass close over the keyholes and are secured by padlocks, beneath one of which a bell pull is concealed. The roof is nearly flat and is covered with half-inch plates of iron, which in 1867 took the place of the tin before employed. There is a skylight similarly protected, and the chimneys and ventilators are arranged along the edges of the roof. Behind are a pair of small windows barred with iron, and close to the ground are two or three scuttle holes communicating with the cellar." This building is valued at thirty thousand dollars; the new and more elaborate structure of the Scroll and Keys is worth fifty thousand.

" The attempt to make an outsider realize the overwhelming fascination which a senior society exerts upon the mind of the average Yale undergraduate would be probably useless. An election thereto is valued more highly than any other college prize or honour, and in fact these honours derive a good part of their attractiveness from their supposed efficacy in helping to procure the coveted election. There is nothing in the wide world which seems half so desirable." Membership in Bones or Keys is really valuable because it introduces a man to the best graduates of Yale wherever he may be, and secures him entertainment by the ablest undergraduates when he visits New Haven. Both the societies have developed in their men great pride and generosity which is expressed in a somewhat different way by the two organizations. The members of Skull and Bones avoided displays of their feelings, while Keys men rather ostentatiously exhibited the same. This attitude toward the public is typical of the two societies, Bones gathering in the real ability, leaving Keys the men of brilliant social qualities. Bones, being the older, has always stood highest in the opinion of the Yale world.

The attitude of the neutrals or the non-society men toward these two organizations was that of bitter hostility. The neutrals form a rabble on the night of election, which ranges about the college yard, barring up entry doors, raising false alarms, and otherwise disporting itself. A bogus society, called, in mockery of the Bones, the Bowl and Stones, amused itself ridiculing the usages and symbols of the senior societies by singing comic songs, printing and posting derisive handbills, and offering bogus elections to simple-minded classmates. At one time the neutrals went so far as to smash bottles of ink upon the front of Bones Hall, and tore the chains from their staples. They frequently steal the ice cream prepared for inaugural banquets.

Efforts have been made in other institutions, notably Columbia (Axe and Coffin), Michigan (Owl and Padlock), and Wesleyan (Skull and Serpent, and Owl and Wand), to imitate the senior society system of Yale. None of these imitations has been of any particular importance, for while the copying of the outer signs and names of the Yale system is easy, to gain their peculiar position and prestige is quite another matter. At Yale the existence of the lower-class societies facilitates the sifting of men so that the ablest students are well-marked characters by the end of the junior year. Harvard is the only other institution in the country where such societies would have been possible, and Harvard,

12

as we have seen, developed social clubs on the basis of congeniality rather than any society system properly so called.

No discussion of the fraternity system would be complete which failed to take account of the violent controversy which the introduction of this form of student organization has produced in American colleges. Students and professors have both been divided in their attitude upon the issue involved. Men of equally high standing and large experience are found who take a pronounced position on each side of the controversy; while the conflict of opinion is not now as sharp and bitter as in the formative period, yet the antagonism persists in perhaps three fourths of the American colleges. In a number of the smaller denominational institutions the fraternity is still excluded by a faculty enactment, while in others lodges are tolerated because it is believed that their exclusion is impossible. In the larger universities, particularly the State universities of the West, the fraternities and neutrals struggle for the supremacy in college politics.

The writer has known two men of the same antecedents and intelligence, graduates of the same college, at practically the same period, whose ideas on the fraternity question were as wide apart as the poles. One, after carefully reviewing his college career, gave it as his deliberate opinion that his fraternity experience was the most valuable portion of his college training; he considered the system almost without defects. To the other, the fraternity system was the chief cause of dissipation, rowdyism, and neglect of studies. A feeling of partisanship almost as deep as this pervades the literature of the subject; most of the articles in books are either attacks or vindications, eulogies, or disparagements. In the present section we shall merely aim to present the question historically, reviewing the chief items in the controversy.

As we have seen in the section relating to the debating societies, the introduction of fraternities tended to dissolve the old associations. The more conservative college men attached to the debating society found themselves at a disadvantage in college politics and so proceeded to organize open societies of their own, which professed to be the legitimate successors of the debating clubs. The struggle between the secret and anti-secret societies for the possession of promising men waxed fierce during the forties and fifties. At times this conflict seemed to overshadow all other student interests.* The same disadvantage which forced the open society men to combine in each college made co-operation between this element in the different colleges advisable. In 1847 the social fraternity of Williams united with the equitable fraternities of Union, Amherst, and Hamilton to form the Anti-Secret Confederation. Eleven years later the name was altered to that of Delta Upsilon, which has since been retained. Since 1860 the anti-fraternity feature of the Delta Upsilon has for all practical purposes disappeared and its methods and practices are identical with those of the other fraternity, except for the fact that its constitution is open to the public. For many years it was regarded with contempt by the secret fraternities, but of late this feeling has largely disappeared.†

The general attitude of the college authorities of the period may be followed from a number of letters by American college presidents, which Edward Hitchcock

---

* Hitchcock, Edward. Reminiscences of Amherst College, p. 321.

† Baird, W. R. American College Fraternities, first edition, pp. 67, 68.

prints in his Reminiscences of Amherst College.* Observing that a fraternity man expelled from one college found a ready welcome among his brethren in another, Hitchcock issued a circular letter to Northern college presidents, asking opinions as to the advisability of joint action in an effort to crush the entire fraternity system. Nine replies are printed, without giving the names. No president says a good word for the fraternity, although óne correspondent apologetically remarks that the society which exists in his college is supposed to be harmless. While they all agree as to the danger, the majority doubt the expediency of compulsory measures, testifying from experience that such action would probably intensify the evil. Some of the chief objections urged against the fraternity were that it divided the college into factions, thereby promoting envy and jealousy, and that they were unfavourable to religion. The unfortunate effect of the dissensions provoked by the fraternity on the old literary societies was mentioned by some of the writers. This discussion led to no action, and is valuable chiefly as showing the general attitude of college administrators.

However, many of the colleges attempted to uproot the fraternity system. In 1851 the faculty of the University of Michigan made the effort to crush all student secret societies, expelling the fraternity members from college.† This action aroused the Masonic order and other secret societies throughout the State and led to the downfall of the anti-fraternity administration. Princeton abolished fraternities in 1855, and remains the only

---

* Hitchcock, Edward.   Reminiscences of Amherst College, pp. 321–325.

† McLaughlin, Andrew C.   History of Higher Education in Michigan, p. 44.

institution of the first rank to persist in this policy. By the early seventies the fraternities which had been surreptitiously organized attempted to gain control of the Princeton halls, and it was only the strong influence of President McCosh which finally destroyed them. Princeton men have claimed an immunity from factions and petty jealousies because of this action.* It is said, however, that secret fraternity chapters have existed at Princeton during many periods of its recent history. In the late fifties Harvard also declared against fraternities. Many small colleges and State fraternities in the South and West followed the lead of Harvard and Princeton, and it was not until the late seventies that the opposition was relaxed. On the other hand, Pennsylvania, Columbia, Cornell, and to a certain extent Yale, have uniformly regarded the fraternities with favour.† The majority of small colleges in the East have taken the same attitude.

While chronologically the further discussion of this problem belongs to the next period, the fierce decade of controversy from 1870 to 1880 is so intimately connected with the storm and stress period that it may be considered in this connection. A digest of the chief controversial articles of importance will be followed by an account of the struggle between the opposing forces in two or three typical institutions of importance. In the conflict the fraternities have generally stood on the defensive.

The most comprehensive attack on the fraternity system ever made was published in 1874 with the title College Secret Societies; their Customs, Character, and

---

* Wallace, G. R. Princeton Sketches, p. 195.

† Schelling, Felix E. Organizations within the University, in F. N. Thorpe's Benjamin Franklin and the University of Pennsylvania, p. 418.

Efforts for their Suppression. This work, of which
H. L. Kellogg was editor, emanated from a committee appointed by the National Christian Association
in 1873. The committee issued two *questionnaires* to
the colleges of the country; the first solicited their
opinion concerning the relation which " Freemasonary
and kindred orders sustained to the moral and political
welfare of our country." The colleges replied that such
orders were enemies to political purity and social morality. A second circular, with which we are more immediately concerned, related to secret societies in
colleges. Forty-eight institutions situated in twenty
States replied. Three of these favoured fraternities;
the remainder show a " general and deep-seated convic-
tion that their nature and tendency are wholly evil."
The editor, therefore, states in his preface that the
book is designed to lead parents and guardians to a
hearty co-operation with college boards for the extinction of fraternities.

The first chapter of the book treats of the origin and
history of the fraternity system, and is both unsatisfac-
tory and unreliable. In the second chapter the fraternity system is described, accounts of initiation and
copies of by-laws previously printed in the newspapers
are inserted, together with a stinging arraignment of
secret societies. The author, Mr. Kellogg, describes an
attempt on the part of the Greek-letter champions to
break up an anti-fraternity meeting. He next outlines
the attempts to check and destroy the fraternities previous to the Cornell tragedy of 1873, which episode fills
the entire fourth chapter. The story of this affair is soon
told. A young man of good family while waiting blindfolded for an opportunity to be initiated into the Kappa
Alpha fraternity, accidentally walked off the edge of a
cliff and was killed. The fraternity unwisely endeavoured to suppress all accounts of the affair, with the

natural result of arousing the suspicions of the public.* It led to a bitter attack on the fraternities. Chapter V is the most valuable part of the book, as it contains testimony from professors and students in regard to fraternal secrecy. The answers strike an impartial reader as unrepresentative and prejudiced, as may be supposed from the parties and the character of the work; the conclusions in the last chapter are worthless.

The work contains considerable valuable testimony however, and gives an insight into the reasons for opposition to the fraternity. The two elements of antagonism which seem to have predominated were the religious distrust of the supposed immoralities and waste of time consequent upon fraternity life, and democratic hatred of anything with pretensions to aristocracy or selectness. Two papers of value previously published, one by Dr. Howard Crosby, in The Congregationalist for 1869, and the other by Prof. J. R. Jacques, of the Illinois Wesleyan University, read before the Central College Association in 1868, were reprinted in this publication.

Dr. Crosby wrote from a student connection with the Delta Phi fraternity. From personal experience, he objects to college secret societies because they encourage immorality and destroy confidence between parent and child. " They are a pretence, and thus at war with true candour and manliness. However harmless in their active operations or undertakings, however well composed in membership, the habit of secrecy is insidiously weakening to the foundations of frank truthfulness in the youthful mind. Sham is not only a mean thing, but it blocks the way to truth. A lazy soul finds a quasi success in sham and gives up the pursuit of the true. A lad who receives honour among his comrades

---

* Kellogg, H. L. The Secret Society System, pp. 51, 52.

because he wears a mystic skull and bones upon his breast will proportionately lose so much of his zeal for scholarship or all else that constitutes true worth." *
He also urges against the fraternities that they exalt the social above the intellectual, tend to cause insurrections against college authorities, destroy the regular literary societies, and increase the expense of college education.

Professor Jacques makes nearly the same charges against the system, emphasizing the difficulties in college government created by the presence of the fraternities. In his experience they embolden students against the faculty and tend to a laxer standard, warping and blindly influencing the president and professors with a vague fear of rebellion against wholesome discipline. With the other anti-fraternity writers of this period he makes the moral objection paramount. " They tend to breed that secretive disposition which is the very opposite of truly candid, generous, magnanimous character, besides affording opportunities for stealthy planning and plotting to accomplish the proposed ends; they divert attention and confidence from honest work, manly measures, eternal right, triumphant truth, to the tricks of a temporizing and compromising policy which need the secret conclave and sleepless cunning." †

Much of this criticism is of a condition of affairs which has long since passed away except in a few frontier colleges. The fraternities were in most cases newly established, with no reputation to lose. Each chapter was virtually independent, a condition favourable to recklessness. Many of the colleges were small and weak, pervaded with an intense evangelical fervour,

---

* Quoted by H. L. Kellogg. College Secret Societies, p. 32.
† Ibid., p. 36.

and maintaining an almost inquisitorial discipline. An antagonism in which neither of the contending parties appeared to advantage was the natural outcome.

E. E. Aiken's Secret Society System represents a more mature standpoint.* The abstract ethical objections are relegated to the background, and the author makes his case rest on the supposed effects of the fraternity life upon the students. He objects to the exclusiveness and what he calls the ostentatious secrecy of the fraternity, and because of its effect on non-fraternity men. To quote his own words: " There is something terrible about the silent exclusion, stern and cold as death and about as hopeless, by which the neutrals are left out of what they believe to be the controlling powers of the college." † Concerning secrecy, he observes that it belongs to a juvenile mind and a juvenile state of civilization. It is the meat of petty rather than large minds, and of the feminine rather than the masculine cast of thought. The matter-of-course secrecy of the home is contrasted with the ostentatious secrecy of the fraternity. The privacy of the fraternity is advertised publicly, as if two friends should publish that they were about to exchange confidences and warn everybody off, thus violating the very spirit of privacy.

The disintegrating effect of the fraternity on the social life of the class is treated at length. President Porter of Yale, and President Robinson of Brown, who made a special report on the fraternity question, are quoted in support of this view. Says President Robinson: " Fraternities and the management of class affairs

---

* E. E. Aiken. The Secret Society System, New Haven, 1882. The book is more immediately directed against the peculiar system at Yale, although the author by no means confines his criticism to his Alma Mater, and five sixths of his arguments are intended to apply to fraternities in general.

† Ibid., p. 64.

lead to habits of intrigue and the practice of the low
arts of the politician. Combinations and bargains are
often made to secure the election or defeat of candidates
for parts in exercises of class day at the end of the college course which are inconsistent with the disingenu-
ousness of youth and scholars." The fact that members of the faculty have belonged to fraternities excites
the suspicion of the neutrals, who often regard them as
working secretly to advance their organization.

" Real friendship," argues Mr. Aiken, " is not the
result of formal compacts and societies; the spiritual
bond is the true one, covenants of friendship are unnecessary, compacts are made for different ends. In a
social club it is very hard, in the first place, to make
formal lines correspond to natural relations, a difficulty
much increased when the club is not formed by them
whom it is to unite, but by others; and, secondly, an element of selfishness creeps in which is likely to demoral-
ize the organization." " I hate the prostitution of the
name of friendship to signify modish and worldly alliances," writes Emerson. " Society is spoiled if pains are
taken, if associates are brought a mile to meet. Like
living for happiness, seeking friendship defeats its own
end. Then, again, club life gives undue· prominence to
social and physical enjoyments as such, and consequently is not calculated to further the true ends of
college life."

The case against the fraternity is well summed up in
a paragraph by President McCosh, of Princeton, which
we here insert in full: " They foster in youth when
character is forming a habit of underhand action and
underhand procedure which is apt to go through life.
It should be one of our aims to rear open and manly
character. There is always a tendency in these secret
organizations to meddle with college management, to
check certain plans of the college authorities, and in-

fluence elections to college honours. They often tempt young men to drink and dissipation. Nearly every professor acknowledges them to be an evil, but is afraid of them." *

The two ablest justifications of the fraternity have been written by Mr. W. R. Baird, in his American College Fraternities, and by ex-President Andrew D. White of Cornell. Of the two, Baird represents the polemic attitude, as he answers point for point the arguments advanced by the opponents of the system; President White the affirmative side, stating the benefits to be derived from fraternity life.

Baird begins his chapter on College Fraternities— Have they a Right to live?—by a review of some of the anti-fraternity literature, including the books of Kellogg and Aiken. His representation of these works, while not incorrect, is misleading, because he emphasizes certain details in his opponents' arguments to the exclusion of more important issues. While more skilful than his opponents, Baird is equally lacking in candour, and betrays an ignorance of other student organizations, particularly of the debating society. His chapter is in truth a special plea for the fraternity. He defends fraternities under the following heads: secrecy, political relations, moral relations, fraternities and faculties, anti-fraternity laws, and expensiveness.

In discussing secrecy, Baird declares that it is a minor factor in fraternity life; that in most respects the fraternity, instead of being a secret, is in many respects a distinctively public organization because of the display of badges and the publicity of their banquets and conventions. Their secrecy consists of but two elements: the members hold meetings with closed

---

* McCosh, James. Discipline in American Colleges, North American Review, vol. cxxvi, p. 440.

doors, and do not tell the meaning of the Greek letters by which they are known. The fraternities are merely called secret, and differ fundamentally from other secret organizations.

As to the relations of the fraternities with the college faculties, Baird claims that where opposition exists it is due wholly to the fact that the faculty refuses to recognise the fraternity as a useful social party existing within the college. When the authorities conclude to recognise the fraternities, they find the chapters only too glad to assist in maintaining order. The fraternities tend to mitigate class hostility and to banish hazing, and in numerous other ways to benefit the college. If, however, the faculty passes anti-fraternity legislation, they create the very evil they seek to counteract by driving the students to form secret lodges which have no reputation to lose and do much damage.

The only charge against the fraternities which has the slightest foundation in fact is that of expensiveness. Most of the money, however, is spent by a class of students who would get rid of it in any event, perhaps in some less legitimate way. "We can say from personal experience and after careful inquiry that the fraternity expenses in any one chapter rarely exceed twenty dollars per annum in a city college with a comparatively small society, while any increase in the size of the chapter reduces the expense proportionately. In country colleges, where living is cheaper, the total expenses will rarely amount to more than half that sum. In return for this outlay the members receive lasting benefits in the way of business and social training. They have the help of the upper classmen and the use of a costly library, perhaps, and usually the privileges of a chapter house.*

---

* Baird, W. R.   American College Fraternities, p. 349.

" In college politics the fraternities have not caused the formation of cliques as such, for they existed years before the system was developed, and depend for their formation upon the inherent conditions of human nature. The single fraternity is too small to act as a clique, and the only method of procedure would be to form combinations. The societies themselves strongly disapprove of such combinations, and many of them have legislated against the practice; the general sentiment prevailing among fraternity men is that interference in politics is a mistake. The fraternities have introduced neither cliques nor politics into college life: they found them there and have left them." If fraternity men are elected to offices it is because they generally comprise the most prominent and deserving students. The author, however, weakens the force of his vindication by remarking, further on: " The *esprit de corps* engendered by membership in the fraternities, and which we deem a most valuable feature in their organization, may at times degenerate into political allegiance, but it is not the first or only time that a good thing has been put to a bad purpose."

To the charges of immorality sometimes levelled against the fraternity, Baird replies that fifteen per cent of the membership of the fraternity is composed of clergymen, including bishops of the Methodist and Episcopal churches, and more prominent divines in other denominations. These men are identified with the societies after graduation and advise their sons to join them, which would be hardly the case if the chapters were the seats of dissipation.

To ex-President White there are great advantages in the permanency and public character of the fraternity. Unlike a merely temporary club, it has a reputation to make and maintain. The badge which each member wears fixes his responsibility; if he is less than a gentleman he disgraces his fraternity. In time each chapter comes to have a body of graduates who naturally scan closely their brethren in college, and are the first to condemn any conduct which would be likely to injure the fraternity. No chapter can afford the approval of its graduates because of its dependence on them for incoming members and financial support. The fraternity pride can be appealed to in case of discipline. When a man is failing and in danger of suspension the university authorities can call in the senior members of the fraternity, dwell on the injury that the man is doing the order, and insist that they either reform him or remove him. This succeeds when all other measures have failed. Fraternity pride also prevents social occasions from degenerating into carousals. The fraternities throw healthful restraints around their members which prevent degeneration.

The chapter house is an excellent substitute for the home. Its possession brings to the undergraduate a healthy sense of responsibility. He no longer indulges in carelessness, uproar, and destruction which characterize dormitory life. All properly constituted chapters contain steady, earnest men who exercise a thoughtful care over the younger members. Socially the fraternity is likewise advantageous to its members. " Simple receptions and entertainments show a growing away from one of the main objections to the association, the growth of a petty, narrow, contemptible clique spirit." *

While the fraternities take part in college politics and bear the same relation to student life which the guilds held in the mediæval municipality, such a condition of affairs is inevitable in the present conditions of American life, where a dozen students can not be

---

* White, Andrew D. College Fraternities, The Forum, vol. iii, p. 247.

brought together without developing party politics. The real dangers from which the fraternities should guard themselves are the growth of a narrow clique spirit and extravagance. These should be fought against at every step, although so far as they exist within the fraternity they are simply bubbles on the great stream of American life.

Dr. White saves his strongest language for colleges which endeavour to suppress the fraternity. Such efforts he says must always be futile. When it has been attempted, badges were worn for years beneath the students' coats, meetings were held by stealth, and a system of casuistry adopted by the members when questioned, which was injurious to the students from a moral point of view. Such secret chapters are cut off from all connection with their graduate members and gradually degenerate. Moreover, a general repressive policy defeats its own purposes and deprives the college authorities of the power to rid themselves of any particular fraternity which is really evil; for when an attempt is made to drive out all fraternities, they will stand by each other to the last. "They will simply conceal their badges and band themselves as a wretched, occult, demoralizing power. On the other hand, if each fraternity is allowed to exist on its own merits, any one thought injurious by the college faculty can easily be driven out. It is one of the easiest things imaginable. I myself have driven out an old and widespread fraternity which was doing evil to its members, by a simple public statement why members should keep out of it." *

Charles Kendall Adams, likewise President of Cornell, expresses more moderate ideas. He sums up his experience by saying that good societies are beneficial,

---

* White, Andrew D. College Fraternities, The Forum, vol. iii, p. 248.

bad societies injurious. According to him, three or four of the Cornell chapters have a beneficial effect on their members; two or three others are at least doubtful in their influence. The fraternities usually keep the black sheep among their own members from excesses, but not always. They give their members a certain polish, but on the other hand they interfere with the highest scholarly progress of the very best fellows.*

The second characteristic of the period under discussion was the increasing interest taken in athletics. Not only were athletic games more frequent, but the interest manifested itself in the creation of formal athletic organizations and in the inauguration of intercollegiate contests. The years from 1840 to 1870 were the formative period in American student athletics.

It was some time after the wave of athletic interests struck the colleges before the typical athletic sports—boating, football, baseball, and track athletics—emerged from a number of competing games. At Princeton, in the period from 1840 to 1865, handball and cricket were in vogue. The first regular athletic organization at that college was a cricket club, formed in 1857. By 1870 it had disappeared from the field. The first regularly organized and equipped gymnasiums at Yale, Princeton, and Amherst were put in operation during this period.†

Boating was the first organized sport to gain a permanent foothold. As early as 1843 the first racing boat was purchased by a Yale undergraduate, and the first club formed. From that time on there has never been

---

* The Academy, Syracuse, vol. ii, p. 373. This article contains opinions by Presidents McCosh, of Princeton; Seelye, of Amherst; Adams, of Cornell; Prof. T. C. Burgess, of the State Normal School, Fredonia, N. Y.; and Prof. Oren Root, of Hamilton.

† Princeton Book, p. 443.

less than three student boat clubs at New Haven. In
1852 the so-called Yale Navy was formed, which elected
a commodore or admiral of the fleet, who had charge
of all boating arrangements. So great was the interest at this period that in 1859 the entire college was
divided into twelve clubs of twenty men each. This
elaborate organization, which was taken from the English, proved much too cumbersome; class crews were
found to be greatly superior to the boat clubs, and in
1868 the entire scheme was dissolved. The Yale University Boat Club was substituted. The boating interest at Harvard came later, and it was not until 1852
that the first intercollegiate boat race between the two
colleges took place on Lake Winnepesaukee. Six miscellaneous contests on three different courses and with
varying conditions occurred between 1852 and 1860.
In 1864 racing under standard conditions was begun
between Harvard and Yale on Lake Quinsigamond near
Worcester. In a great majority of the earlier races victory inclined to Harvard. Elated by five successive
victories over Yale, Harvard in 1869 sent a crew to
England, which was beaten by the University of Oxford.
The conditions were unfavourable to the visiting crew,
as the race was rowed over a difficult course.*

The intense spirit of athletic rivalry which has
played such an important part in developing college
sport in America seems to have been in evidence for the
first time at these contests on Lake Quinsigamond.
Here for the first time we note the hard training, the
great popular excitement, the special trains, the cheers
and colours of contending colleges, the recriminations
and charges of unfairness, the newspaper sensationalism, and the fierce exultation and abandon of victory
with which the modern student is so familiar. As local

---

* See Harvard Book.

13

opinion favoured Harvard, Yale objected to the continuation of these races, which led to the inauguration of the Rowing Association of American Colleges, which belongs to the next period.*

The formal organization of baseball came a decade later than boating. The first regular nine was formed at Princeton in 1858, at Amherst in 1859, and at Yale in 1865. Princeton was the first college to advance the new sport vigorously. In 1862 the Nassaus, as the Princeton nine was called, became the champions of New Jersey, and defeated non-academic athletic clubs. Two years later interclass rivalry in baseball was instituted at the same institution, and from there made its way to other colleges. The first of the regular series of the Harvard-Yale baseball games was played in 1868. The primitive conditions of the game may be imagined when we learn that Princeton beat Columbia by a score of fifty-nine to thirteen, and that the figures of the second Harvard-Yale game were forty-one and twenty-four. Instead of being supported by a general athletic association, the baseball players constituted themselves a society, with the regulation president, vice-president, secretary, treasurer, and three directors.

A rough form of football was one of the traditional amusements of college men as far back as pre-Revolutionary times. The old custom of a freshman-sophomore game was continued at Yale until 1858, when it was prohibited by a municipal ordinance of the city of New Haven, because such contests invariably took place either on the Common or in the streets of the city. A football club was organized at Princeton as early as 1857, but soon died. In 1864 the sport was revived

---

* Good descriptions of these early contests are found in G. H. Tripp's Student Life at Harvard, and Hammersmith's Harvard Days.

and was said to be the most popular of all athletic games; 1868 saw the first university club, which was beaten by Rutgers in the following year. It was not until three years later that the rules of the game were written down, oral tradition serving until this time. The early Princeton game differed in many points from the present form of the sport. Football was revived at Yale in 1870, by D. S. Scharf, an old Rugbyan, and in 1872 a football association was formed. During this period there was no uniformity in the game, each section in the country having its own rules. Harmony was not secured until 1876, when the Rugby rules were formally adopted by a convention of American colleges which met in New York.

By the end of the period, in 1870, athletics had won a recognised place in college life. Boating was efficiently organized in the two chief New England colleges and sporadically cultivated elsewhere; baseball was found in all the colleges of first rank in the East; football was exciting considerable local student interest, but was in a more backward state of development; track and field sports received little recognition. In boating, competition was fierce, and discussion of the advisability of mitigating some of the severity of the contest appeared in the newspapers and elsewhere. The other sports were too new and undeveloped to have given rise to serious criticism.

CHAPTER V.

§ 1. CLASS DURING THE MODERN PERIOD.

SOON after 1870 new influences began to be felt in the superior education of the country. Most prominent among these forces has been the elective system which has tended to destroy that community of interest upon which the class depended for its vitality. The rapid increase of students resulted in sinking the individual in the mass and in limiting the circle of collegiate acquaintance. A student could no longer take a personal interest in all his classmates, for they were so numerous that he could scarcely know them all by sight. Then the very multiplicity of interests and organizations in many modern colleges militates against that closeness of association which made the class so powerful. These influences have been strongest in the larger colleges and universities, particularly those situated in large cities where the *esprit de corps* has always been weakest. Because of its size and the free extension of the elective system, Harvard affords an excellent opportunity of observing the result of these new tendencies. By 1880 the Harvard class ceased to be the preponderating social unit, and ten years later it was said that even for administrative purposes class lines were tending to disappear. Two students might enter Harvard from the same

196

school and by the same examinations, and never meet again in any academic work during their entire course. One might graduate in three years, the other in four, so they would be placed in the catalogue of graduates as belonging to different classes.* At Yale conditions have by no means changed so rapidly. The men study for two years together before there is any appreciable break along elective lines. The students gather by classes in the chapel; their voluntary prayer-meetings are class gatherings. They row and play football by classes. Even the college journals, secret societies, and debating clubs are conducted on class lines.† Yale, however, is exceptionally conservative here as in many other respects. The conditions in the great universities of the West much more nearly approximate Harvard.

In all the colleges and universities the class exists as an organization. In the larger institutions it has ceased to be a social power and is chiefly remembered by the old customs and traditions which are connected with it. These are carried through in a half-hearted way, which contrasts in a marked manner with their former vigour. In the smaller colleges which train three fifths of the youth, the class remains with much of its old-time power and vigour. The changes in form and spirit which have taken place in the last thirty years can be most satisfactorily indicated by outlining the conditions at the present time. The class of to-day is strongly institutionalized. It possesses a written constitution, stating its aims, defining its powers, and providing for a full corps of officers. These are the usual officers of all voluntary associations: the president, vice-president, secretary, and treasurer, with the addition of athletic

---

* Thayer, W. R., in Harvard Graduate Magazine, vol. iii, p. 468.
† Welch, L. S., and Camp, W. C. Yale: her Campus, Classrooms, and Athletics, p. 37.

officers, the managers of the various teams, and a number of ornamental officials, such as historian, orator,
poet, jester, whose duties are nominal. The ornamental officers vary greatly among the different institutions. The students of Adelbert College elect a *magis-
ter equorum;* the position is usually filled by the most
unpopular man in the class. The " toughest man " in
the class is often chosen chaplain, and the most eccen-
tric individual either jester or sergeant-at-arms. The
term of the offices is six months in the Western colleges
and one year in the Eastern institutions. Class meetings
occur at intervals of a month or more, except in the first
and last years of the course, when class functions are
most prominent.

The value attached to class offices as college honours varies in the different colleges. The presidency is
nearly always sought after, and is particularly prized
during the freshman and senior years. To be president
of one's class, however, carries with it more prestige
among the outside public than within college walls.
Whenever the offices are considered highly desirable,
political canvasses are organized to gain possession of
them. The issue is generally either between the fraternity and the non-fraternity element, or between different combinations among the fraternities. In a body
as small as the average college class the personal popularity of the candidate is an element that must always
be reckoned with, regardless of social affiliations.
There is usually but little competition for the minor
offices, although a good treasurer is quite as essential
to the prosperity of the organization as a good president, and is much more difficult to discover.

When we turn to the functional activity of the class
we discover that a great change has taken place in the
last thirty years in the manners of the undergraduates.
Hazing and rushing are gradually disappearing. Testi-

mony from such institutions as Tufts,* Harvard, and Yale in New England, Adelbert and Pennsylvania in the central group of States, Wisconsin, Nebraska, Beloit, and Leland Stanford in the West, all point in the same direction. It is evident that the old customs are largely perpetuated from a sense of duty to the traditions of the past. An excellent example of this is seen ·in the sophomore-freshman rush at Harvard known as Bloody Monday. Occasionally there are relapses to violence with serious results, like the accidents at Cornell and the Ohio Wesleyan, but they form the exception. The gradual disappearance of violence has been commonly credited to athletics. It may be questioned, however, whether other factors, such as the greater age of students upon entering college, and the general mildness of manners characteristic of our time, have not been equally potent in producing the result.

The class has certainly come to have a recognised place in athletic organization. Each class is represented by its nine, eleven, and track team, and various interclass contests are scheduled. A special effort is directed to developing freshmen teams in order to discover athletic capacity among the newcomers. Contests with freshmen teams of other institutions are encouraged for the same reason. It rarely happens that there is any very live interest in athletic games between the classes, although the attempt is frequently made to generate some artificial enthusiasm. Public attention is so focused on the college team that few students care what becomes of interclass cups and championships.

The rôle of the class in the social world is becoming more important. To class day and the junior exhibition have been added junior proms (or promenades),

---

* Start, A. B. History of Tufts College, p. 65, contains an interesting account of the abolition of hazing in that institution.

senior hops (balls or dances), freshman banquets, and
sophomore cotillions. These are the great public social events of the college year, but in many institutions they have long since ceased to belong exclusively
to the class which gives them. In a few institutions,
like Beloit College, such social occasions are prohibited
by the faculty; in a few others, fraternities and cliques
control them. In some of the larger institutions the
class occasions have ceased to be representative, as the
wealthy element predominates. The expense of the last
junior " prom " at Yale was so heavy that a large portion of the class were prevented from attending.

In the great majority of American colleges the class
publishes the annual or year book. Positions on the
editorial board of this publication are eagerly competed
for. The class in its official capacity occasionally presents farces and even more serious dramatic efforts. In
some colleges it is customary for each class to produce a
farce caricaturing the faculty or certain of its unpopular members.

In general, the influence of the class has declined.
Instead of the strong, spontaneous, all-powerful association of former days, the modern class is simply one
among the many organizations of college life. Yet the
picturesque side of class activity seems appreciated as
never before. That somewhat mysterious sentiment
known as " class feeling " does not appear to be on the
decline. At the University of Nebraska it is reported
as being on the increase, in spite of the elective system.
Correspondents from Vanderbilt, Leland Stanford, Lafayette, Beloit, and Bates testify to its growth. There is
undoubtedly a strong feeling among the colleges of the
country to the effect that the peculiar flavour of college
life should be preserved. This tendency is seen in the
movement for the maintenance of a distinct academic
costume—the cap and gown; in the revival of old cus-

toms,* and in the invention of new ceremonials.† Such a movement has a significance to a student of democracy, but that it will succeed in re-establishing the conditions which made the old common life of the class so effective seems impossible.

§ 2. DEBATING SOCIETIES IN THE MODERN PERIOD.

There exists a class of institutions, small in number but respectable from their academic standing, in which there are found no student organizations aiming directly at practice and public speaking. Such practice in these colleges is gained either from courses in forensics from oratorical and declamatory contests for medals and other prizes, or else it is not obtained at all. Most of these colleges are located in the extreme East, although occasionally one may be discovered in the South and West. Typical institutions of this class are Brown, Trinity, and Wesleyan, and in the West the University of California.

In the second class are placed those universities which have recently organized special debating clubs on a new plan and chiefly as auxiliaries for intercollegiate debating. Practice for beginners and the mass of students is obtained in a series of class debating clubs which serve as supports for a university debating club or debating union, which is reserved for picked men and advanced students. Such organizations are solely for the purpose of obtaining practice in debate, and are entirely lacking in *esprit de corps* and social features. Harvard and Yale are the best representatives of this class of institutions, although some of the smaller colleges have attempted to imitate them. At Harvard the system was adopted after considerable experimentation,

* Columbia University Quarterly, vol. i, p. 389.
† Start, A. B. History of Tufts College, p. 71.

which began in 1879, with an attempt to reproduce the Oxford Union. The name remained until 1897, but the society was something entirely different.

A great majority of American colleges belong to a third class, which retains the old debating society, but with essential modifications. Discussions here are likely to be on political and social topics, and extemporaneous discussions are most popular. The social features have dwindled to a tithe of their former greatness. The collective membership of the societies never includes half of the students, and frequently not more than seven or eight per cent. In many colleges these societies serve as a rallying point for the non-fraternity element, although membership is never exclusively confined to it. In such institutions the societies usually furnish a majority of candidates for the intercollegiate debating and oratorical teams, and their membership is from the more substantial element among the students. This general characterization applies to Wisconsin, Cornell, Nebraska, Minnesota, and Leland Stanford among the larger institutions, and Lafayette and Western Reserve among the well-equipped colleges.

In the fourth and last class of colleges the debating society still remains one of the potent factors of student life. It maintains its position as a social centre. Society rivalry waxes keen and society anniversaries are numbered among the important events of the academic year. Princeton alone, of universities of the first rank, adheres to this system, largely by reason of its conservative conditions and hostility to fraternities. However, it is commonly reported that, notwithstanding their magnificent halls and official recognition, the Princeton societies are losing their hold from year to year. The remaining institutions of this class are local in character—small colleges, and colleges existing in peculiar environments, where for various reasons the fraternity has not yet entered in sufficient strength to be a disturbing factor. The institutions of this class are usually denominational colleges.

To understand public speaking in American colleges during the last quarter of a century it is necessary first to survey a number of parallel movements. Firstly, there has been an important change in the ideals of public speaking. Oratory as a fine art is on the decline. Public speaking is coming to be considered merely as a means to an end; form is being subordinated to substance. Clearness and accuracy are valued above oratorical fervour and redundancy of expression. In many quarters high sentiments and passionate declamation are likely to produce amusement. To characterize a public man as a great orator savours of irony. This revolution has been brought about by the increased attention to science in modern education, and by the general improvement of public taste. The movement is confined to the critical portion of the professional classes, and has scarcely touched the vast mass of the population who are as susceptible to oratorical appeals now as in the past.

The smaller colleges of the West—which, as we have before indicated, remain in close touch with the ideals of the middle class—specialize in the line of popular oratory. Besides inter-society contests, State and interstate leagues are formed as an additional stimulus. Ten States and one hundred colleges were represented in an oratorical league which existed in the Mississippi Valley in 1895. This league by no means represented the complete strength of the movement, because many State and local leagues were unrepresented for geographical reasons. There has been a discernible tendency for reform associations, particularly the Prohibition party, to adopt the intercollegiate oratorical association as a means of propaganda. One representative from each college is chosen for the State contest. The intercollegiate contest takes place between the candidates who have been successful in the local competition. Women often take a high rank in these exhibitions.*

The limitations of these contest orations are obvious. Confined to two thousand words or ten minutes, the youthful orator must immediately plunge into invective paradox, antithesis, and solemn warning, which might well become experienced statesmen at the end of a three hours' speech in the Senate, but which sounds absurd when delivered by a sophomore who has never voted or studied the elements of economics. Most of these orations are high-keyed and artificial. The temptation to phrase-making, to spectacular displays of rhetoric, proves too much for the majority of competitors in these contests. They usually pay but meagre attention to the accuracy of the facts on which their pleas are based, and their presentation lacks all that strength which comes from reserve and moderation, while to an outsider who for the first time listens to one of these displays the effect is somewhat startling. After a time one detects the scanty fund of commonplaces, and tires of the reiterated appeals to do something, to stand alone, accompanied with references to Thermopylæ and Brutus, Luther and Calvin, Washington, Lincoln, and Grant. While space will not permit us to include quotations from these addresses, some idea of their aims may be obtained from their titles. Among the orations delivered at the interstate contest in 1895 were the following: " American Literary Genius," " The Better Personality," " The Statecraft of Napoleon," " The Province of Law," " The Hero of Compromise,"

---

* For an account of these contests see article by Albert Shaw, College Oratory in the West, Review of Reviews, vol. xi, p. 665.

"Fidelity to an Ideal," "Our Nation's Safeguard," "A Plea for Shylock," and "Social Progress."

A competent critic is likely to condemn the entire practice as mischievous and worthless. He is wearied by the hazy thinking and disgusted by the platitudes. With the editor of The Nation, he knows that one may talk for hours and say nothing on any subject similar to those enumerated above, and that the perfection of the type would result in nothing better than a half-poetic rhapsody worthy of Ossian.* And it is not to be denied that an excessive indulgence in this type of public speaking destroys a man's capacity for accurate thinking, and tempts him to premature expressions of opinion on subjects of which he is ignorant; views which he afterward feels himself bound to defend. More serious yet, excessive rhetorical display causes a young man to mistake high-sounding combinations of words vague and meaningless for real concepts.

Admitting that such perversions are common and should be guarded against, is there not, after all, something to be said for the oration? Is not youth a period of large ambitions, of high aspirations and dreams; and can it be complete if all opportunities for the expression of these sentiments are eliminated? To the writer it would appear that the oration has a legitimate function in the preparation of youth in the higher schools. Indulgence in the rhetorical impulse is necessary if in the future the public man is to rise above mere technic and detail to a higher plane. High sentiments and he-

---

* Godkin, E. L. Collegiate Oratory, The Nation, vol. xxvi, p. 38. The speeches consisted mostly of commonplaces and platitudes taken in a loose way from the most accessible books and poorly put together. Not one bore the evidence of careful preparation as regards facts and logic. All the speeches kept pretty clear of fact and avoided anything like an argument; none contained any sign of wide, accurate reading.

roic points of view are as legitimate and influential expressions of the human spirit as accurate generalizations. A certain modern tendency to depreciate everything but mere organized facts is born of a shallow rationalism and a mechanical commercialism; such a tendency is based on a mistaken conception of the needs of active life. However, to be of value from a pedagogical standpoint, the oration should be based on fact, and should represent the real opinions of the speakers; otherwise it degenerates into the cant and affectation of sentiment.

Intercollegiate debating on a large scale is the result of the last decade.* Contests between high schools and academies have taken place for many years, and it was from these that the idea of intercollegiate debating originated. The present movement began in 1889, when Harvard sent the first challenge to Yale. Despite considerable ridicule, the proposition was accepted, and into the association thus formed Princeton was afterward admitted. Other important leagues are the Pennsylvania-Cornell combination in the central States, the union of Michigan, Wisconsin, Chicago, and Northwestern in the West, and the California-Stanford alliance on the Pacific coast.

In 1893 † a scheme was proposed by which all the colleges of the country were to be united in one alliance. Each month a question for debate was proposed by the alliance, which was to be discussed by the individual institutions. The advantages ascribed to this plan by the promoters were numerous; it was thought that such a demand for knowledge on certain subjects would be created that the popular magazines could be induced to

---

* Ringwalt, R. C. Intercollegiate Debating, The Forum, vol. xxii, p. 633: Sketches of the history of intercollegiate debating.

† See Carl Vrooman, The Arena, vol. x, pp. 677-683.

print a large number of articles dealing with the questions. The plan aimed chiefly at arousing a more general student interest in debating matters. Questions of
great interest, dealt with monthly by the ablest men
in the institution, would gather larger audiences and
thereby stimulate interest. The men were to choose
sides according to their convictions, instead of being
assigned questions at random. This change would put
an end to simulated sentiments and unreal passion, and
place the entire debate on a substantial basis. A record
of the votes taken on the different questions was to be
preserved as an index of student opinion. The plan
came to nothing, but contains some just criticism on the
methods then in vogue.

The constitution of an intercollegiate debating
league is simple and elastic; a committee from each college arranges the details, the colleges alternately propose the questions for debate, the second institution
having the choice of sides, thus insuring the acceptance
of a proposition with two well-balanced aspects. No
graduate of either college may serve on the board of
judges, and no judge may be chosen except by the unanimous consent of both committees. Within the university itself the different debating societies choose representatives, who compete before a committee of the
faculty which selects four men. In some colleges men
outside of the colleges compete, while under the system
which prevailed at Harvard for a number of years, any
member of the university might compete in a five-min-
utes speech. This plan was found ineffective, because it
afforded the committee no adequate data from which to
make their judgment.

The debaters chosen, a serious course of training is
at once undertaken: either the debaters or their special
advisers in the faculty issue a bibliography of all the
books and articles bearing on the subject for dis-

cussion. The debaters then cover the field in a thorough course of general reading. When this is completed they meet, compare notes, and divide the field, each man being apportioned some particular line of argument and investigation. The preparatory process being completed, they prepare a logical outline or skeleton of their line of argument, which is given to the coach for criticism. From this time on the coaching forms the principal element in the training.* The chief coach is usually a professor in the department of history or English, and supervises the entire process, and is assisted by instructors in elocution and others. Under this expert direction the contestants write down and commit a set speech, although at times this is not intended to fill the entire time at their disposal. During the period of preparation the training is severe and rigorous; the debater is criticised and exercised on all points of doubtful strength; he is daily forced to meet in impromptu argument the ablest men of the college, whether professors or old debaters. The influence of modern athletic training is evident here; in some cases the influence has been direct.

In the debate each speaker has either fifteen or twenty minutes for an opening speech, and in some cases is allowed five minutes in which to refute the arguments of his opponents. In other debates the third speaker only hazards the risk of reply. Instances have been known in which one side attempted no extemporaneous speaking whatever, and yet won the contest. The questions chosen usually involve some public issue, but so worded and limited as to confine the discussion to the

---

* See Ringwalt, R. C., Intercollegiate Debating, Forum, vol. xxii, and Albert Bushnell Hart's Introduction in Brooking's and Ringwalt's Briefs for Debates, for an account on the different steps in the training of debaters.

expediency aspect of the problem. The speeches are fluent, logical, well-arranged expositions. They are usually framed too closely in a common plan to sustain interest; their collective effect is likely to be monotonous. Notwithstanding the moderate tone of the speakers, the debate is often the occasion for great enthusiasm. Delegations of students make noisy demonstrations, and the winning team receives " tremendous ovations." Considerable local fame in the line of newspaper biographies falls to the lot of the intercollegiate debater. He sometimes receives a more substantial reward in money prizes which are divided among the successful contestants. The existence of such inducements illustrates the essential artificial character of intercollegiate debating. Its popularity is confined to a small portion of the students. The faculty and the outside public foster debating, but it is not a native interest of the majority of students.

Intercollegiate debating, with its careful training and statement of facts, forms a valuable antidote to the tendencies of American stump-speaking. A distinguished critic has referred to our national style as turgid and inflated, as marked by rhetoric, which is Rhodian rather than Attic, overloaded with tropes and figures, and aiming to conceal poverty or triteness in the thought by profusion of ornament, and appeals to sentiment too lofty for the subject or occasion.* It is when contrasted with such a style that we are able fully to appreciate the training which the college course in forensics and the intercollegiate debate are offering to the youth of to-day. The careful preparation, the absence of display, the analysis of argument, lay the foundations for a new style of public speaking. It is when con-

---

* Bryce, James. The American Commonwealth, vol. ii, chap. cxi. American Oratory.

14

trasted with the speeches delivered in legislative bodies and printed in the Congressional Record that the merits of the new mode of training become apparent. A competent observer has said that the average intercollegiate debater speaks with more clearness and accuracy than the ordinary member of Congress.

But the new movement has not been without its critics. The complaint most commonly heard is that the coaching is overdone; the debates are gradually becoming contests between rival college faculties.* It can not be denied that the coaching is the most important factor in determining victories, and that success in intercollegiate contests is no test of the vitality of the debating interest in the different colleges. Recognising the danger, Harvard proposed to the Eastern League that action be taken to check this tendency. Failing in this endeavour, the Harvard debaters attempted a reform within their own boundaries. The faculty were no longer to arrange the lines of argument for the debaters, to criticise their speeches, or even to debate with them. General directions as to reading, and suggestions from the teaching body as to elocution, were still to continue. The experiment is comparatively recent, and the results of the two systems have not been thoroughly tested.†

Connected with the preceding criticism is the objection that the present system discourages originality of thought and spontaneity of expression. The speeches are cast in one mould; there is a dead level of mediocrity. An English visitor has recorded his impressions to this effect: He found an intercollegiate

---

* For admissions of and protests against this fact see Harvard Graduate Magazine, vol. v, pp. 398, 545; Brodt, P. E., Debating Societies at Columbia, Columbia University Quarterly, vol. i, p. 52.

† Since this paragraph was written, recent changes in the Eastern League have reduced faculty coaching to a minimum.

debate serious to the point of dulness, lacking in the humorous and satirical thrusts which were found in the best speeches of the Oxford and Cambridge unions.* Ethical objections have been raised to the plan of assigning men positions on debates regardless of personal opinions. Except as a preparation for the bar, it is urged that the ability to maintain any given thesis is of doubtful expediency, particularly in youth, when there is a natural tendency toward sophistry. If the questions dealt with were primarily ethical in character and affected the foundations either of morals or of social theory, such an objection might have some force. However, as most of the debates deal only with the questions of detail and political expediency, this criticism loses much of its cogency.

In conclusion, we may summarize the weaknesses of the intercollegiate debate by saying that it completes the training on too low a level. It gives admirable preparation for public speaking up to a certain point, but the inherent artificiality of the system prevents it from approximating the actual conditions of public speaking, and consequently it is by no means conducive to developing the higher reaches of oratory. Then, again, its resources are concentrated on a few men, to the neglect of the majority. With the present apathy of the collegiate public toward debating, it was probably the only method which would have met with even a moderate degree of success. By enlisting intercollegiate rivalry on its behalf, it has attracted public attention and thus prepared the way for future progress.

---

* Percy Gardiner, in The Nineteenth Century. Impressions of American Universities, January, 1899, p. 110. "The youthful orator seemed to me to equal or surpass our English undergraduate debaters in fluency and ease, but I was not greatly impressed with their debating force. They seemed rather to repeat a prepared theme than to demolish one another, or really grip the subject."

The ideals of intercollegiate debating have been closely interwoven with the courses of collegiate instruction in the department of forensics. The colleges had given considerable attention to public speaking from the pre-Revolutionary period on; but, until recently, such attention was confined to rhetoric, opportunities for display at Commencement, and other exhibitions, and coaching of a somewhat desultory character. The instruction was weak along theoretical lines, and the criticism devoted mainly to the accessories of style and elocution. Contemporaneous with the intercollegiate debating movement an effort has been made to place such instruction on a scientific basis. The specialists in this department have produced a number of valuable handbooks. Rhetorical teaching has departed from its old structural definition standpoint and taken up with the new point of view of function. The struggle for a higher standard in English composition and the rapid growth of scientific treatment of institutional history have aided in the reconstruction of the debating ideal.

As the university courses of instruction illustrate the current tendencies in public speaking, it has been thought worth while to devote considerable space to their consideration. In order to arrive at some tentative conclusions, a statistical study was made of the courses in oratory, forensics, and elocution in seventeen representative colleges. The larger universities and colleges were selected because of their probable more immediate response to modern conditions. The smaller colleges tend more frequently to represent the conditions of the past. Of the seventeen colleges, six—Harvard, Brown, Columbia, Cornell, Pennsylvania, and Princeton—were selected as typical of the East. For the West, not only the leading universities—Michigan, Wisconsin, Minnesota, Northwestern, and Chicago—were chosen, but likewise two large Western colleges, Oberlin and the Ohio Wesleyan. The South is represented by Johns Hopkins, Virginia, and Vanderbilt; the Pacific slope by Leland Stanford and the University of California. In all cases the data were collated from the registers of the year 1898–'99.

Omitting duplications in the professional schools, the seventeen institutions offered one hundred and four courses of instruction in preparation for the different forms of public speaking. By a rough estimate, the average college offered six distinct courses of instruction. Among the different colleges there was a great variation in the amount of work offered, Chicago and Minnesota leading with twelve and ten courses respectively, Virginia giving only one. An equally great contrast was apparent in the emphasis on the subjects of instruction. Chicago seemed to specialize on elocutionary training, Cornell in furnishing immediate opportunities for speakng, Harvard in the theory of argumentation. In many colleges the courses in forensics and oratory are so intermingled with the instruction in English that it was impossible to estimate the actual amount of time given each. Probably the amount of teaching done in an average institution of this class would need approximately the entire services of two instructors.

The classification of these courses, without first-hand acquaintance with their contents, is an undertaking involving considerable risk. The announcements are not always definite in their outline of the courses which are sometimes composite in character; and it is scarcely necessary to add that such statements usually represent what the instructors hope to accomplish rather than the territory usually covered in the class-room work. In consequence, the following conclusions are of service only in the most general way: The entire one hundred and four courses fall into four main divisions—(1) general introductory, (2) elocution and voice culture, (3) forensics, and (4) oratory. Under the heading, general introductory, have been included only those courses which distinctly announce their relation to the work in public speaking; ordinary courses in English have been omitted. Only ten general introductory courses are offered. The next main division, elocution and voice culture, leads with fifty-five courses, sixteen of which are special and given over to the reading and interpretation of Shakespeare, the Bible, lyrical poetry, and hymns. Forensics, argumentative composition, and debating come next in importance with twenty-four courses, six of which consist of actual practice in debating. Most diversified are the courses falling under the general description of oratory. Out of the fifteen courses, six are devoted to general practice and impromptu speaking, five to the survey of the oratorical field, and four lay special stress on the history of oratory and public speaking.

Three or four conclusions may be drawn from this study: Firstly, it seems probable that, in so far as the extent of territory covered is concerned, the instruction is adequate. Some of the universities tend to subdivide the field unduly, while others go to the contrary extreme and advertise more lines of study than can possibly be followed efficiently in one course. Secondly, the predominance of elocutionary training and analytic argumentation is strikingly in evidence, they comprising seventy-three out of one hundred and four courses. On the other hand, the history of public speaking, including its relations to political and social life, is scantily treated. The most common methods are either to dissect two or three speeches, usually those of Burke or Webster, or hastily to survey the history of oratory from Demosthenes to Gladstone, which survey largely consists of striking anecdotes of doubtful origin. Neither of these methods seems to meet the student's need. The most valuable training appears to come from that intangible growth which is the result of close contact with the works of masters. In oratory such an understanding will rarely come from the analysis of lines of argument, or the minute study of one or two speeches.

The relations between the debating society and the college department of forensics are usually cordial, each supplementing the other. In order to determine these relations more accurately, however, a circular note was despatched to the chief instructors in the seventeen institutions before mentioned. Fourteen replies were received; of these, twelve considered the debating society a valuable adjunct of their work, while two conditionally opposed it. At Northwestern and Minnesota the departments have been the means of establishing new discussion clubs. The instructors favour the debating society because it gives the men practice, teaches them tolerance, and offers them a chance to apply knowledge. They criticise the debating society for the lack of critical standards, and for the vague thinking and pompous diction which it is said to foster.

§ 3. The Fraternity in the Modern Period.

During the last thirty years the fraternities have entered upon a new stage of their development; with the storm and stress period of their history behind them, they have been free to perfect the details of their system and to expand. As early as 1871 a movement toward the centralization of the various societies was inaugurated. The old system of control by central or parent chapters when the convention was not in session gave way to central governing boards, usually known as executive councils, composed of alumni, which performed functions similar to those delegated to the boards of trustees in American colleges. In this body is vested the ownership of the fraternity property. The determination of fraternity policy remained to conventions of delegates consisting largely of undergraduates. Many of the fraternities have divided the college territory of the country into provinces, and shown great insight and judgment in the location of chapters. It has been claimed that the action of the larger societies in issuing and withdrawing charters may be taken as an almost sure index of the future of the college.*

In recent years the influence of the alumni has increased greatly, and many of the societies have endeavoured to still further augment this influence by establishing alumni chapters and fraternity clubs. In a few instances the alumni chapters are regularly organized, hold sessions, and send delegates to conventions, but in a majority of cases they are chapters only in name. Fraternity clubs are a more natural expression of interest. Several fraternity clubs have been founded in New York, San Francisco, and elsewhere. Two or three societies have established summer camps in the woods for the recreation of their members.†

The chapters at the stronger fraternity centres are coming to partake more and more of the character of social clubs. The progress of the club idea may be traced in the architecture of the fraternity houses. The earlier structures were built as lodge rooms or temples for general meeting places only, while the more recent buildings are complete club houses, containing public rooms, lodge rooms, and sleeping apartments. Many of the modern fraternity houses are ornate and expensive structures, of which their members are justly

* See The Independent, August 3, 1899, an article by W. A. Curtis, The Decline of the Denominational College.

† W. R. Baird. American College Fraternities, fourth edition, p. 22.

proud. The club idea finds its freest expression at Harvard, where the typical societies are local and unconnected, and therefore in a position to respond quickly to the movement of the age. A recent writer speaks of Harvard club life in the following strain: " The small clubs are not conducive to sustained effort in the public service on the part of their members, but, after all, their seductions are not necessarily irresistible. . . . For superior men who are too active to be pocketed, the clubs are pleasant without being unprofitable. There are usually such leaders among the Harvard clubmen, but they are leaders because it is in them, and rather in spite of the clubs than because of them." *

It may be remarked in this connection, however, that in adopting club life the students of our wealthier colleges have only followed the lead of the society of which they form a part. Of the merits and demerits of club life in general it is not our purpose to discuss here, although it may be added that this tendency does not seem to have attracted the attention of educators to an extent proportioned to its importance.†

Among the geographical types of fraternities, the societies of the Southern group, founded soon after the conclusion of the civil war, have spread rapidly in the last thirty years. Sectional lines are rapidly becoming

---

* Edward S. Martin. Undergraduate Life at Harvard, Scribner's Magazine, vol. xxi, p. 543. Mr. Martin also adds: "The clubs have their uses, but probably the most satisfactory talk that goes on between undergraduates is not the talk of the clubs, but the seasoned communication born of affinity which passes from man to man by gaslight in the college rooms."

† W. R. Thayer traces the rise of the club idea at Harvard in an article, Shall we have a University Club? in the Harvard Graduate Magazine, vol. iii, pp. 474, 475. Some aspects of club life at Harvard are described by C. M. Flandrau in his Harvard Episodes—Wolcott the Magnificent.

obliterated, especially between the West and South; the
Eastern group have been much more conservative than
the other two in expanding, although their chapters are
found side by side with the other two types at such
recent foundations as Chicago and Leland Stanford.
While sectional lines are tending to disappear and all
the general fraternities are becoming national, each society is coming more and more to stand for a fixed ideal
of culture. For instance, Fraternity A makes wealth
the criterion of membership, Fraternity B literary capacity, Fraternity C sporting tastes, Fraternity D all-
round good fellowship or social qualities, and so on
throughout the list. In the older colleges of the East
these characteristics are more firmly fixed than elsewhere, and the same society usually has the same ideal
in different colleges, while in the West the same fraternity may stand for different ideals in different institutions. In the smaller and more newly founded colleges
there are usually certain fraternities which stand for
nothing in particular, and admit almost any one they
can secure to membership.*

---

* In order to make our meaning clearer, we will include extracts from the reports of correspondents in different colleges :

Adelbert College, Cleveland.—" The best fraternities have a distinct social ideal. The better the chapter here, the more unique
and distinct is its characteristics. The poorer chapters seem to be
mere collections of rag ends and left-overs. One fraternity stands
for social prestige, one for athletic prestige and the character of
its men ; a third may be said to stand for scholarship."

Beloit College, Wisconsin.—" The fraternities do not represent
distinct social ideals."

University of Nebraska, Lincoln.—" The fraternities do stand
for different ideals. Some aim for social prestige, some for athletic superiority, some for scholarship, and one or two at a combination of these—that is, at a representation of the entire life of the
university.

Vanderbilt University.—" The fraternities stand for different

In addition to the general college fraternities (men's), twenty-nine in number, which we have described, the vitality of the idea is seen in the rise of women's fraternities, sometimes known as sororities, professional fraternities, honorary fraternities, and secondary school fraternities. There are also a large number of local societies of this type, of which Baird enumerates twenty-eight for men and fourteen for women.* The most noteworthy of these, such as the I. K. A. Society at Trinity College, the Alpha Sigma Phi at Norwich University, and the Phi Nu Theta at Wesleyan, have long histories and were the creations of the same movement which produced the general fraternities. Some of the others are disgruntled chapters of general fraternities which have either seceded or been expelled; a third class consists of chapters which have been recently formed for the purpose of securing admission to some general fraternity. If they fail in their object, they almost invariably disappear, as the conditions of modern college life make the formation of new societies increasingly difficult. As a group the local fraternities are comparatively unimportant, numbering in 1898 5,389 members, to the 142,688 of the general fraternities.

---

ideals to a certain extent, several fraternities emphasize social prestige, others college honours, including places on the college team or musical clubs. Scholarship alone could secure entrance to no fraternity, although some chapters would be more influenced by it than others."

At a prominent Western university a story is told which illustrates the difference between fraternity standards. One of the fraternities having expelled a member for drunkenness, another Greek-letter man observed that his society would expel a man who was not drunk periodically.

*.Baird, W. R. American College Fraternities, fifth edition, pp. 280, 298.

Women's fraternities are almost entirely the product of the present period, for, although the Pi Beta Phi was organized in 1867, it was not a purely academic society for some time afterward. Kappa Alpha Theta and Kappa Kappa Gamma were founded in 1870, and Delta Gamma in 1872. Women's fraternities originated in the coeducational colleges of the West and South, and have never gained a strong foothold in the women's colleges of the East, which usually prefer some form of literary or scientific society. In colleges where women's fraternities exist, they enroll a smaller proportion of their constituency than do similar societies among men. They are close copies of men's fraternities, and are said to differ only in being much more exclusive. In many coeducational colleges there is a tacit social understanding between certain of the women's societies and some few of the men's fraternities.

Professional fraternities have been founded for students in law, medicine, music, scientific agriculture, engineering, commerce, and the Spanish language. The majority of these societies are small and unimportant, being confined to four or five colleges, although one or two are the regular fraternities for engineering and agricultural schools of a high grade. The one exception to the generalization regarding size is the Phi Delta Phi, a legal fraternity founded in the law school of the University of Michigan in 1869. It lacks many of the common characteristics of a fraternity; its chapters are named for great lawyers, and the use of the ritual is not mandatory. Its motto, grip, and password are not communicated to outsiders; otherwise the organization is open. The Phi Delta Phi avoids antagonism with all existing literary societies and general fraternities, drawing its members impartially from all of them. The chapters are expected to draw up a schedule of work, supplementing the regular lectures of the law school.

After graduation the members make use of their connection with the order to obtain an interchange of business and information. Its members are said to be known by their high legal accomplishments.

The honorary fraternities, six in number—the Phi Beta Kappa, the Pi Beta Nu, Sigma Xi, Lambda Sigma eta, Tau Beta Pi, and Alpha Theta Phi—aim only to designate a certain aristocracy of talent. The oldest and most important of the group, the Phi Beta Kappa, did not become purely honorary until the antimasonic movement in the thirties.* For many years after this the chapters met but once a year, to listen to an oration and poem, and to elect members for the ensuing year. The Phi Beta Kappa key became and has remained the symbol of high scholarship in the colleges where the society exists. In 1881 the Harvard chapter initiated a movement for the reconstruction of the order, which resulted in the adoption of a new constitution in 1882. The order is now organized on a modern basis. In 1898 the Phi Beta Kappa numbered forty chapters, with a membership of 19,334. The five remaining honorary societies follow closely the Phi Beta Kappa in their usages, and have only a local importance and small membership.

The academic or secondary school fraternities are treated in Chapter VII, which deals with student organizations of the secondary school and may be passed by in this connection.

In a previous chapter we have discussed the struggles which ensued from the early foundation of the fraternities to the beginning of the modern* period. The task remains of bringing the discussion down to date. In general, it may be said that, while the antagonism between the fraternities and their opponents still ex-

---

* See Chapter III for early history of the Phi Beta Kappa.

ists, much of the bitterness and clamour has disappeared in the last twenty years. Of late, college authorities have been more cautious in antagonizing the societies; the firmly established position of the fraternities has cooled the ardour of their adversaries. A few struggles of importance between faculties and banded alliances of Greek-letter men remain to be noticed.

One of the most interesting tests of strength took place in 1881 at Purdue University, an industrial college founded by the State of Indiana. The faculty for a time permitted the organization of fraternities, but, having satisfied themselves that the societies were endeavouring to change the course of the college, they attempted to crush the chapters by compelling freshmen to sign an anti-fraternity clause. The guardian of a student who was refused admission on this ground carried the case to the Supreme Court of the State and obtained a judgment against the college administration. The anti-fraternity president of the college resigned and was succeeded by an enthusiastic supporter of the Greek-letter cause.

A similar conflict between the professors and fraternities of the University of California, two years earlier, resulted in a defeat of the faculty, although they were strongly supported by a majority of the students. For several years an intense hatred separated the two factions among the students. Fraternity members on two occasions endeavoured to assault non-fraternity men who had attacked their characters in the college papers. The non-fraternity men published a pamphlet tracing the history of each one of the societies then in existence at the university, and charging the fraternity element with dissipation, negligence of university work, cheating in examinations, and the publication of obscene literature. From an examination of the college records the editors of the pamphlet claimed to prove that during ten years 42.28 per cent of the entire membership of the fraternities had been expelled, against 18 per cent of the non-fraternity men.* The decisions in the California and Purdue cases made the position of the fraternities secure in State institutions, but the power of the faculty remained unchecked in private colleges."

At Vanderbilt University the faculty endeavoured to protect the literary societies from what it considered the inroads of the fraternities. At first, secret societies were absolutely forbidden, but they came and remained in spite of prohibition. In 1879 indirect recognition was extended to the fraternities by a rule which debarred their members from competing for the honours of the university, including the medals in oratory, the candidates for which were chosen by the literary societies. Under this *régime* the literary societies became the arena for fraternity cliques and combinations. Four years later the faculty changed its tactics and passed a rule to the effect that the literary societies should certify that the speakers elected to the contests were eligible. The attempt to saddle the societies with the enforcement of the law failed miserably. One society flatly refused, and the other dodged the issue. Finally, elections for honours were transferred to the faculty and fraternities permitted to exist.†

---

* The charges were not vague and general, but given with circumstantial detail. This pamphlet is one of the most interesting documents in American student literature. It is by no means a mere hysterical protest, but is written with considerable force and cleverness. The title runs as follows : " An Account of the Greek-Letter Fraternities of the University of California, republished, corrected, and brought down to date from the Files of the Occident Newspaper for the Year ending June 1, 1883. Berkeley, 1883."

† Merriam, L. S. Higher Education in Tennessee, p. 167.

Numerous colleges still prohibit the organization of fraternities, but, with the exception of Princeton, they are small denominational institutions and are not regarded by the fraternities as suitable locations for chapters. Notwithstanding the fact that none of the best fraternities care to gain a foothold in such places, the majority of the students are often frequently leagued together in secret orders, usually quite temporary, for no better reason apparently than to be in opposition to the college authorities. In colleges of this class the literary societies are still strong and possess an *esprit de corps* which reminds one in many ways of the fraternity. With the increasing wealth of the students, fraternities will in time find their way into the majority of these institutions.

The antagonism between the Greeks and barbarians, or non-fraternity students, has continued a much more constant factor in the legal opposition of college faculties. The strength of the two parties varies widely with different sections of the country and different classes of institutions. In general, the fraternities dominate the smaller colleges, particularly those of New England and the Middle States, although an occasional revolt on the part of the non-fraternity men sometimes occurs.* The " barbarians " are strongest at the large colleges, particularly the State universities of the West, which have always been the seat of a strong anti-fraternity feeling. The issue occasionally comes to the surface in the Harvard class-day elections.† In the senior elections at Yale, class of 1899, the entire non-society ticket was elected.

---

* Start, A. B. History of Tufts College, p. 68, describes such a revolt.

† Harvard Graduate Magazine, vol. iii. p. 209 ; also Thayer, W. R.. Shall we have a University Club? Harvard Graduate Magazine, vol. iii, p. 471.

In one of the large Western universities, where the writer happened to be acquainted with the conditions of college life, both parties were organized in a manner very similar to that of outside politics. The fraternities formed an alliance, and divided the offices in proportion to their strength and influence. The non-fraternity men were still more systematically arrayed. Their forces were divided and subdivided for campaign purposes; each leader had a territory assigned him, where he was held accountable for the vote. In class and general elections (for student-body officials) there were no speeches or outward signs of agitation, but both sides instituted a thorough canvass, and brought their entire voting strength to the polls. In general elections, the greater numbers of the non-fraternity men usually carried the day; in smaller elections their forces were less manageable, they were frequently betrayed by their leaders, and were in consequence at a great disadvantage in diplomacy and in the control of small boards or committees. Realizing this fact, they abolished all such bodies and threw all the important offices open to direct popular election. To prevent chicanery, they endeavoured to secure as much publicity as possible in the management of public affairs. The great lack of the non-fraternity party was competent leaders; the fraternities always endeavoured to pick off their best men. The division of the students into two great parties, while provocative of much wrangling and some narrowness, insures a more competent administration than could otherwise be secured, because it means a certain measure of responsibility. Student politics in such an institution is a faithful copy of outside conditions, in many ways neither better nor worse. A certain type of undergraduates will employ machine methods and stuff ballot boxes as freely as the most veteran politicians; another type of men work for a clean and hon-

15

est administration; the great majority are indifferent, except in cases of closely contested elections.*

The continuous existence of organized parties almost equally strong and pitted against each other in each successive election, as described in the last paragraph, is a somewhat exceptional phenomenon which exists only in large Western universities like Michigan, Wisconsin, Indiana, and Leland Stanford. In most colleges an anti-fraternity movement is a somewhat spasmodic affair, intense and unreasonable while it lasts, but soon over, after which the college settles down to its normal condition. Strange to relate, these movements frequently result in the formation of new fraternities by the most vigorous protesters.

The American † fraternity system has attained to a strength and stability which have rarely characterized student associations. The general fraternities alone (men's) have a membership of one hundred and thirty thousand members. No statistics have been gathered in regard to their property, but a rough estimate places its valuation in the neighbourhood of five million dollars. The prominent fraternities issue an entire series of publications, including extensive catalogues

---

* The participation of fraternities in college politics is sometimes denied. We append the following representative testimony from our correspondents:

Beloit.—" Fraternities control elections for athletic positions."

Lafayette.—" Fraternities enter politics and control class elections to a limited extent by first combining among themselves."

Nebraska.—" Sometimes the fraternities enter politics, at other times they unite with the literary societies."

Vanderbilt.—" Fraternities as such do not enter college politics, although they sometimes influence votes in the literary societies."

† The term American here must not be limited to the United States, as important chapters have been organized in the Canadian universities.

and expensive quarterly magazines, and hold conventions, with hundreds of delegates from all sections of the Union.

In a majority of the colleges of the country the fraternities aim to select the ablest, most socially gifted, and wealthiest men. Of their social pre-eminence there can be no question; in all the colleges from which we have received returns the fraternity members are the society leaders. From the list of alumni published, it would seem that a majority of the graduates of American colleges in the last forty years who have become famous were in their student days members of fraternities.

We have no means of accurately determining the percentage of undergraduates who belong to fraternities in the different colleges of the country. The following estimates made by recent graduates of the colleges in question will give some idea of the proportion. From Adelbert College it is reported that 40 per cent of the men belong to fraternities, Beloit 33⅓ per cent, Lafayette 50 per cent, Vanderbilt 50 per cent, Leland Stanford 25 per cent, and Nebraska 20 per cent; in a few of the New England colleges considerably more than one half of the undergraduates. From the character of the fraternity principle, all the students of a college could not be included under its operation. To state the difficulty in Baird's language: "Experience has shown that if the bulk of the students in any college belong to the fraternities, fraternity life in that college is apt to be dull and the chapters weak; and in consequence an election to a fraternity is taken as a matter of course and a little-prized honour." *

The general scheme of organization and manage-

* Baird, W. R. American College Fraternities, fourth edition, p. 16.

ment as well as the type of symbolism are common to all the fraternities, and yet each preserved its separate and independent character, all alliances having been thus far of a local and temporary character. In 1883 an attempt was made to bring about a loose form of federation under the name of a Pan-Hellenic Council. A college fraternities congress was held by representatives from several fraternities in Chicago during the World's Fair (1893). A similar meeting took place at Atlanta some time afterward. Thus far the agitation for federation has only resulted in a yearly meeting known as the Pan-Hellenic Banquet, where topics of common interest to all fraternity men have been discussed. Pan-Hellenic clubs composed of fraternity graduates have been formed in a number of large cities.*

---

* We have treated the causes underlying the success of the fraternity idea only in the most general way. Below we append quotations from two correspondents, one a Greek and the other a non-fraternity man, bearing on this important point:

Fraternity Opinion.—"The chief fascination seems to me to be due to the well-known adolescent curiosity and unrest. Fraternities are to college men types of adult societies, such as Masons, Odd-Fellows, etc., and they look upon them as stepping stones from youthful to adult organizations. Anything with an element of secrecy appeals to adolescents. To many, no doubt, the desire for the support of a crowd of influential fellows in political and social affairs is the chief motive which impels them to fraternity membership. To others the desire to be in it with the popular 'set,' and to avoid being referred to as 'non-frat,' appeals most strongly. Again, the means for furnishing pleasant pastimes, such as billiard and pool tables, cards, etc., which fraternity rooms afford, together with the convenience of a pleasant loafing place, are strong allurements."

Non-fraternity Opinion.—"The chief motives [in joining fraternities] seem to be two—the social impulse toward good fellowship and the desire 'to have a time' and 'be out with the boys'; and secondly, the instinct to be a power, which leads men to join

Some observers have predicted for the fraternity a future similar to the English college, and have advocated the location of permanent graduate tutors in the chapter houses. One fraternity is said to have even made a move in this direction. The surface objections to a widespread adoption of such a plan are numerous. Many chapters could not bear the expense; to others it would seem like the invasion of " shop " on the privileged field of leisure. Such a plan does not make for specialization, which is now the watchword of superior education in this country. This scheme is largely bound up with the future of the small college, because it is only in the small college that such a supplement to the curriculum is needed, and nowhere else are the fraternities sufficiently strong to inaugurate such an undertaking. Present tendencies point to the expansion of one class of colleges into universities, and the absorption of the weaker by the secondary schools. If such a revolution comes to pass in superior education, it will necessarily cut the ground from under the fraternity tutor plan.

---

because they hope to gain a 'political pull,' and want 'to have a gang that will be your gang.' "

A third correspondent puts the case in a somewhat different form :

" The source of the fascination which the fraternity idea exercises is found in the desire for mutual companionship on the part of young men having similar ideals. Young men of the college age are apt to group themselves together, according to their likes, dislikes, ambitions, and customs. They feel a longing for an influence like that of the home which they have left. They recognise that there is a certain strength in organization, and a mutual aid and benefit in close companionship with twenty of their fellows."

§ 4. ATHLETIC ORGANIZATIONS IN THE MODERN PERIOD.

Athletic sports with their numerous organizations and contests have been the most prominent feature in American student life during the past twenty-five years. The greater portion of the public know a college almost exclusively through its athletic records, for three fourths of the news items concerning student life deal with sport. In the comic journals the typical college man is the football player with his long hair and limp. While within academic precincts athletics is only one of numerous interests, and many students have only the most superficial connection with the games, still, of all undergraduate concerns, intercollegiate contests play by far the largest part in the daily life and talk. The successful captain of the eleven or the crew usually stands forth the most popular and influential man of his class and the ideal of the younger students. In writing the history of the modern athletic movement we shall first indicate the relative position and popularity of the various games, and then pass on to a discussion of the problems arising from athleticism.

In 1870 boating was the only sport which had gained for itself a well-recognised status. In that year the last of the first series of intercollegiate contests between Yale and Harvard had been won by the latter, which opened the way a year later to the formation of the Rowing Association of American Colleges, which included all the colleges of importance in New England, with two or three outside institutions in New Jersey and New York. Six races took place under the auspices of the association, the first three on the Connecticut River at Springfield, the remaining three at Saratoga Lake, New York. Membership in the association shifted from year to year; one year seventeen colleges were represented by crews, the next there were only seven contestants. The old antagonism between Harvard and Yale dominated the association, the minor colleges taking sides with either one or the other. This rivalry, together with the difficulty of managing and judging so many crews on the same course, led to much doubtful diplomacy and frequent controversies. Many of the smaller colleges maintained crews with great difficulty and expense, and, as soon as the novelty wore away, neglected to send representatives. The final stroke to the association was given in 1876, when Harvard and Yale withdrew.* Since 1876 no attempt has been made to revive boating on a large scale. Most of the colleges of the country are unfavourably located for participation in the sport, while the expense and difficulty of preparation place it beyond the reach of many of the small colleges. The Harvard-Yale races have continued from 1876 to the present, and are considered athletic events of the first magnitude, second only in interest to the great football games in the autumn. Cornell, Pennsylvania, the national Naval Academy at Annapolis, and more recently Wisconsin, have cultivated boating with great care and considerable success. Of all the forms of intercollegiate athletic competition it is the least extended and is practically confined to six or seven institutions of the first rank in the Eastern States, and is without a following in the West and South.

Baseball, the next sport to be extensively developed, is the most widespread form of athletic competition; in small and obscure colleges it is the only game played. Its universal diffusion among all classes of people, and

---

* The following colleges won in the years designated: Massachusetts Agricultural, 1871; Amherst, 1872; Yale, 1873; Columbia, 1874; Cornell, 1875; Cornell, 1876. An effort was made to continue the association by Brown, Dartmouth, Bowdoin, and Trinity, but without success. For a full account of the entire episode see Yale Book.

the ease with which match games can be prepared for, are responsible for its popularity among college students. From the standpoint of the spectators it is greatly inferior to football, lacking the mass movements and general attitude of conflict which give zest to the latter. The fact that professional baseball in the cities has become a business has worked injury to the game as an amateur sport. Nearly every college in the country has its nine, the achievements of which are watched with considerable interest in the spring of the year, but in most cases without that extreme absorption which characterizes football enthusiasm. It is worthy of note that some of the small colleges, particularly Catholic colleges with an Irish *clientèle,* are able to compete in this sport on terms of equality with larger institutions.

Football is now the college sport *par excellence* of the country. Its popularity as an organized game in the colleges dates only from 1880, and for a number of years its votaries were largely confined to the Eastern States. Since 1890 the colleges of all sections of the country have adopted it, and it has also been diffused downward to the academies and high schools; even in many sections to the elementary schools. The small boys on the streets, who fifteen years ago played only baseball, now devote much more time to its rival, although football is not so well adapted to their physique and playing grounds. The colleges of each State and section of country have their local contests, which are considered of momentous importance. The games between certain larger institutions of the first rank are regarded as of national importance, and their details are telegraphed from one end of the country to the other. The most important group of institutions is composed of the five great universities of the East—Harvard, Yale, Princeton, Pennsylvania, and Cornell. In the middle West, Michigan, Wisconsin, Minnesota, Northwestern, and Chicago form a second group of inferior importance. The games between Virginia and Vanderbilt in the South, Missouri and Kansas in the far West, California and Leland Stanford on the Pacific coast, stand midway in importance between the contests of widespread interests and those of simple local importance.

Football owes its popularity to the element of physical combat which plays so important a part in the game. In this it appeals to one of the strongest human instincts, an instinct which under different conditions has insured the success of gladiatorial combats, bull-fighting, and prize fighting. Walter Camp has drawn an interesting comparison between football and war,* pointing out that the problems in strategy and training which confront the football coach are practically identical with those which a general has to overcome. More than any other form of athletics, football is confined to the schools; it has not yet become a business, like bicycling and baseball. The fact that the games are *bona fide* exhibitions of skill is not without effect in establishing it in the good will of the public.

Track and field sports were the last branches of athletics to receive serious attention. As early as 1872 we have records of organized field days.† Until recently this department of athletics excited less interest than football, baseball, and boating. Now in many colleges

---

* See Camp and Deland, Football, chap. v. In this book the practical and technical details of the game are discussed with force and brevity by the best-qualified man in the country. The growth of the American game and a comparison of it with the English and Canadian games is the theme of a chapter of unusual interest.

† See Yale Book, vol. ii. p. 451; Princeton Book. Felix E. Schelling, Organizations within the University. in F. N. Thorpe's Benjamin Franklin and the University of Pennsylvania, pp. 4, 7.

it ranks above baseball, and is looked upon with favour by the authorities because it enlists a much larger number of men in its pursuit than any other sport. In international contests, American athletes have distinguished themselves in this line, whereas they have uniformly failed in boating, the only other form of athletics in which international competition is possible.

These four great departments of athletics form an upper hierarchy of college sports; the relative rank of a college is determined by its success here. The public athletic organization of the college provides for training only in the four branches. They do not by any means exhaust the list of athletic interests, most of which are represented by clubs of a more private character. In many colleges lawn tennis numbers more devotees than any of the official sports.* In the larger colleges clubs are formed for walking, gunning, bicycling, polo, golf, cricket, and new and unusual forms of sport.† The prosperity of these organizations fluctuates from year to year, and depends much on the position which the game in question holds in the estimation of the outside public. In nearly every case they are to be commended because they afford healthful exercise without those adventitious rewards and excitements which unduly intensify the better recognised departments of sport.

An enumeration and description of the various sports, and an account of their organization, are by no means a history of college athletics. Such a history must include the relations of athletic sports to the cul-

---

* While usually the tennis club has no official recognition, this is by no means always the case ; in some colleges it is recognised as a sport of the first rank, and success in it highly valued.

† Welch and Camp. Yale—Athletics, chap. vi. "Outside activities" treats of miscellaneous athletic clubs at Yale.

ture and characteristics of the people, and is a more difficult task. The space at our command will not permit
the detailed consideration of the movement from year
to year; so, without any attempt to write annals, we
shall endeavour to describe the condition of athletic
sports, particularly football, which existed in 1890. The
unhealthy features of competitive contests which appeared as early as the sixties in boat-racing reached a
climax in football at this period. The ideal of college
sport prevalent among undergraduates and trainers was
to win at any cost, and in consequence unworthy strata-
gem and diplomacy were resorted to; overtraining was
common, extravagance and the employment of professionals by no means uncommon.

When we come to consider athleticism more in detail we see that the outside public through its representative, the press, was in a large degree responsible for
these extravagances. To quote from an able article
by Professor Taussig, of Harvard: " During the autumn
a veritable craze seizes the community on the subject
of football, and for weeks the most important question
before the public seems to be whether eleven youths
dressed in red, or black and yellow, will prove themselves more expert in rushing a football than eleven
other youths dressed in blue." * The public flock by
thousands to the matches and give substantial proof of
the keenness of their interest by paying extravagant
prices for seats.

The newspapers of the time exploited college athletics to a degree previously unheard of and out of all
proportion to the importance of the sports in question.
For weeks before every important game, the names and
faces of all the players appear in every newspaper, with

---

* Taussig, F. W. A Professor's View of Athletics, Harvard
Graduate Magazine, vol. iii, pp. 308, 309.

a detailed account of their skill, and "after a period of training during which the boys are led to believe that their doings are of real importance to the civilized world, they come to the game far more overwrought mentally by the nervous strain than overworked physically." * The writer has before him a three-page newspaper account of a great football game in the West. It contains twenty columns of printed matter and seven columns of illustrations, including cartoons and pictures of the captains and coaches of the two opposing teams. The article consists of two long accounts of the game—one popular for the general reader, the second technical for the football enthusiast. Besides these main features, there are biographies of all the players, the opinions of the captains, coaches, and the presidents of the two universities on the outcome of the struggle. In a personal note the emotions of the gray-haired father of one of the players are described in detail. Such a cheap notoriety tends to place the football player on a level with the prize-fighting and bicycle-riding profession.†

The result of the notoriety and fever of expectation are seen (1) in the recruiting of men, (2) the extravagant outlays of money, (3) the overtraining of teams, and (4) the fierceness and intensity of the contests. The prob-

---

* Hemenway, Augustus. Important Suggestions in Athletics, Harvard Graduate Magazine, vol. vi, p. 192.

† Emmons, in the Harvard Graduate Magazine, vol. iii, pp. 318, 219, has described the effect of newspaper notoriety on the rising athletes of the secondary school: "A schoolboy finds his photograph and a sketch of his life put before the public, and he is described as a future star. The consequence is that the first few weeks, which ought to be spent developing him into a player, are spent in reducing, what is the natural result of his publicity, 'a swelled head.'" This remark applies with equal force to college athletes who are successful in the early years of their course.

lem which first confronted the captain long before the
season began was the task of securing as many promising athletes from the secondary schools as possible.
While the college preferences of many men were fixed
either by family tradition or academic considerations,
a considerable number of the best players remained
without pronounced ties, some of them too poor to bear
the expense of a college education in the natural course
of events. The most successful captain or manager
was he who by any means succeeded in attracting this
floating class of athletes to his college. At times the
captain visited the different preparatory schools, and by
flattery and the promise of social favour secured some,
while more substantial considerations were offered
others. Usually a direct money proposition was not
made directly, but positions with nominal duties and
high salaries were thrown in the way of the promising
full-back or tackle. Recruiting was not confined to the
fitting schools, but extended to the small colleges which
found their best men drawn away by the inducements
of the larger universities. Men of brawn, with no particular scholarly interest, were registered as specials in
some one subject; this permitted them to play on the
team. Athletes of value received instructorships from
the faculty which enabled them to play for an indefinite
number of years.

The managers of the large teams could afford to be
extravagant in their outlays for players as well as for
the legitimate expenses, because the public interest in
games made it easy to collect large sums of money,
sometimes exceeding one hundred thousand dollars in
a single season. So strong was the athletic feeling
among the undergraduates that any manager against
whom the charge of parsimony could be brought was
looked upon as little better than a traitor. The regular
expenses of outfitting, training, table, and coaches, were

swollen by additions of every device or indulgence which could be thought of. Probably little of the money was directly embezzled, but much of it was ineffectively spent and invested in schemes of a very doubtful character. The appropriation of large sums for needless indulgences for the team prevented the proper expansion of athletic interest among the body of the undergraduates by cutting off the possibility of improved athletic facilities.*

Excessive physical training of the players during the period previous to the great games also characterized college athletics at this period. Four or five hours of the hardest physical exercise, taken under conditions of great excitement and stimulation, unfitted the athletes for any more than nominal participation in the intellectual life of the college. To quote President Eliot again: † "In the three sports above mentioned [boating, baseball, and football], the training and practice occupy too large a portion of the college year and too many hours a day. No student can keep up his studies and also play his full part in these sports as presently conducted. The faithful member of the team

---

* For a strong presentation of this point see article by Walter Camp.

† Likewise this quotation from one of President Eliot's annual reports: "There is something exquisitely inappropriate in the extravagant expenditure on athletic sports at such institutions as Harvard and Yale, institutions which have been painfully built up by the self-denial, frugality, and public spirit of generations that certainly did not lack physical and moral courage, endurance, and toughness, yet always put the things of the spirit above the things of sense. At these universities there must be constant economy and inadequacy in expenditure for intellectual and spiritual objects; how repulsive, then, must be foolish and pernicious expenditures on sports!" Annual Report of President and Treasurer of Harvard College, 1892-'93, p. 14.

or crew may manage to attend his lectures or other college exercises, but has rarely any mind to give to his studies. His nervous energy is exhausted either by severe bodily exercise or by the excitement of frequent contests. This evil, which is comparatively new, has rapidly increased within recent years." * It is now admitted that such training overshot its own mark, and placed a team in the field at Thanksgiving which was already stale. On the mental side, too, the process was carried too far, for frequently a team entered the decisive game of the year in an overwrought, almost morbid state, from which a return to normal life was difficult.

The same intensity, involving an eager desire to win at any price, which we have observed in the preparatory steps, characterized the contests. Football, a game so rough as to be dangerous for all except the strongest and best-formed players, presented many openings for unfairness and brutality. It was no uncommon event for a team to enter a game with the set purpose of disabling a skilful player of the opposition sufficiently early in the contest to deprive their opponents of the advantage of his capacity. Violations of the rules when undetected, tricks, stratagems, like clothing a team in well-oiled leather suits, were all considered legitimate methods of winning a victory.

Hitherto we have not entered into a discussion of the physical injuries consequent upon football when played by fair and honourable methods; but as this issue has played an important part in the controversy, it can not be ignored here. Walter Camp would have us believe that serious injuries are few—a fact which, when

---

* Report of the President and Treasurer of Harvard, 1892–'93, pp. 13, 14.

we come to consider the violence of the exercise and the number of opportunities for accidents, is an evidence of the strong physique which the game bestows upon the player. The degree of risk is much overestimated by the newspapers, and is not greater than in most sports and pastimes. The most serious accidents are due to the extreme youth of the players and to the lack of competent coaching.* Camp quotes Mr. W. C. Church, in The Century, who, having made a study of reports from sixty-seven different colleges in thirty-seven States, claims that serious accidents are of rare occurrence. Francis A. Walker supported this view. His words are: " There is much exaggeration in the public mind regarding this matter [physical injury], and instances of permanent injury from athletics are fewer than popular rumour or maternal anxiety would make them out to be. The experience of football players of the last fifteen years . . . proves that this form of athletic contest works little enduring injury among thoroughly trained competitors." †

Against these statements may be placed the testimony of President Eliot, who says: " In most manly sports danger is reduced to a minimum, but in football the recent development of the game has made it more and more dangerous without making it more skilful or interesting. The danger to life in this country is not yet great, but the exposure to a class of injuries which decrease the serviceableness of the body throughout life is decidedly increased. Such injuries are sprains, wrenches, congestions of the brain, breaking of bones, loss of teeth, and the enlargement and stiffening of the joints. The objection to football is not that it in-

---

* Deland and Camp.   Football, pp. 42, 43.

† Walker, F. A.   College Athletics, Harvard Graduate Magazine, vol. ii, p. 11.

volves some risk, but that the risks are inordinate and excessive." *

If the writer may be permitted to intrude his opinion among those of experts, his judgment would be that while men of a certain heavy build are able to play football with impunity as regards accidents of a serious nature, there are many men now actually playing the game in American colleges who are taking large risks of injury because of their light frames, the softness of their bones, and other physical deficiencies. It has been the writer's observation that physical mishaps of the kind specified by President Eliot are much more common among football players than any other class of athletes. The written testimony of football players or officials to the contrary should be largely discounted, because, in many cases, from an affection for the game, they minimize or conceal their hurts in order that it may stand well with the public. The entire subject is one that should be thoroughly investigated through a series of years by a committee of scientific men, preferably by the directors of physical training in the colleges. Until some such inquiry is undertaken, we must be content with general impressions like the above.

The evils of athleticism extended further than the specific disadvantages here described. There can be little question but that the exaltation of physical prowess tended to the disparagement of intellectual discipline and acquirements among a large number of college men who were by no means confined to the strictly athletic class. In the larger colleges there was little in undergraduate life to make able and earnest students feel that intellectual work was really an important part of life. The predominance of athletic ideals strength-

---

* Annual Reports of the President and Treasurer of Harvard College, 1892-'93, p. 15.

16

ened the impression already strong among the lower classes that " colleges were, after all, institutions where the children of the well-to-do pass three, four, or sometimes five years of agreeable leisure, rescued from utter boredom by some slight enforcement of attention to books, but not involving serious exertion, or yielding any valuable training for the duties of later life." * The fact that a small number of this class of students exist in every college gave enough colour to this view to make it a dangerous half truth, and to present a mistaken impression of the part which the college plays in the education of citizens.†

---

* Taussig, F. W. A Professor's View of Athletics, Harvard Graduate Magazine, vol. iii, p. 310.

† President Eliot's view of the evils connected with football may be compared with the account just given : " The disadvantages of college athletics are the result of wanton exaggeration, and not necessarily inherent in the sports themselves. When thus exaggerated they interfere with instead of clarifying and maintaining mental activity ; they convert the student into a powerful animal, and dull for the time being his intellectual parts ; they present the colleges to the public, educated and uneducated, as places of mere physical sport, and not of intellectual training ; they make familiar to the student a coarse publicity which destroys his rightful privacy while in training for intellectual service, and subject him to insolent and vulgar comments on his personal qualities ; they induce in masses of spectators at interesting games an hysterical excitement which too many Americans enjoy, but which is evidence not of physical strength and depth of passion, but of feebleness and shallowness ; they tend to dwarf mental and moral qualities permanently, and to unduly magnify physical prowess." Annual Report of the President and Treasurer of Harvard College, 1892–'93. p. 20.

Another view of the situation by the historian of athletics, Dr. E. M. Hartwell, is here inserted for the purposes of comparison : " The best interests of rational and effectual physical training have suffered much in this country, and suffer still from the disproportionate influence exercised by athletic ideals upon the

The excesses of athleticism provoked an unreasoning reaction on the part of the press and the public; the opposition seemed anxious to rival the athletes themselves in exaggeration and extremes. Football was denounced as brutal and barbarous; it was compared with bullfighting and prize fighting, and in some instances the Legislatures were invoked to stop the game. A bill to this effect actually passed the Georgia Legislature, but was vetoed by the Governor. In California and other States similar attempts were made. The religious papers were particularly strong in their denunciations, which was more than could be said of

---

scholastic and collegiate youth; and from the undue prominence accorded athletic contests and contestants by an uncritical public and an injudicious press. It is natural for youth on the threshold of manhood, segregated from their elders under conditions peculiar to school and college life, to be headstrong and self-sufficient. They are eager to distinguish themselves in the eyes of their fellow-tribesmen by the display of individual prowess, and for the time being are apt to be animated by narrow and distorted views, or to be insensitive or averse to enlightened or even civilized opinion. They are strongly swayed and frequently overmastered by the spirit of rivalry, which is largely inseparable from athletic sports, so that at times doubtful and discredited methods seem admissible if not admirable, and foul means fair. . . . So sudden and rapid has been the rise and spread of athleticism, that the generation of men who have recently left the stage on which our athletic youth now figure so prominently and grotesquely number but few who are qualified by insight and experience to serve as the exemplars and advisers of their juniors. . . . Hence our athletes have been left in the main to their own crude and boyish devices, which tend, when unchecked, toward extravagance and professionalism. The powerlessness of our educational leaders to originate, and their failure to adopt effectual measures for evolving order out of the athletic and gymnastic chaos over which they nominally preside, constitutes one of the marvels of our time." On Physical Education, in the Report of the United States Commissioner of Education, vol. i, 1897-'98, pp. 558, 559.

the dailies, which by their sensationalism had largely created the evil. The New York Nation led the attack, assailing intercollegiate contests in a keen and indiscriminating manner, and exhibiting all the bad aspects of games from overtraining in preparatory schools, to the employment of graduate coaches. (See bibliography, under " Godkin.") Many of the points made by the Nation and the religious press were legitimate, but so strong was the animus of the writers, and so wholesale their denunciation, that they excited only the contempt and derision of the athletic faction. The direct result of this reaction and criticism was *nil;* indirectly it accomplished much in stimulating the college authorities to decided action and in encouraging the more conservative element among the undergraduates.

The reform in college athletics has been worked out from within, and is due to the efforts of a few public-spirited college presidents, professors, and graduates. In most colleges the amateur standing of the athletes is maintained by one or two vigilant, well-informed men, usually members of the faculty. Without such men, abuses creep in and steady degeneration ensues. There has always existed a large number of undergraduates, perhaps a majority, in favour of clean sport, but their zeal has been so negative and halting that they were easily overridden by an enthusiastic, unscrupulous minority who were out to win. The neighbourhood of 1890 has been suggested as the period when matters reached a climax, and from which an improvement may be traced. This generalization is only true of a certain group of large colleges on the Atlantic seaboard, and only true there in a qualified sense, as progress has not been either rapid or uniform. The reform wave struck the colleges of the West and South somewhat later. The returns to a circular letter (hereafter to be described) showed that in some colleges the struggle with professionalism is now being fought out for the first time. The writer does not mean to convey the impression that a thoroughgoing reform in athletic methods has taken place since 1890 in the Eastern colleges; such language applied to many of them would seem absurd. All that he means to say is, that before 1890 college athletics were deteriorating; since that date there has been a slow return to more healthful ideals.* How this return was brought about it is now our purpose to describe.

During the period of the worst excesses of athleticism the machinery of administrative control was greatly lacking in centralization and continuity. On the side of the students there was an athletic association, nominally consisting of all the students, but in reality dominated by the athletic element. The officers of the association were those common to all free associations—president, vice-president, secretary, and treasurer—and were elected by the members. The athletic managers, however, who possessed the substance of authority, were commonly selected by either the athletic teams or captains.

The most important function of the association was to provide financial support; otherwise the teams prac-

---

* It is a difficult matter to estimate the amount of professionalism in American college athletics at the present time. Of thirty colleges replying to a circular letter through their physical directors, only two admitted that it was a serious issue. Eleven reported slight traces of it, and thirteen declared themselves entirely free from illicit practices; four of the replies were so general as to be useless. Such evidence is not entirely valueless, but the replies have such a strong tendency to err on virtue's side, that little reliance can be placed upon them. In two or three of the colleges reporting themselves as free from the taint, the writer has personal knowledge of flagrant violations. In a majority of the larger colleges the letter of the law as described later is lived up to, but public sentiment usually justifies liberties with the spirit which are by no means conducive to clean sport.

tically managed themselves. The athletic committee
of the college faculty formed the only check to their
proceedings. These committees must be credited with
good intentions, but suffered from lack of knowledge, because their members had usually completed the college
course in the pre-athletic period. At best their authority
could only be exercised in a negative, veto manner; they
might check and regulate, but had no power of initiating
measures, or of securing accountability in the details of
administration. A more powerful, stable, and representative body was called for by the needs of the time.

The want was met by the creation of a permanent
committee of composite membership, consisting of representatives in equal proportions from the faculty, the
alumni, and the undergraduates. The undergraduate
members were usually either the managers or captains
of athletic teams. In this body the supervision and ul-
timate control of athletics was rested. The committee
selected a graduate treasurer, who supervised and au-
dited the accounts of all organizations, using the university grounds or buildings. The committee itself
made disposition of the athletic funds as it saw fit. In
addition to its close financial control, the committee determined the eligibility rules of players, the regulations
to be followed in intercollegiate contests, and the mode
of electing captains and managers. By this centralizing
authority, and establishing an executive body which was
empowered to bind all members of the university for a
series of years, a definite policy was for the first time
made possible. Harvard initiated the central committee
plan, and by this instrumentality was able to exert a
strong leverage on the athletics of the country.*

---

* See article by Augustus Hemenway, Important Suggestions
in Athletics, Harvard Graduate Magazine, vol. vi, for a history of
the Harvard committee on athletic sports.

At the present time (1901) an eligibility code has been generally agreed upon by all universities of good athletic standing in the country; any departure from it subjects an institution to immediate suspicion. From the point of view of the university, the code declares that only *bona fide* students in good standing, who give notice of their intention to remain throughout the academic year, shall be permitted to play on the university athletic teams. Such students must take a required minimum course (usually ten hours a week), and any failure in scholarship shall deprive them of the privilege of participation. No student entering from another college shall be permitted to play until he has been at least one year in residence. The rules are ironclad in their opposition to professionalism: a student who in any way, either individually or as a member of a team, has accepted remuneration for playing, or for training athletes, is excluded from representing the college. Every student must also pass a physical examination, and receive a certificate entitling him to take part in some particular sport. Students may not play on university teams for more than four years. It is not necessary to add that rules do not enforce themselves, and that the athletic standing of a college is in no way determined by its rules.*

A reasonable degree of uniformity has been reached in the regulation of sport; it is far otherwise in regard to organization. A circular letter on the present con-

---

* All these provisions are found in the rules regulating athletic sports at Harvard, Columbia, and Pennsylvania. See Committee on Regulation of Athletic Sports, Regulations on Athletics, Harvard University. Rules governing students participating in athletics in Columbia University, 1898. University of Pennsylvania, Constitution and Functions of the University Athletic Committee, Eligibility Code, 1898.

dition of athletics, sent out by the writer and answered by the directors of physical training in thirty colleges, showed the greatest diversity in the methods of management. Three types of government were discernible: the highly centralized, of which Harvard is the best example; the dual plan of student athletic association and faculty committee; and exclusive student control, tempered by graduate advice. The class of institutions with the centralized organization is strongest in the East, where it is represented by Amherst, Bowdoin, Bates, University of Maine, and Wesleyan, all of which have the graduate, undergraduate, and faculty elements represented on their board of control. Tulane University, Louisiana, is the only college away from the Atlantic seaboard which reported the existence of a board of this type. Dual management prevails throughout the West and South, and is much the most common form of organization. A few colleges noted for the strength of their student traditions, like Princeton, Yale, and Virginia, almost eliminate faculty interference, although the graduate element is sometimes present in great force.

The difference between the first and third types may be seen by comparing Harvard and Yale. At Harvard the committee on the regulation of athletic sports supervises the election of captain, in whom it invests all delegated authority. The captain is elected by the players who have taken part in the important contests of the preceding year, but the committee may at any time annul such an election. The manager and coach are appointed by the captain, subject again to the approval of the committee on the regulation of athletic sports. The captains and managers of the various teams are held responsible for the observance of the rules communicated to them by the committee; the captain is particularly responsible for the enforcement of the regulation in regard to physical examinations. The members of the team must be passed upon by the committee before the first game of the season. No team may be taken away for a long journey without a written authorization from the committee, which must also be consulted by the manager before arranging schedules.*

At Yale the entire control falls to the managers and captains of the four university teams. The captains are elected, as at Harvard and elsewhere, by the members of the previous year's team, but the managers are chosen by the university at an annual mass meeting. "The four managers, together with a graduate treasurer, compose the financial union, and all funds are received and disbursed through this agency which acts as common pool. Each manager, however, prides himself on the showing of his association, for all the moneys are credited to the individual organization which turns them in, and the expenditures of each are kept in separate accounts, and an annual report of these is published in the columns of the Yale News. There have been graduate advisory committees, both general and for separate organizations; but their functions have not been onerous, and in fact the general advisory committee has not acted for many years, although in the early eighties it was called upon several times for advice, which it rendered satisfactorily. Each manager is practically omnipotent in his special branch. He is his own master, and responsible only to the university." †

As the noise and dust which resulted from the conflict between the athletes and their critics gradually disappear, the gain to the student community from the

---

* Harvard Regulations on Athletics, article iv, pp. 5, 6.
† Welch and Camp. Yale, p. 453.

movement becomes more evident. One of its great services has been the stimulation of many students to participation in some form of physical activity. The great match games have been a widespread advertisement of the existence of physical culture in the land. The evils which result from the exaggeration of college sport affect only the few men who train for the contests; the benefits are felt by hundreds who have never seen the track or oval. Professor Taussig, in an ingenious paragraph, argues that intercollegiate games do not increase the interest in physical training, but, on the contrary, " it is the intercollegiate contest that springs from the spirit of exercise, not the spirit of exercise from the contest." * While this clause states what ideally should be the correct order, as a matter of fact it seems that athletics have flourished in proportion as the competitive feature has been emphasized. In many colleges the chief motive power is not an interest in physical training, but a craving for distinction, an ambition to beat some one. Among nations of Anglo-Saxon descent the desire for exercise is chiefly the result, not the cause, of competitive contests.

The physical ideal which athletics exalt is calculated to counteract some of the most dangerous tendencies in modern life which tends to produce neurotic and luxury-loving individuals. The great co-operative games call not only for swiftness and strength, " but make for courage, coolness, steadiness of nerve, quickness of apprehension, resourcefulness, self-knowledge

---

* Taussig, F. W. A Professor's View of Athletics, Harvard Graduate Magazine, vol. iii, p. 307. For the opposite view, see Annual Report of the President and Treasurer of Harvard College, 1892–'93, p. 17, and Walker, F. A., College Athletics, Harvard Graduate Magazine, vol. ii, p. 13.

and self-reliance, qualities useful in any profession." *
The great public contests not only develop these qualities, but afford as well impressive examples to the minds
of the spectators. These games have diffused a greater
desire for bodily excellence, and a greater admiration
for such manly qualities as courage and fortitude among
the schoolboys of the country. In an age when industry and politics—the two great interests of American
life—are becoming more mechanical, it is no small thing
to have an admiration for the physical virtues spread
abroad among all classes of the population.

The social training which comes from college athletics has been often spoken of in the highest terms, and
elaborated in great detail. It is pointed out that in
the competitive struggle between colleges, something
akin to patriotism is developed; that men sacrifice opportunities of individual distinction for the good of
the team, that the few are trained to command, the
many to intelligent subordination. That under proper
conditions these games might be made important
means of social control has been fully established by
English experience, as described in a preceding chapter. However, it may be doubted whether these results
are actually obtained in many American colleges at the
present time. The students are not habituated to the
athletic tradition sufficiently early in life, and the atmosphere of trickery, sharp diplomacy, and even strong
personal animosity among members of the same teams,
is unfavourable to the cultivation of the social virtues.

From the standpoint of the public, college athletics
may be said to have made a great contribution to popular amusement. In the growing monotony and inten-

---

* College Athletics. Francis A. Walker, Harvard Graduate
Magazine, vol. ii, p. 13. See also in this connection an article by
Luther Gulick, Pedagogical Seminary, March, 1899.

sity of American life, an out-of-door attraction which arouses a deep and healthy enthusiasm in the community at large is a genuine contribution to civilization. The rapid spread of football in the West and South was probably to a great extent due to the feeling that it supplied a long-felt want. Among the students also, competitive sports give an added charm and interest to college life. Without athletics there would hardly be those strong emotional reactions, the passionate love for certain colleges and colours, and equally strong detestation for certain others, which now form such a strong and attractive element in undergraduate life.*

The two problems which confront college athletics to-day are, (1) the realization of a higher ideal of sport which involves the relegation of the now all-important factor of intercollegiate competition to a secondary position, and the substitution therefor of an adequate conception of physical culture, and (2) the extension of the benefits of organized games to a much larger number of undergraduates.

The growth of a healthier ideal must of necessity be a work of time, and is dependent on the rise of more rational views among the graduates, the faculties, and the intelligent public. The attempts to limit athletic contests to college grounds, and to multiply games within the college, are steps in the right direction. The diffusion of an active athletic interest among all the undergraduates would be a most important move toward the goal. A great responsibility here rests upon the

---

* It is sometimes urged in behalf of athletics that they fill a man's time to the exclusion of vice and dissipation. During training there is necessarily an improvement, but in general it may be said that the reaction against the severe rules of training is likely to carry men into dissipation who had hitherto avoided it. This only applies to members of the team and others who specialize in athletics.

secondary schools which mould the student's tastes during his most impressionable period, when his instincts lead him to games and physical activity. All the burden can not be shifted from the colleges, which might do much more than they are attempting at present to make athletics general.

At present, probably twenty per cent of the undergraduates, or one student in five, participates sufficiently in athletic games to be appreciably influenced thereby. At Harvard a careful study made in 1897 showed that twenty-one per cent of the undergraduates passed the examinations entitling them to take part. It is hardly reasonable to suppose that all these men trained regularly.* On the other hand, many men played handball and tennis without securing permits. If we make these two classes balance each other, our general estimate would hold true of Harvard. A circular letter†

---

* Report of President and Treasurer of Harvard College, 1897.

† The circular letter asked the following questions :

1. What proportion of the students can be accommodated on the athletic grounds ?

2. What proportion of the students train in the various activities during the different seasons ?

3. What organizations control athletics ?

4. Have you had any difficulty with professionalism ?

The letter was sent to forty colleges in all sections of the country. Twenty of the largest and most influential institutions were chosen to represent one class, and twenty small colleges in New England and the West stood for another class. The following thirty institutions responded : Of the larger colleges—California, Columbia, Cornell, Harvard, Johns Hopkins, Leland Stanford, Minnesota, Nebraska, New York, North Carolina, Pennsylvania, Princeton, Tulane, Vanderbilt, Virginia, Wisconsin, and Yale; from the group of smaller colleges—Amherst, Bates, Bowdoin, Cornell College, Des Moines, Hillsdale, Iowa College, Grinnell, Maine, Parsons, Tabor, Wesleyan, and Whitman. Comparing the two groups, there appeared to be no generic difference in regard

sent to the directors of physical training in American colleges produced the following results: Out of twenty-eight institutions replying, seven reported less than twenty per cent of students taking part in athletics, twelve reported that from twenty to twenty-five per cent participated, six placed the estimate between twenty-five and fifty per cent, with three above the fifty-per-cent line. New York University led with eighty per cent, while the University of Nebraska stood at the foot of the column, with only seven per cent. When allowance is made for the tendency on the part of the physical directors to have their institution stand well and consequently to give themselves the benefit of all doubts, it will be seen that twenty per cent is probably a fair average.

The replies to question 1 of the circular, in reference to athletic accommodations, were somewhat surprising. Fifteen colleges could furnish athletic privileges to all their students, five could accommodate from fifty per cent upward, and only nine could care for less than fifty per cent. In a number of instances it was evident, from the tenor of the response, that the college possessed sufficient bare ground for athletic purposes,

---

to interest in athletics, the variations between colleges being equally prominent in both groups. The small colleges seemed to be better equipped in regard to athletic grounds, but even here the difference was not marked.

Some of the percentages for the different colleges may prove of interest: Amherst about one fourth, Bowdoin fully fifty per cent, Cornell College from ten to fifteen per cent, Wesleyan at least twenty-five per cent, California twenty per cent, Columbia twenty-five per cent, Pennsylvania from one third to one fourth, Vanderbilt thirty per cent.

The answers to questions 1 and 2 have been previously noted. It should be remembered that these are but estimates at best, and that they do not include private athletics or gymnasium work, which in some institutions is compulsory.

but nothing would warrant the statement that it was sufficiently improved for games.

Concise replies to this question would at any rate be difficult, because the serviceability of the playing fields depends to a certain extent on the arrangement of instruction. Grounds sufficient for a student body, if they could be used all the time, would be insufficient if the students could only utilize them between the hours of four and six in the afternoon. Taking all these facts into consideration, we are justified in concluding that few American colleges could meet the demands of the undergraduates for out-of-door activity if all the students desired to join in the games.

The first step in the creation of an active athletic interest among the students is therefore a sufficient improvement of facilities to make their participation possible. The next move would probably be, as we have before suggested, the multiplication of internal contests and organizations, which would in time lead to an increase in their importance. Such a change is by no means easy when all the interest is concentrated on intercollegiate contests. Progress here, as elsewhere, must necessarily be slow. In fact, the two lines of improvement which we have suggested—the clarifying of the athletic ideal and the diffusion of athletic interest—are interdependent; neither is possible without the other.

§ 5. SELF-GOVERNING ASSOCIATIONS IN THE MODERN PERIOD.

On a previous page we noted the antagonism between faculty and students, and the double standard of honour engendered thereby—a standard which justified a student in lying to the authorities, in cheating at examinations, and in indulging in disorders and excesses of various kinds. " The professors are employed to catch us; it is our business to escape by any means in our power," was the instinctive thought of the American undergraduate, although not more than ten or fifteen per cent of the students customarily took advantage of the double standard to cause trouble. About 1870, experiments in student self-government were inaugurated, which aimed to enlist the eighty-five or ninety per cent of law-abiding students in the active maintenance of order. President Warfield, of Lafayette, in a recent article has expressed the standpoint of the innovators: " Give the seventy-five or more per cent of orderly students a voice in the determination of college conduct, teach them how to use that voice, encourage them to think that their reputation and the reputation of the college are at stake, and by an energetic public opinion they will more effectively suppress the disorderly element than any law that can be applied will ever do." *

Before passing on to the history of the self-governing idea in different colleges, it may be observed that the more recent experiments are not continuous with the schemes in operation during the Revolutionary period. The houses of students, students' courts, and juries passed away without leaving any appreciable impression on college tradition. The only exception to this generalization is the honour system of the University of Virginia, which has not only survived in its parent institution but has also influenced student life in many other colleges.†

Probably the most comprehensive scheme of student

---

* Student Co-operation in College Government, Educational Review, vol. viii, p. 450. The same position is taken by James C. Mackenzie, Honor in Student Life, School Review, vol. vii, p. 72.

† Adams, H. B. Thomas Jefferson and the University of Virginia, p. 156.

self-government ever attempted in the United States was that inaugurated at the University of Illinois in 1868. At the opening of the college, the president laid the question of discipline before the students in a short address, pointing out the need of better relations between faculty and students than those which existed in adjacent colleges, and emphasizing the civic bearings of the problem. The students considered the proposition for some days and then declared it their unanimous desire to proceed with the scheme of organization. A committee was appointed, and soon reported a constitution which divided all the functions of government into the executive, legislative, and judicial of the Federal Constitution. The entire body of students were to represent the legislative branch; a president, vice-president, secretary, treasurer, and marshal served as the executive branch; and a court of three judges tried all offences. Laws for preserving order, regulations against gambling and drinking intoxicants, against violations of sundry rights of students and trespassing on college property, were passed, and fines, ranging from a few cents to five dollars, were levied for violations of the code. The new government went into operation with great seriousness; students of a mature age, conspicuous for scholarship and ability, were chosen officers; good order was established and maintained with little difficulty, notwithstanding the efforts of a few turbulent students to discredit the entire plan.

In a few years the number of students increased to such an extent that the general assembly of students became too unwieldy a body for ordinary business, and a senate of twenty-one members was substituted. In the development of the scheme two defects became evident: (1) abrupt changes in policy between administrations which brought about a perpetual state of flux in discipline, and (2) much self-conceit among the student

17

officials. When the novelty of the experiment wore away, the serious task of governing became irksome to the officials, and the execution of the law lax, until the rapid increase of offences aroused the slumbering rulers. These conditions in time produced factions. The laws would be executed vigorously by the strong men of the college for a time; then the law breakers and their sympathizers would defeat the law-and-order party in the elections and an entire change of policy would take place, only in turn to produce another reaction in favour of severity. The possession of so much power seemed to intoxicate the young and weak; the student officials had such an exalted conception of their own wisdom that they refused to accept counsel from older heads. On the slightest appearance of interference they threatened rebellion, and serious outbreaks were avoided only with the greatest difficulty. Notwithstanding these two serious defects, the experiment was considered a success for some years, because it secured good order without the intervention of the faculty.*

The defects became more pronounced with advancing years; the students objected to the espionage of their fellows, and the need of some method of balancing their authority became increasingly evident. At the same time the legality of the plan began to be questioned. The Attorney-General of Illinois decided that the student government possessed no legal right to assess and collect fines. This decision made the co-operation of the faculty necessary to the continuation of the plan. Student rule existed for a few years longer under the protection of the authorities, but was finally abolished in 1883 by a vote of the students themselves.

---

* Gregory, John M. An Experiment in College Government, International Review, vol. x, p. 517.

Out of three hundred and fifty students only seventy-six voted for its continuance.*

In 1873 more limited powers were vested in the students of the University of Maine, then known as the Maine State College. The framework of government was much simpler than that in the University of Illinois. The members of a student council were elected by the different classes, subject to the approval of the faculty, which might veto objectionable candidates. The general place of the council was to serve as an intermediary body between faculty and students. Its more specific duties were to secure the maintenance of order on the different floors, neatness of halls, and the observance of public regulations within and without the public buildings. In the operation of the plan each new council has found its work easy if it managed successfully the first one or two cases of disorder which came before it. If the council thus demonstrated, in the language of the street, that " it meant business," there was no further trouble. The historian of the council claims that it has contributed to a better understanding and more harmonious relations between faculty and students than could have otherwise existed, that it has rendered discipline easier and more effective, and has had a tendency to prevent misdemeanours. When violations have occurred the council has disposed of the minor cases satisfactorily without the intervention of the faculty, and thus saved the professors time and temper. Among the students the plan has developed the habits and principles of self-government, so important in all the periods and relations of life.†

---

* Peabody, Selim H. An Educational Experiment. Proceedings of the National Educational Association, 1889, p. 543.

† Fernald, M. C. Co-operative Government, in Proceedings of the National Educational Association, 1890. p. 686. This writer enumerates the requisites of a successful self-governing plan :

In 1866 the University of South Carolina altered its discipline to fit into a self-government plan, and in 1870 Indiana University followed its example, meeting with considerable success for a few years. The movement reached the lower schools. The New York Evening Post for December, 1880, published a series of articles by a successful city teacher, describing the experiments in student government which he had been cautiously conducting for a number of years.*

More celebrated than these early experiments was the Amherst senate, inaugurated in 1883. For the old *in loco parentis* theory of college discipline it substituted a voluntary contract between faculty and student. It was based on the assumption that a student's relations to his fellows was a very important one, and that in this relation the undergraduates have a far better opportunity than the faculty for judging of a man's conduct. The senate consisted of ten members—four from the senior, three from the junior, two from the sophomore, and one from the freshman class. A veto on the proceedings of the senate was vested in the president of the college, but he did not belong to it or attend its sessions. The senate supervised class suppers, student publications, and for a time athletics, which was later placed under a separate board. Often, when

---

(1) His earnest and hearty acceptance by both students and faculty.

(2) The insistence that only the best men, who are reliable and have the courage of their convictions, shall hold places in the council, so that the membership of this body shall be regarded as an honour as well as a responsibility.

(3) The cordial and hearty support of the council by the faculty, so it shall be known that all reasonable actions, rulings, and assignments of penalties on the part of the council will be sustained.

* Stevens, W. L. Self-Government in Colleges, Popular Science Monthly, vol. xix, p. 697.

a veto was threatened, the students became excited and supported the senate to a man. Differences of opinion between the president and senate were usually compromised, only one veto occurring in eight years. The senate was abolished in 1894 by a new college administration which was out of sympathy with the self-government idea. The general influence of the Amherst system was toward a more wholesome manliness.*

In order to ascertain the extent of student self-government in American colleges, the writer issued a circular letter to forty institutions—twenty small colleges in New England and the West and the twenty largest American universities. Out of the thirty-two colleges replying, eighteen had experimented with some form of student control. Three of the attempts had been marked failures and at the time of the report had been discontinued. The small colleges seemed to display a somewhat greater interest in the problem than the universities. No geographical difference between the East and the South and West could be discovered. Five distinct classes of self-governing schemes were discernible, viz., (1) student courts for those caught cheating in examinations, (2) advisory committees to the faculty, (3) committees having more or less general disciplinary power, (4) committees for the maintenance of order in some one dormitory, and (5) student body associations differing from the four preceding forms in having no connection with discipline.†

---

* Bigham, John. An Instructive Experiment in College Government, Educational Review, vol. iii, p. 162.

† The circular letter was issued February 7, 1899, stating in full the purpose of the investigation. The colleges replying were, from the group of small colleges, Amherst, Bowdoin, Bates, Coe, Grinnell, Maine, Middlebury, Parsons, Tabor, Trinity, Vermont, Wesleyan, and Williams; from the universities, Brown, California, Chicago, Cornell, Harvard, Leland Stanford, Michigan, Minnesota,

The honour system of conducting examinations is said to enforce itself in the Southern colleges. The professor takes no precaution against dishonesty, and in some cases goes so far as to leave the room while the papers are being prepared by the students. Any student detected in cheating is taken severely in hand by his fellows, who sometimes compel him to leave the college.* The sentiment of honour in the Southern sense hardly exists in the Northern colleges; Southern students in the North are often considered quixotic because of their tendency to take offence quickly.† The average Northern undergraduate, however scrupulous he may be personally, is likely to think that his responsibility ends there, and that other men are quite capable of managing their own concerns. Consequently, in the

---

Nebraska, New York, North Carolina, Northwestern, Pennsylvania, Princeton, Texas, Tulane, Vanderbilt, Virginia, Yale.

* That the system sometimes fails in its operation even in its home, the South, is seen by the following quotation :

" But there is no doubt a certain amount of cheating on examinations. In every assemblage of men there are a few of the baser sort who are insensible of appeals made to their higher nature, but these are seldom hardy enough to brave the strong public opinion that exists on the subject by open and flagrant cheating. A number of years ago one of the Greek-letter fraternities expelled two members on the charge of cheating. More recently some students in one of the professional departments on the campus were accused of crookedness in examination. One or two of them were indicted, tried before a student jury, and acquitted."—L. S. Merriam, Higher Education in Tennessee, pp. 165, 166.

† The writer does not mean to convey the impression that Northern students are more unscrupulous and untrustworthy than their Southern contemporaries. There are certainly no data which would lead to this conclusion. The sentiment of honour is an aristocratic product fostered in the South by family pride ; it is the result of ante-bellum conditions. The North has always been essentially democratic.

application of the honour system to Northern conditions it has been necessary to emphasize the formal side with its tribunals for detecting and punishing guilty parties. The attempt has been made to put the control of examinations on a more constitutional basis. It is made the duty of each student, who sees another cribbing or cheating, to report the fact to a student jury. At Cornell the jury, or court, consisted of ten undergraduates, elected in the ratio of four seniors, three juniors, two sophomores, one freshman, and the president of the university. The rules adopted at the University of Vermont grant the accused the right of being confronted with the witnesses against him, and make a unanimous vote of the jury necessary to convict. All fraternity brothers are excluded from service while a member of their society is on trial. If adjudged guilty, the name of the person is published in the college paper and posted on the university bulletin board, and he is deprived of the right to vote in class or public meetings, and to hold any office within the gift of the class or student body.*

The replies to the circular letter showed that seventeen colleges out of the thirty-two reporting had adopted the honour system, including Grinnell, Maine, Middlebury, Tabor, Vermont, Williams, Cornell and Princeton, California and Leland Stanford, after a short trial, abandoned the method. As to the success of the plan in the North, reports are conflicting. At Princeton and Cornell we have the word of the highest authorities that the honour system has wrought a great moral change in student life.† The introduction of

---

* See Broadside Student Honour System, University of Vermont, February 28, 1898.

† Mackenzie, J. C. Honour in Student Life, School Review, vol. vii, p. 74.

student control of examinations at Cornell was the means of establishing a self-governing committee, which has jurisdiction over all cases of college discipline.*

Notwithstanding the notable utterances in favour of the honour system in Northern colleges, one may well doubt whether its introduction has ever accomplished more than a healthy agitation of the subject in the student community. A temporary improvement often follows its adoption because of the agitation, but the moral strenuousness originated is usually short-lived, and cheating soon resumes its normal proportions. A graduate of a prominent New England college (Williams) is responsible for the statement that there was neither more nor less cheating after the adoption of the honour system than before. At Leland Stanford University the system was adopted by a sweeping majority and with much enthusiasm; mature and representative students were selected for the committee, but the entire matter disappeared completely from view because no

---

* From a report of the working of the new system by the four senior members of the class of 1894 we take the following : "It was scarcely to be expected that all dishonesty in examinations would disappear the moment the new system went into effect. Such was not the case, though there was a considerable improvement both in the amount of cribbing and the general attitude of the students toward it. During the first year the committee was obliged to investigate eleven cases of cheating in examinations, and the guilty parties were suspended from the university for two or three terms each."—A New Feature of College Life at Cornell : The Student Self-Government Council, p. 2 (pamphlet).

The following note from President Schurman, dated April 4, 1900, explains itself : " I should add that upon the subsequent reorganization of our faculties the system fell into abeyance so far as the organization is concerned, in consequence of a failure on the part of the students to express a desire for its continuance. The spirit of the system still prevails, nevertheless, at Cornell University."

one reported cases of dishonesty. There was nothing for the committee to do, and it soon disappeared. Public sentiment held it dishonourable and belittling for a man to report on his fellows, and before this feeling the honour system was powerless. In brief, the strong sense of personal honour is the peculiar product of Southern life and conditions and can not be developed in a different environment by copying the forms through which it works. Before deploring this fact too deeply it is well to remember that the value of the honour system may be easily overestimated. In at least one Southern college (University of Georgia), while it is highly dishonourable for a student to cheat in examinations, public sentiment permits him to crib in a daily recitation.

The second and slightest form of student control is through an advisory committee to which the faculty turn for consultation in the crises of college discipline. The supporters of this plan, usually college presidents, felt that there should be some method of ascertaining student sentiment in such a way as to prevent those misunderstandings which always result from a cleavage between two separate standpoints. Advisory committees are found at Bates, Vermont, Wesleyan, and Pennsylvania, and are reported satisfactory by both the parties concerned. These bodies are usually known as conference committees, and are elected by the members of the different college classes in the ratio before noted in the Amherst senate—four seniors, three juniors, two sophomores, and one freshman.

In four colleges which have reported—Bowdoin, Maine, Tulane, and Cornell—certain definite powers are lodged with the student councils, the composition of which is similar to that of the preceding class. The Bowdoin plan vests the greatest authority in its student jury, which has " absolute and final jurisdiction over all cases of public disorder and all offences committed by the students against each other." * The president of the college is in no sense a member of the jury, his relation to it being for the most part like that of a judge to a civil jury. He may present to them any matter of business, may assist them in any way they may desire in the discharge of their duties, may point out to them omissions or errors in their ascertainment or appreciation of facts, or remonstrate with them for the undue levity or severity of their decisions. But he can not control their legitimate action as jurymen, except as provided in the articles of agreement, and he can not call upon them to perform any duty as jurymen not plainly committed to them in these articles. The institution of student juries† has relieved the tension between faculty and undergraduates on the subject of hazing which in 1883, when the departure was introduced, threatened the prosperity of the college. In other respects the new system has secured fair results. " The members of the jury, as was expected, have not been far in advance of their constituents, and have quietly ignored things they could not control. But the system has slowly done great good in moulding public sentiment among the students, and in teaching the much-needed lesson that they themselves are largely responsible for the good government of the college."‡

The preservation of order in Tulane University is

---

* Article VII of the Articles of Agreement between the Faculty and Students of Bowdoin College for the Administration of Justice, adopted June 1, 1894.

† See Article VI of the Agreement. The Bowdoin jury consists of one member from each undergraduate class, one member from each chartered fraternity of three years' standing, and one member from the non-fraternity students.

‡ Smith, C. H. Modern Bowdoin, in The Congregationalist, June 21, 1894.

handed over to the officers of the four college classes. The time and place of the election of class officers are specified by the faculty, and in case the class refuses to elect, the president of the college may appoint. The entire body of class officers constitute an academic board with the senior president as *ex-officio* president, the junior president as *ex-officio* vice-president, and the sophomore president as *ex-officio* secretary. The academic board has recognisance of all cases brought before them by class officers and matters touching the general discipline and welfare of the students. They report their findings to the faculty with necessary recommendations. A long list of prohibitions dealing with a great variety of offences, such as smoking on the campus, and entering drinking saloons, follow in the handbook.*

Chicago, Pennsylvania, and Vanderbilt have forms of student self-government, the operation of which is confined to certain dormitories. The students in each house of the dormitories at Pennsylvania elect one of their number as representative; these representatives form a board which meets regularly and acts with the parietal committee of the faculty in matters concerning the order and comfort of those in the houses. Every group of six or more students living together as an organization at the University of Chicago is organized as a house with a set of officers. Each house has a head, appointed by the president of the university; a chancellor, chosen from the faculty by the students in the house; and a house committee, elected by the resi-

---

* Student's Handbook, Tulane University of Louisiana, p. 2. The handbook contains this somewhat naïve statement from the faculty: " The classes should select representatives who enjoy the confidence of their comrades, and whose influence on them would, on any occasion of anticipated excitement, be strong enough to allay feeling and prevent disturbance."

dent students. Each house is governed by a body of rules adopted by a two-thirds vote of the members of the house and approved by the university council. In 1898 there were twenty houses, eight of which were fraternity chapters, the remaining twelve being dormitories on a small scale.

The four different forms of student self-government which we have described were all intended to deal primarily with discipline and only incidentally with general student activities. The student-body organization which has recently become popular in the West, aims, on the other hand, to unify and make representative all student interests. No organization bearing the college name shall be a close corporation or possess an exclusive membership; all college societies must be equally open to the various elements of their university constituency who have the requisite qualifications for membership. The scheme of centralization and control which such a theory necessitates has been worked out with great detail and thoroughness at the Leland Stanford University. The outlines of this scheme we now present.

Each year the students elect by ballot a president and other executive officers, and seven members of an executive committee; the two corresponding to the mayor and council of an American municipality. The president of the student body is *ex-officio* chairman of the executive committee which exercises control of the general policy of all student concerns, but supervises most closely the athletic organizations, and the musical and debating clubs. Perhaps the môst important officer of the administration is the salaried treasurer, who must be a graduate, and has the financial management of every game or exhibition given by an undergraduate organization of the university. In fact, centralization has been in direct ratio to the money interests involved;

the operations of the athletic teams and musical clubs with their large outlays are closely watched and controlled by the central authorities. Other organizations practically manage their own affairs and are never interfered with.*

Technical athletic questions are left to an athletic committee of seven, which has only power to recommend, and makes no appropriations. The athletic element has at times fought for a separate athletic association and predicted dire results from student-body control. The athletic management seems to be neither better nor worse than in other colleges where the undergraduate element predominates. (Leland Stanford University is a recent foundation, and as yet has had no considerable body of graduates.) The financial management has greatly improved under centralized control. Here, as elsewhere in the administration of the system, the student-body officials must exercise due caution, because at any time it is possible for a member to appeal from the president and executive committee to a mass meeting of the students, who may overrule the action of their representatives.†

---

* The organizations over which the president and executive committee exercise control, in addition to the regular athletic teams, are the following : The Palo Alto (college daily), Sequoia (college weekly), Students' Guild (charity dispensary), Glee, Mandolin, and Banjo Clubs, Orchestra, Women's Athletic Association, Tennis, Gymnasium, and Fencing Clubs, Sword and Sandals (dramatic club), and the Debating League. The constitutions of these societies, as well as of the associated students, were published by the executive committee in 1896.

† The present constitution of the associated students is a slow growth. As first organized in 1891, the student body gave little power to its chief officials, and the real authority was lodged in numerous boards which were elected from the different classes and responsible to no body in particular. Owing to newness of the university and consequent lack of traditions, the special boards

While the experience with this highly centralized form of student control has been brief, yet on the whole it has been satisfactory. Not only has immediate efficiency been gained, but a wider and more zealous interest in their own affairs has arisen among the students. Critics of the scheme have called attention to the fact that much time is spent in voting and electioneering, and that doubtful methods of political manipulation are not uncommon. These evils are undoubtedly visible; and as society is at present constituted they are likely to be found in any plan which gives real power to the students. As a counterpoise of these, we must recognise the existence of public sentiment which prevents excesses and favours a sane spirit of compromise.

We may fairly conclude that the majority of the self-governing plans have been moderate successes; they have not revolutionized discipline, nor changed the character of the American youth, but they introduced a certain sense of responsibility among the undergraduates; they have promoted harmony between student and professor, helping the one to attain a greater measure of self-discipline, and relieving the other of

---

fell into the hands of cliques, and in some cases unfit men were chosen for responsible positions like managership of teams. The officials who had athletics in their charge were in many cases prodigal of money and careless in business methods. The first important move in the direction of efficiency was made in 1895, and provided for the election of a salaried graduate treasurer. The separate boards were abolished, and their functions added to those of the central executive committee. To insure publicity the constitutions and accounts of all college organizations were published. A year later the central financial control was extended to the musical clubs. For details, see History of the Student Body, by the writer, in the Stanford Sequoia, April 22, 1898, vol. vii.

burdensome duties. The success of these experiments has been by no means uniform. In some colleges they have fallen dead (Northwestern); in others (Harvard), finding no cases coming under their jurisdiction, the student legislators have endeavoured to manufacture them and have become promoters of discord rather than harmony. Their success has usually been proportioned to the tact and wisdom of the authorities with whom they have dealt. These student self-governing bodies must be regarded as incidental rather than essential creations of the American student spirit. Many of the most representative colleges have been without them. They do not belong to the class of great representative student institutions with the class organization, the debating society, the fraternity, and the athletic club.

§ 6. RELIGIOUS AND POLITICAL ORGANIZATIONS OF STUDENTS IN THE MODERN PERIOD.

The modern period has witnessed a complete change in the methods and organization of the student religious societies. The earlier praying circles and societies of inquiry were intended as aids to the devotion of their members; they were simply prayer-meeting associations. The societies in one college had no relations, formal or otherwise, with those elsewhere. The organization which in the present generation has taken their place—the Students' Young Men's Christian Association—is characterized by advanced methods and highly organized machinery. It also gives much attention to the social side of college life. The old type of religious society still persists in the denominational organizations, like the St. Paul's Society of Harvard and Princeton (Protestant Episcopal), the Catholic Club of Harvard, and the Oxford Club of Yale (Methodist Episcopal).

In the year 1858 the first two college Young Men's Christian Associations were organized at the University of Michigan and the University of Virginia. During the two following decades some twenty-five associations were formed in the colleges of the United States and Canada. Many of these societies sprang up spontaneously and were not connected with the general association, in some cases hardly knew of each other's existence. This state of affairs continued until 1877, when the representatives of twenty-one colleges met in convention at Louisville, Kentucky, and organized the students' division of the general Young Men's Christian Association. A college secretary was appointed and organized propaganda work undertaken for the first time. The growth of the student division has been rapid. From twenty-six associations, with thirteen hundred members in 1877, the collegiate branch had come to number in 1895 four hundred and seventy-five societies with thirty thousand members.*

The leadership and supervision of the college Young Men's Christian Association fall to five general secretaries, who spend the greater portion of their time in travelling about from one college to another, establishing new associations, delivering addresses, conferring with the local leaders in regard to the best methods of work, and holding conferences for the training of young men in the service of the church. Some of these conferences are local, bringing together delegations from colleges of a certain restricted section; others aim at training particular officials, like the presidential conferences held in Pennsylvania, Ohio, and Missouri; a third class take the form of student summer conferences

---

* The Intercollegiate Movement, a pamphlet, p. 6. The Young Men's Christian Association has not in all cases located its college branches in institutions of a distinctly superior grade. Many normal schools and secondary schools have regular branches.

which prepare men for the different departments of the association, such as Bible study and foreign missions.* The Young Men's Christian Association publishes a large number of pamphlets and one magazine devoted to Christian activity in colleges. The college department of the Young Women's Christian Association is modelled on the college Young Men's Christian Association, and its branches are much more strongly supported than those of the Young Men's Christian Association.

The local college association meets weekly for devotional exercises; in some institutions this meeting takes the form of a public gathering in the chapel; in others the men gather together in a comrade's room for an hour or so some evening in the week. At times, speakers from a distance, usually clergymen, or Young Men's Christian Association secretaries, are introduced. In addition to these devotional meetings, the modern association exercises numerous other functions; it issues a handbook of instructions to freshmen, cares for students in illness or distress, finds positions for the poor, and offers courses in Bible study to all who care to take them. In many colleges the Young Men's Christian Association gives a yearly reception to freshmen at the beginning of the first term.

The proportion of students belonging to the Young Men's Christian Association and participating in its work varies greatly with the different colleges. In a small denominational college in a country town or small city, like Bates College, Maine, two thirds of the students may belong, and half of them take part; whereas in a large university located in a metropolis not more than ten per cent of the students sometimes connect themselves with the college religious society. Of course,

---

* For an account of the work of the secretaries and conferences, see Year Book of the Young Men's Christian Association of North America, 1897, pp. 24-26.

18

in such an institution the membership of the Young Men's Christian Association by no means represents the strength of the active Christian element, as many students prefer to work in the churches. The Young Men's Christian Association handbook reports a membership of 25,284 students in 415 colleges which contained 105,051 male students, making the approximate ratio one in four.* The same colleges report 40,081 students who are members of Protestant evangelical churches.

During the last fifteen years many of the strongest local branches have erected college association buildings. By 1895 twenty-one such buildings, costing more than four hundred thousand dollars, had been constructed. The associations of Yale, Cornell, and Princeton led in this movement. The existence of a building set apart for this purpose is said to render the work of the local society more permanent, and to give the association a much higher standing in the student community. In colleges without facilities for physical training a portion of the structure is utilized for gymnasium purposes. " Everywhere the possession of a building prepares the way for stronger organization and more efficient methods."† The emphasis placed upon this material agency indicates a tendency to place a large and ever-increasing reliance on physical and mechanical agencies. The machinery of organization is everywhere brought to the front by the Young Men's

---

* Fifty branches sent no statistics. The reader need hardly be reminded again that the classification of normal schools and secondary schools as colleges to a certain extent destroys the validity of these figures.

† See pamphlet by John R. Mott, College Young Men's Christian Association Buildings (New York, 1895), for a description of the buildings erected up to that time, and for a consensus of opinion from college officials as to their usefulness.

Christian Association, and in some colleges it would seem that a disproportionate amount of time and energy is expended in making the machinery go.

In the last ten years, American ideals and methods of organization in this field have been transplanted to Europe. The World's Student Christian Federation, consisting of eleven different religious organizations, has been formed largely through the efforts of the American association. Delegates from these national societies have met in convention at Vadstena, Sweden, in 1895, and Eisenach, Germany, in 1898.* Next to the United States and Canada, Great Britain and the Scandinavian lands support the new movement with greatest energy. The Federation hopes to keep the various higher institutions of the world in communication with each other and to increase the practical efficiency of Christian propaganda in quarters where it had been permitted to languish. Both in Europe and America the new movement has sought to promote Bible study and interest in social problems in addition to its own field of devotional activity. " Comparing the student Christian movement in Europe with that in America, we find

---

* The members of the Federation, with the date of their admission, are as follows:

American and Canadian Y. M. C. A.	1895
Australasian Student Christian Union	1896
British College Christian Union	1895
College Y. M. C. A. of China	1896
Student Christian Movement of France, the Netherlands, and Switzerland	1898
German Christian Students' Alliance	1895
Intercollegiate Y. M. C. A. of India and Ceylon	1896
Students' Y. M. C. A. of Japan	1897
Scandinavian University Christian Movement	1895
Students' Christian Association of South Africa	1896
Students' Christian Movement in Mission Lands	1895

in Europe stronger thought, in America greater practical efficiency."*

We have previously referred to the denominational societies which supplement the Young Men's Christian Association in some of the large Eastern colleges. Yale possesses a Berkeley Association (Episcopalian), an Oxford Club (Methodist), and a Catholic Club. At Harvard the Unitarians are represented in addition to the three denominations having organizations at Yale. The five religious associations of Harvard are known as the United Religious Societies, and at times issue a call for public meetings under their joint auspices.† Denominational clubs and societies, however, are the rare exception; there are probably not more than thirty of them in the country. The student members of the Protestant Episcopal Church most frequently organize separate associations. The Catholic youth are largely educated in church colleges, where they are formed into sodalities by the priest in charge.

In the larger universities the Christian spirit finds many different ways of expressing itself. The forms of activity vary with the college, each institution impressing something of its own individuality on the religious societies. To give the reader a sense of this variety it will be necessary to sketch the main features of religious work at a few typical centres of learning. We have chosen, as representative institutions of the different classes, Harvard, Yale, and the University of Minnesota.

The Christian association of Harvard is the centre

---

* From James B. Reynolds. Facts and Forces in the Religious Life of the Universities of Europe, p. 25, in a pamphlet entitled The Christian Movement in the Universities of America, Europe, and Asia.

† See Harvard Graduate Magazine, vol. iv, p. 416, for notice of such a meeting on the Armenian question.

in the university for men of religious feeling and positive belief. " It is inclined to be broad in its interpretation of positive belief," and the spirit of critical inquiry, which marks Harvard thinking in all fields, is by no means absent here. The association invites all to fellowship with it, " even those who may at times feel that they have little more in common with us than their doubts." * Two meetings are held each week—one on Sunday evening, which is largely of a devotional character; and another on Thursday evening, which provides time for more critical biblical discussion, and is addressed by professors, university preachers, or leaders in Christian activity. Further critical study is carried on in Bible classes. Monthly socials with entertainment by the college musical societies afford social diversion to a certain class of students.

Apart from devotions and study, the chief interest of the Harvard religious organizations lies in participation in outside philanthropy and charitable work. Realizing the need of wise charity administrators, the five religious societies of the university provided a clearing house for philanthropy and benevolence which receives applications for charity and endeavours to fit men to the work. A charity expert was hired who handled the cases directly. " The effort is made to appreciate the whole make-up of the man. His age, his tastes, his home, his college standing, his future plans— all these help to determine the kind of work best suited to his ability. A teacher is sent to lecture to workingmen; a Westerner was given a knowledge of the organization of the Boston charities; medical students are sent to children's hospitals." †

---

* Harvard Graduate Magazine, vol. i, pp. 608, 609.
† Calkins, Raymond. Volunteer Charity Work, Harvard Graduate Magazine, vol. iii, p. 327.

Another unique charity managed by Harvard students is the Prospect Union at Cambridgeport, which serves as a university extension centre. Early in the nineties it had a membership of two hundred working-men and clerks, who were instructed by a score or more of students. Besides the regular course of instruction, the Union provided a public lecture every Wednesday evening, which lectures were delivered chiefly by the members of the Harvard faculty. By means of these instrumentalities the Union endeavoured to bring college men and wage earners into mutual sympathy; and in consequence the organization was consistently democratic in its principles and methods. Its expenses were provided for by light fees and by concerts given by the Harvard musical societies.*

The Young Men's Christian Association of Yale is distinctly more aggressive and evangelical than its contemporary at Harvard. Its object is forceful action rather than clear, critical thinking. This aggressiveness is seen in the methods used to reach the incoming freshman class each year. The Association aims to place before the newcomers " an attractive form of Christianity and to render them every possible service which will render the new life less strange and place the possibility

---

* For full account of the Prospect Union, see Harvard Graduate Magazine, vol. i, p. 462. The Prospect Union is thus described by one of the characters in C. M. Flandrau's Harvard Episodes: " The Prospect Union," explained Haydock, in the deliberate way that was often taken seriously, " is a most admirable educational institution carried on in Cambridgeport by the Harvard undergraduates. It is elaborately designed to make the lower classes—the laboring man—dissatisfied with his station in life. I am proud to say that I once went there every Friday night for six months to teach two bricklayers, three dry-goods clerks, and a nigger how to appreciate the beautiful works of the late Mr. Keats. I spoiled their lives, and they all love me."

of remaining in college within the reach of those in financial straits." * Dwight Hall, the Young Men's Christian Association headquarters, is thrown open a week before the opening of the college session, and every assistance is afforded the freshman in the way of finding suitable boarding places, and in securing employment for those who have their own way to make. A committee of fifteen, chosen from those who have been identified with religious work in the preparatory schools, is made responsible for their comrades, who are divided into squads of twenty-five or thirty for this purpose. The importance of the devotional study of the Bible is emphasized by a series of meetings, and men are encouraged to engage actively in some form of Christian effort.

The religious services of the week are two in number, as at Harvard, but differently arranged. A general gathering of all the students takes place on Sunday evening—a meeting formerly addressed by such men as Drummond, Moody, Gordon, and McKenzie. On Sunday noon the religiously disposed members of each class gather together for a class prayer meeting. Each of the three upper classes elects four deacons, to whom is delegated the entire management of the religious interests of the class. The ablest and most prominent members of the class are said to be frequently elected to this office.† The deacons from all classes form a board of governors for the Young Men's Christian Association. The Yale association provides workers for the missions, speakers for out-of-door and jail meetings, conducts a boys' club, and manages a special mission of its own in

---

* From Work for the Entering Class at Yale, by Henry B. Wright, general secretary of the Yale Young Men's Christian Association, in The Intercollegian, vol. xxi, n. 1, p. 18 (October, 1898).

† Welch and Camp. Yale, p. 60.

one of the tenement-house districts. Yale has supported Moody in his Northfield work more strongly than any other college in the country, and trains many men for the foreign mission field.

The somewhat ostentatious aggressiveness and strength of the religious element in the university led to a reaction in the early nineties. The disaffected accused the Young Men's Christian Association, or Dwight Hall element, of endeavouring to control class politics. One entire class was divided into two well-marked factions, known respectively as Dwight Hall and Holy Poker. This antagonism has since passed away.*

The control of the Young Men's Christian Association of the University of Minnesota is vested in a board of directors consisting of four members of the faculty, three business men, two alumni, and two undergraduates. Such an arrangement secures more stability than is possible in a purely undergraduate association. The board of directors employ a general secretary, who spends his entire time in the work of the society. The student association works through sixteen committees, the enumeration of which will give some idea of the scope of their activities. They are the committees on religious meetings, reception, membership, Bible study, missions, invitation, finance, music, educational department, employment bureau, loan library, reading room, buildings and attractions, intercollegiate relations, care of the sick, and handbook.†

In a State university the entire province of religious instruction is avoided in order to prevent the possibility of sectarian entanglements. The Young Men's Christian Association endeavours to meet this need by offer-

---

* Welch and Camp. Yale, p. 61.

† The Student's Handbook of the University of Minnesota, p. 14, Minneapolis, 1898.

ing courses in the study of the Bible. A course on the Life of Christ, based on Sharmon's Studies in the Life of Christ and Burton's Harmony of the Gospels, is offered to freshmen. The sophomores study the life of Paul and the apostolic Church, and the seniors Old Testament history, while there are more special classes in the study of missions and in training for evangelistic work. The young women's association affords similar opportunities to the women of the university.

The association conducts an employment bureau for needy students. Statistics during the year 1897–'98 showed that about fifty students were assisted to permanent positions, and many more furnished with odd jobs. A loan fund was established, made up of contributions from students and friends of the Young Men's Christian Association, upon which the association paid three per cent interest. Needy students may borrow small amounts from the loan fund at reasonable rates. Free classes in the preparatory subjects are also maintained by the association; these courses enable the freshmen to make up their entrance conditions, and to review such subjects as beginning·Greek, Greek grammar, Virgil, and algebra.

Students from the local association join those from other colleges of the State in making evangelistic tours among the small towns in bands of five, under the direction of the State Young Men's Christian Association. The expenses of such students are paid, enabling them to devote all their time to active service. In the winter of 1898 eighty men went out on such tours from the colleges of the State, twenty-three of these from the State university; three hundred and ninety-eight conversions were reported. Before attempting such services, men are trained in preparatory Bible classes.*

---

* Student's Handbook, University of Minnesota, p. 20

The student volunteer movement for foreign missions has been closely connected with the college religious societies and has been largely instrumental in arousing them to more aggressive action. Interest in missions before the rise of this movement had been somewhat sporadic in colleges. Early in the century Williams College and Andover Theological Seminary were the seats of an intense missionary ferment on the part of a few students. In 1883 a revival at Princeton led to the formation of a foreign missionary society there.*

In the early eighties the missionary boards experienced considerable difficulty in securing well-trained candidates for the foreign stations. It was a transition period; the heroic age of missionary endeavour seemed to have come to an end; the lofty exaltation which came from the prospect of martyrdom and meeting unknown dangers could no longer be depended upon to draw men into the service; the old Puritanic *motif* of saving the souls of the heathen from damnation was losing its force, while the newer desire to elevate the condition of primitive peoples had not come to the front. D. L. Moody saw the needs of the situation, and invited delegates from the Christian associations of the colleges to meet at Northfield for a summer conference in 1886. The enthusiasm of the convention accomplished the desired result; out of two hundred and fifty-one delegates at the conference, an even hundred volunteered for the foreign service. The principles of the movement and the form of organization were evolved in the next two or three years.

The student volunteer movement aims to agitate, to

---

* Beach, Harlan P. Historical Sketch of the Student Volunteer Movement. in The Student Volunteer, vol. vi, No. 3, p. 37 (December, 1897).

stimulate, to inform, rather than to act as a missionary board. " It has never sent out a missionary and never expects to "; it is simply a recruiting agency and works in entire accord with the missionary societies of the churches, and has received the indorsement of the leading denominations. Its function has been to arouse an interest in missions and to enrol a sufficient number of well-trained candidates to meet the successive demands of the various mission boards of North America. The management of the movement includes all colleges, normal schools, and professional schools within the scope of its operations; but no members are enrolled from schools of a secondary grade.

The control of the movement is invested in an executive committee composed of the official representatives of the four great student organizations of North America: the Intercollegiate Young Men's Christian Association, the Intercollegiate Young Women's Christian Association, the American Inter-Seminary Missionary Alliance, and the Canadian Intercollegiate Missionary Alliance. Five travelling secretaries are employed who spend their time in visits from college to college. In the summer institutes held by the Young Men's Christian Association, the volunteer movement conducts a missionary institute which trains leaders for volunteer bands, mission-study classes, and other missionary activities. Every four years, or once in each student generation, the movement holds a large convention which brings together thousands of delegates from all the colleges of the country. The executive committee publish a monthly periodical—The Student Volunteer—and a large number of pamphlets, a list of which will be found in the Bibliography.

The management of the movement hope eventually to have a volunteer band in every American college and professional school. The local band is composed only

of those students who have voluntarily pledged themselves to the foreign mission cause. The volunteer
band prepare themselves by a course of study for active
service and also endeavour to interest the students of
the college in missionary effort. Experience has shown
that an organization of this kind for mutual encouragement is necessary. "In institutions where the volunteers have remained separate and unorganized, their
own interest has usually waned, the missionary spirit
of the students as a whole has usually decreased, the
volunteers have become the object of much criticism,
and practically no recruits have been enlisted." * The
bands spend more energy in practical propaganda, such
as bringing in recruits, circulating missionary literature, and visiting churches in the interests of the cause,
than to study.†

A perusal of their literature gives one an impression
that they have no very exact comprehension of the pedagogical and anthropological problems involved in religious endeavours among primitive and alien peoples.
It may be said of the entire movement that it abounds
in devotion and enthusiasm rather than knowledge.
Not that there is anything fantastic or visionary in the
volunteer methods; the common-sense, business principles which Mr. Moody introduced into all his enterprises are found here also; but there seems to be no
adequate realization of the fact that the evangelization
of alien races is a task of almost infinite complexity and
difficulty.

The most tangible result of the student volunteer
movement is found in the large number of candidates
offering themselves to mission boards; there were five

---

* Lyon, D. Willard. The Volunteer Band. p. 11.

† See Lyon, The Volunteer Band. pp. 26-52, for a description
of this work as it should be conducted.

in 1898 to every one ten years earlier. By the 1st of January, 1898, eleven hundred and seventy-three volunteers had gone to the mission fields and four thousand students had pledged themselves to similar action when their preparation was completed.* Of this number, one third are women. The resources of the church missionary societies have been strained to the uttermost in the attempt to accommodate those who desired to go, and in the last two or three years have declined many eligible candidates. The student volunteer agitation has performed another signal service in promoting the systematic study of missions. In 1894, when the volunteers for the first time turned their attention to mission-study classes, there were only thirty such organizations in the country. In three years the number increased to two hundred and seventeen classes, with twenty-three hundred and sixty-one students, a half of whom were enrolled volunteers.† The classes brought about the accumulation of missionary literature in the different college libraries.

The intangible results of the movement are much more difficult to follow. In many colleges, particularly certain State universities, there has undoubtedly been an entire change of attitude on the subject of missions. The idea so prevalent in the eighties among undergraduates that all forms of aggressive religious endeavour were superannuated survivals of mediævalism, out of place in the present enlightened age, is fast giving

---

* Report of the Executive Committee of the Student Volunteer Movement, p. 7, 1898.

† Ibid, p. 6. The reader will note that this activity does not meet the criticism expressed on the previous page. The reading of the lives of missionaries and hortatory addresses is by no means a study of the scientific problems involved in mission work, although it is of course fruitful in adding to the stock of intelligence of the worker.

way either to appreciation or to acute dislike. The movement has stimulated the churches, aroused the religious societies of the colleges to their responsibility, and has extended its influence to foreign countries. Its success in the present age in reviving the ideals of militant Christianity in the same institutions that by subjective criticisms were undermining the foundations of religious belief, is one of the striking signs of the complexity of modern social forces.

CHAPTER VI.

STUDENT ORGANIZATIONS IN AMERICAN SECONDARY SCHOOLS.

BIBLIOGRAPHICAL NOTE.—No adequate or comprehensive treatment of the social activities of secondary schools exists ; the literature is fragmentary and very recent ; however, some important articles have appeared on high-school self-government in the School Review. W. A. McAndrew describes the experiment at Pratt High School, Brooklyn (School Review, vol. v, p. 456) ; C. W. French, that of the Hyde Park High School, Chicago (School Review, vol. vi, p. 35) ; and C. H. Thurber the condition of affairs at Warren, Pa. The constitutions of the respective self-government corporations are given in full in these articles. For the purpose of comparison, the account of self-government by the pupils of the John Creerar Grammar School, Chicago, is of value. It is published as Appendix H of the Report of the Educational Commission of the City of Chicago. Henry W. Thurston, of Chicago, issued a syllabus on Training for Citizenship in the Public Schools, one section of which dealt with civic training through student societies. The results of this investigation, which are of importance, are presented in the School Review, vol. vi, p. 577. Isaac Sharpless (School Review, vol. vi, p. 145) and Endicott Peabody (School Review, vol. iii, p. 502) discuss the *pros* and *cons* of secondary school athletics. Florence Milner's School Management from the Side of Social Life (School Review, vol. vii, p. 215) treats of the relation of the school to social functions.

The greater portion of the information contained in the following chapter was obtained from a topical *questionnaire* on Student Life in Secondary Schools, issued in November, 1898, which reads as follows :

1. To what extent are the following lines of student activity represented in your institution ? (*a*) Class system, (*b*) literary and

debating society, (c) preparatory school fraternities, (d) athletics, (e) student body organizations, (f) press, (g) miscellaneous.

2. Name any activities or institutions peculiar to students of a secondary grade.

3. To what extent is the student life in your institution influenced by college ideals?

4. What difference have you noticed between the same institutions in colleges and preparatory schools?

5. In what way is student activity supervised or aided by the teachers or governing authority?

6. What is your estimate as to the value of these institutions in secondary schools?

Answers were obtained from forty-one institutions of a secondary grade. In most cases the replies came from the principals, in a few instances from either secretaries or teachers. Of the forty-one schools, sixteen were academies, ten high schools, and fifteen normal schools. The great majority of the normal schools from which returns were received are in reality secondary schools, paralleling the courses in high schools and academies and preparing students for college. If the normal schools were given over largely or exclusively to professional training, their inclusion in the list would be indefensible. The schools reporting represent every grade of instruction and all sections of the country, although the large schools outnumber the smaller ones, a fact of which account must be made in evaluating the results. The list of schools reads as follows: Academies—(1) Phillips Andover, (2) Phillips Exeter, (3) Friends' Academy, New Bedford, (4) Groton School, (5) Sawin Academy, Sherborne, Mass., (6) Wesleyan Academy, Wilbraham, (7) Adelphi Academy, Brooklyn, (8) Lawrenceville School, New Jersey, (9) William Penn Charter School, Philadelphia, (10) George School, Newton, Pa., (11) Harry Hillman Academy, Wilkesbarre, Pa., (12) Jacob Tome Institute, Port Deposit, Md., (13) Abingdon Male Academy, Virginia, (14) Winchell Academy, Evanston Ill., (15) Belmont School, California, (16) St. Matthew's School, San Mateo, Cal. The high schools were—(17) Springfield, Mass., (18) Lowell Mass., (19) Gloucester, Mass., (20) Cambridge English High School, Massachusetts, (21) Albany, N. Y., (22) Jamestown, N. Y., (23) Indianapolis, Ind., (24) Ashmore, Ill., (25) Davenport, Ia., (26) Iowa City, (27) Sioux City, Ia. Normal schools were—(28) Fitchburg, Mass., (29) Westfield, Mass.,

(30) Worcester, Mass., (31) Indiana, Pa., (32) California, Pa., (33) Carbondale, Ill., (34) Cedar Falls, Ia., (35) Mankato, Minn., (36) Winona, Minn., (37) Peru, Neb., (38) Albion, Idaho, (39) Cheney, Washington, (40) Chico, Cal., (41) San Jose, Cal.

Returns showed great differences between the different types of secondary schools. Two academies and one high school reported the total absence of student organizations of any type, while a number of large public academies almost duplicated the organizations of a vigorous college. The great majority of American secondary schools occupy a middle position, having the typical organizations of the college—the class, the debating society, fraternity and athletic association. These societies are usually less vigorous than those of the college, and include in their scope only a minority of students.

FOR the purpose of studying their student associations, we may divide the secondary schools of the country into four classes: first, large academies and fitting schools; second, large city high schools; third, small country high schools and academies; and fourth, normal schools.

Student life is much the more important element in schools of the first class. The reasons for this superiority are clearly seen; they are boarding schools, family life is eliminated; the entire social activities of the pupils centre in the school. The teachers are more likely to be college men and consequently more in sympathy with student societies, and frequently they live in the school in charge of their pupils, which facilitates intercourse. The head master being in many cases vested with large discretionary power and sure of his position, is more likely to take a liberal view of his functions than the principal of a high school, who is often hampered by the public sentiment of the community, the whims of schoolboys, and the insecurity of his office. The evidence which we have collected shows that the head masters of these schools value student societies much more highly than high-school officials, and

19

view them as a legitimate factor in training, and not a nuisance to be managed and abated. For these reasons the best class of academy and fitting schools have developed a stronger *esprit de corps* than the high schools, and possess a much more vigorous community life; a much larger percentage of the boys take part in the social activities than elsewhere. As might be anticipated from their close connection to the colleges, the associations in the academies and fitting schools closely approximate those of the superior institutions. The list of societies at Phillips Exeter or Phillips Andover almost duplicates that of Harvard or Yale. Athletics are likely to predominate in these schools, although class spirit and organization are relatively much stronger than elsewhere. The debating societies are usually weaker than in high schools and normal schools.

In the city high schools the students are largely left to their own devices. The principal supervises them sufficiently to prevent the debating societies from becoming elements of disorder, and the athletics from being involved in scandals which would find their way to the newspapers. In a few exceptional cases the debating societies are turned into something which nearly approaches class-room exercises. Teachers are likely to think that they are paid for teaching so many hours a week, and to resent any change which looks like an additional demand on their time. So, in general, the initiative rests with the students. A small percentage of the boys and girls interested in public affairs gather together for weekly discussions; another small percentage of the physical *élite* form the teams and athletic associations. The majority of the students have only the training which comes from two or three class banquets, a sense of proprietorship in a school paper which usually excites more interest here than in colleges, and occasionally a students' association.

Both the athletic and debating societies stand in need of a vigorous public sentiment. The temptation involved in handling large sums of money is often too much for the athletic manager, who is frequently a bright boy from a family where a low sense of honour prevails. The amount of financial crookedness which goes on in connection with the athletics of an average American high school would surprise the general public if known. There is naturally no way of ascertaining the exact facts of the case, as the interest of the school and the parties implicated demand their suppression. These defalcations are due to the absence of any feeling of accountability or responsibility, rather than to innate depravity. In the contests, the spirit of competition rages stronger than in the colleges, and more liberties are taken with the proper standards. The debating society, if all the members are immature and no outside influence is felt, oftentimes degenerates in its proceedings to mere wrangle and chicanery, and is more productive of conceit and wire-pulling than of any more desirable products.

It is difficult to generalize respecting the small rural academies and high schools; the data at our command are too slight and the variation too wide. Still, it is the personal impression of the writer that, so far as formal organizations are concerned, their position is in a majority of cases lower than that of the large city high schools. The principals and teachers are overburdened in the attempt to teach a large number of subjects, sometimes as many as seven or eight in one day; the labour of discipline is also relatively greater than in larger schools. The number of pupils to whom either debating or athletics spontaneously attracts is often too small for any efficient organization. Here again the teachers sometimes turn the debating into a class-room exercise. In small schools the formal organization side is less essential than elsewhere. The entire high school may be, and usually is, in the country, one large society; play arises without formal games. Nowhere is the influence of the principal so powerful to mould the opinion and practice of the school.

Normal schools have their own peculiar tendencies; they are conditioned by the character of their students, who are more mature, earnest, and hard-working than those attending other types of secondary schools; the majority come from homes of the lower middle class and are ambitious to make their way in the world. In many parts of the West and South the ideals of the normal schools are determined by a class of men and women of the college age, who have already spent some time in the active service of teaching. For these same reasons normal students are extremely practical; they demand some substantial return for every moment of time expended. In consequence of this, debating societies and Christian associations are their strongest organizations, although recently many of them have put athletic teams in the field. These teams are usually weak and poorly supported, and by no means arouse the enthusiasm which similar teams command elsewhere. Class feeling is also weak before graduation, although in many normals annual reunions bring the alumni together frequently.

Normal school authorities differ widely in their attitude toward student organizations. A recent committee, consisting of prominent normal teachers appointed by the National Educational Association, indorses student societies strongly. " Under proper management and care the literary life of the institution can be much elevated and encouraged by the students through self-help and self-dependence, as exhibited through literary societies. . . . Teachers should be trained to write and to speak. They should be at home

on the page of the periodical and on the platform. . . .
These literary societies should control their own internal affairs; they should do more to develop their members than to entertain audiences, and they should have
great encouragement from the faculties and boards of
trustees, as after-years will demonstrate the fact that
no work at the school gave a student better command
of himself than active membership in the literary society." The Christian associations are indorsed in the
following language: " Wherever the student organizations known as the Young Men's Christian Association
and Young Women's Christian Association are encouraged and authorized to exist, there great benefit has
always come to the moral and religious life of the
general student body." * Of the fifteen normal school
teachers and principals replying to the *questionnaire*,
two expressed themselves as strongly opposed to student
societies. One writer argues as follows: Students in
secondary schools are forming habits of study, and
therefore should devote as little time as possible to outside interests. These two correspondents represent the
driving element which sometimes comes to the front in
normal schools; the other principals speak of the organizations in terms of the highest praise.

Leaving now the different classes of schools, we will
discuss the different forms of activity more in detail.
The class organization was formed in thirty-eight out
of the forty-one schools reporting. Usually the class
organizes upon entering, and continues organized
through the four years of the secondary school course.
In other cases the class does not organize until the second year, as associations of first-year students are

---

* Report of the Committee on Normal Schools, Z. X. Snyder,
Chairman (Section IV), The Inner Life of the Normal School.
Proceedings of the National Educational Association, 1899, pp.
861, 862.

frowned upon by the authorities.   One principal states
that in his high school the lighter elements of the class
always rise to the top during the first year of organization; the management falls into undesirable hands, and
a waste of time and money ensues.   Three first presidents of classes were successively expelled from the
school.   During the remaining years the class is well
managed.   In a third class of schools the class remains
unorganized until the term before graduation, when
the prospect of parting draws the members together.
Many principals report an increase of interest in the
class as the senior year is approached.

Class interest manifests itself in the form of rivalry,
athletic contests, and social events.   The amount of
rivalry differs greatly; sometimes it is almost entirely
absent, then again it extends to pins, colours, and yells,
and at times even takes a more violent form and results in rushes, and occasionally in schemes for rebellion
in case of extreme discipline.   Class rivalry in athletics exists to some extent wherever a large number of
students take part in the sports, but it is always secondary and subordinate to interscholastic contests.

The chief function of the class, particularly in the
high school, is to promote social intercourse by dramatics, informal dances, and more formal receptions.   In
many schools the juniors give an annual reception to
the seniors.   In towns and smaller cities the school is
the natural centre of social life, and meetings between
the different classes and teachers often produce good
feeling and give the students a needed experience of
social conventions.   In a larger city conditions are different; society is stratified, and many of the students
would not meet each other elsewhere or ever enter
the inside of each other's homes.*   Here social af-

* " Pupils in city high schools have too much social life as it is.
I am unwilling to take the responsibility when I must work in the

fairs in connection with the school are of doubtful expediency. Such affairs, unless closely watched by the teachers, tend to become more and more expensive, and consequently involve an undue drain on the finances of many pupils.

In a majority of the schools the class organization is accepted as a matter of course, but no attempt is made, except in a few institutions, to utilize the higher class as an instrumentality for elevating the standard of the lower, as in the English public schools since Arnold's day. At Phillips Exeter class lines are important and somewhat rigid; for a student to be transferred from one class to another is no ordinary disgrace. He feels that he has lost his proper status. Class feeling is in every way strengthened and encouraged by the authorities, and is considered the basis of a proper school spirit. The head master of the Belmont school, California, is endeavouring to make use of the position of the senior class to stimulate its members to set the proper standard of morals and manners. The Groton school has transplanted the sixth form rule from England; it is said to succeed admirably.

The tie of class in many normal and high schools is likely to be stronger after graduation than before. The more restricted social life of the graduates of these schools enables them to keep alive a keen interest in the doings of their classmates. Class banquets and reunions are of common occurrence. However, like all such organizations in secondary schools, they have not the stability and sustained interest which characterize college associations of the same type.

Out of the forty-one secondary schools which re-

---

dark and not know what elements I am bringing together. I am unwilling to thus risk tangling the threads of Fate."—Florence Milner, in School Review, vol. vii, p. 216.

plied to the *questionnaire*, thirty-one reported debating societies in active operation. The principals and teachers, with one exception, regarded these organizations with favour; the one exception thought that the pupils were already overburdened with the work of the curriculum.* In the fitting schools, from one fourth to one half the boys belong, on the average; in some few schools, all the boys. A much smaller percentage of high-school pupils were members, usually from five to twenty per cent, although the writer has known of exceptional schools where fully eighty per cent belonged. The evidence shows that debating clubs are most numerous and highly prized in normal schools, where their membership often includes practically the entire student body. They are also strong in the preparatory departments of Western denominational colleges.

To give the reader an idea of the working of these societies, we include two quotations, one from the head master of an academy, and the other from the principal of a leading high school, describing the operation of these societies in their respective schools. The account from the co-educational academy runs as follows: "Four literary and debating societies flourish in the school. The two of them for the boys are more than fifty years old, and do very good work. They elect their own officers, prepare their own programmes, fur-

---

* This testimony corresponds with the result of a *questionnaire* investigation made by Prof. Henry W. Thurston, and reported in the School Review (vol. vi, p. 577, 1898) under the title, Training for Citizenship in the Public Schools. Of the seven correspondents who specifically mention debating societies in his report, six favour and one condemns them. The one criticism runs as follows: "Such societies are a source of disorder in a building and often conflict with authority, and children of that age [secondary-school age] are not fit to exercise authority."

nish their own halls, and succeed in developing considerable forensic ability. Each of these societies numbers among its members public speakers of prominence. There is never an occasion of anxiety to the management of the school except rarely, when interest in them flags on the part of the members because of outside sports, as football or baseball. One evening each week is given up exclusively to this work. The girls in their organizations have more time for music and essays; debate with them is incidental. Society feeling is not so strong among them."

One high-school principal * writes: " Our pupils have a flourishing debating society which is well attended once a fortnight, and well managed, considering the age of the pupils. I am always present as a visitor, and am frequently invited to serve them in a variety of ways. Some marked power is developed each year in a number of individuals. The majority take little part, being younger pupils. The burden of work is done by a few older boys who attend. The results are good. The kind of debate preferred is the ' drash debate,' in which the audience is requested to send in slips bearing a subject and the name of a proposed debater. These are arranged in order by a presiding officer and the proposed debaters called out, one after another. This cultivates readiness, but places ' smart speeches ' of short duration in prominence. The prepared debates are sometimes excellent, particularly if some rivalry enters in, as in class debates, when one class is pitted against another, or prize debates with other schools."

The first Greek-letter society for schools of a secondary grade was the Alpha Phi, a literary society which was merged into a fraternity in 1876, and established

---

* Prof. Ray Greene Huling, of the Cambridge English High School.

chapters in a limited number of schools in eastern New York, New Jersey, and Delaware. Baird enumerates nine other societies of this class, all of them confined to some small section of the country, and some of them limited to a single chapter. Among the most prominent are Alpha Zeta, among the high schools of eastern New York; the Gamma Eta Kappa, in central California; and the Omicron Kappa Pi, in Chicago. No statistics have been published of the membership of these societies.* Local societies modelled on those of Yale are found in some of the most prominent preparatory schools of New England, particularly Phillips Exeter and Andover.

The opinions of the head masters and principals of high schools, as far as we have collected them, condemn secondary school fraternities. Nine of our correspondents objected to them and none defended them, although they were permitted to exist in six schools. Almost all the private secondary schools prohibit them, and the high schools discourage their formation. Where they are permitted, as at Exeter and Andover, one member of the faculty must be chosen a member, and have access to all the meetings of the society, which he closely watches. A correspondent from one school, where four such societies exist, writes as follows: " I regard all [student] institutions of value except the Greek-letter fraternities. I should be very glad to see them all die. They are not, however, an unmixed evil, and undoubtedly do a good deal toward rubbing off the corners and making the immature student more manly, provided the influence exerted is judicious; but there is such a very large opportunity for injudicious influence in the fraternity organization that I am disposed to

---

* For a detailed account, see Baird, W. R., College Fraternities, fifth edition, pp. 362–365.

believe that the defects of the system are greater than its virtues." A prominent Western head master writes: " I distinctly discourage school fraternities, and none therefore exist in the schools. There was one for a time, but it stirred up such ill feeling that it split the school into two strong factions."

Of all the activities mentioned in the *questionnaire*, athletics seems to be the most highly valued by the teachers, and to excite the greatest enthusiasm among the boys. In the language of one head master, " athletics serves as the most valuable outlet for animal spirits which would find an outlet in objectionable ways; and then to the amount of training necessary to build up a good football team calls for hygienic attention and restraints that are of great value, I think; and then, too, they are promoters of school spirit which I think is well worth the while." The uses of athletics have been enlarged upon in the section treating of athletics in English secondary schools, and it is only necessary here to state that the best American head masters and principals follow in the path which English precedent has established. Of the forty-one schools on our list, thirty-two reported full, well-organized athletic teams. The different athletic games are mentioned in the following order of frequency: football (19), baseball (18), tennis (7), track (6), and boating (2).

Athletic organization is a close imitation of college models. Thus the athletics of the Cambridge high schools is managed by a committee composed, like that of Harvard, of equal representation of students, graduates, and professors. In the majority of schools the scheme or organization is more simple; one member of the school-teaching force, usually either the head master or professor of physical training, makes it his business to superintend the school games, coaching the teams, accompanying them on trips, and acting as treasurer of the student athletic association. The efficiency of the student management depends on the manager and captain. " If either of these men is a leader, even though he may not have very much technical ability in the particular game, the season is an assured success." Interscholastic associations with rigid rules barring out illicit practices are found among those schools situated near the large centres of population. They closely follow college models.

The abuses which have been frequent in secondary school athletics have been due (1) to inadequate supervision and control on the part of the authorities, and (2) to the desire of the school to advertise itself. The high schools have laid themselves more open to the first charge, the private secondary school to the second. The dangers besetting all forms of amateur athletics in America are doubly great in case of the secondary schools, owing to the immaturity of their students. In many high schools the initiative in and entire management of competitive contests has been left to boys of sixteen or seventeen years, which has naturally resulted oftentimes in sharp practice and embezzlement of funds. The second evil is by no means as serious, although here and there a head master may be found who will wink at sharp practices until the season is over. As the athletic prestige of a school has a tangible cash value, it speaks well for the morals of the teaching profession that this form of perversion is not more common. In many schools the only students to compete are those who have hopes of gaining distinction thereby. In only one school was participation in athletics compulsory. On the average, perhaps fifty per cent of the students in the best academies take part in games, while in most high schools such activities hardly reach more than ten per cent of the student body.

Five schools out of the forty-one reported the existence of some form of student self-government. With one exception, where English precedent was followed, these constitutional governments seem to be recent foundations and the result of the movement which has swept over the country in the last five years, and includes schools containing at least fifty thousand students in its scope.* The movement originated in the interest produced by the George Junior Republic, a unique institution in central New York. Mr. George, the founder, took a number of boys from the lower classes of New York city into the country for a vacation colony, and there established a complete imitation of a municipal government, with president, judges, legislature, and police. The Republic was by no means a mere play institution, as the citizens were subject to fines and imprisonment. The Republic issued a special currency which was redeemable in hard cash, so that the community possessed a firm industrial as well as political backing. The plan was heralded abroad as a striking success, and some of the large New York and Chicago dailies began to establish similar colonies.†

The schools were not slow to recognise the value of the suggestion, and many of them adopted constitutions providing for the maintenance of discipline by the pupils. A number of these constitutions have been published in the School Review, with a brief account of the experiments. From these, we choose an account of the scheme at the Hyde Park High School, Chicago, as typical.‡

---

* The estimate is made by Albert Shaw, in an article, The School City, Review of Reviews, December, 1899.

† For best account of the experiment, see Commons, J. R., The Junior Republic, American Journal of Sociology, vol. iii, p. 281.

‡ French, C. W. School Government, School Review, vol. vi, p. 35.

The theory of the new experiment demands the extension of democratic principles to the schoolroom, and this in the interests of good training for citizenship. The antithesis between democracy in the management of local community affairs and autocracy in the schoolroom is dwelt upon at length. We are told that the school is a distinct community by itself, with the interests and possibilities, if not with all the functions, of the larger community outside. The political incompetency evident in many communities is held by the thinkers of this school to be the legitimate result of the abuse of authority in the schoolroom.

In the Hyde Park High School " each room elects in regular form a representative to a body which is partly legislative and partly executive in its function, and is called a senate. This body elects a president and secretary, appoints the necessary committees, and assumes the control of order in the halls and the care of furniture and buildings; it formulates a code of laws and appoints a corps of tribunes to execute them. The laws are read to the students in each room and carefully explained, so that the reasons for their adoption and the methods of their enforcement are clearly understood, and then they are posted in conspicuous places. Whenever classes are passing through the halls, the tribunes are stationed at strategic points throughout the building to see that the rules are enforced."

The senate appoints a court of three judges to whom all cases of lawbreaking are reported, and before whom the serious ones are tried with the customary procedure of prosecution and defence. The judges very wisely make their administration reformatory rather than punitive in its purposes, and seldom find it necessary to inflict a penalty.

We are told that the whole body of students, with few exceptions, are intensely loyal to the idea. They take pride in the recognition of their rights and feel that they are individually responsible for the welfare and good name of the school. " The old spirit of forced submission to authority is passing away, and in its place is coming a voluntary submission to the general rules of good behaviour as embodied in the laws which they themselves have made. Excellent order is maintained by the student tribunes, and in no case has the student citizen refused to give his testimony in any case where the integrity of his institution was at stake. In general, such evidence has been given in a manly and womanly way, and no stigma has been attached to the witness."

In the Pratt High School, Brooklyn, the students distinctly objected to being put in a position of spying on one another, or of punishing their fellow-students. The constitution is somewhat more complex than that of Hyde Park. It was framed on the model of the Federal Constitution, and delegates authority to an executive (principal of the school), a senate (teachers), an assembly (seniors), and the judiciary (equal members of teachers and seniors). "The plan has worked beautifully. It has a beneficent effect on both teachers and students. Every student knows he is free to appeal to the school court when he regards the requirement of teachers and principal as unjust. Every teacher and the principal feels that any whimsical or unduly severe exaction is subject to review by the instructors and three students; and as a result there has not been one appeal since the plan was instituted." *

The published testimony in general agrees with the examples here given, although there are some exceptions which will be referred to later. However, it may be said that the experiments are too recent to justify any

* McAndrew, W. A. High School Self-Government, School Review, vol. v, p. 458, 1897.

authoritative conclusions. The various schemes have been in the hands of sympathetic friends who, by their own example and inspiration, probably contributed largely to the results achieved. Then the published accounts are special pleas; they " put the best foot foremost." Conversation with unsympathetic teachers or assistants brings out many counterbalancing facts which are overlooked in the printed accounts. However, the experiments do show that the strong play impulse in children, which frequently takes the form of imitating adult activities, may be appealed to by a sympathetic principal and made the means of arousing a strong interest in the problems of government.

In addition to the important forms of activity which we have discussed, there are numerous miscellaneous clubs of minor importance among students in secondary schools. Our *questionnaire* reveals the existence, in the forty-one institutions studied, of twenty school papers, eleven religious associations (confined to boarding schools), eleven musical clubs, seven reading circles, six camera clubs, four chess and whist clubs, and two dramatic associations. These societies have a distinct value in affording opportunities for social diversion to students of peculiar tastes who would otherwise be excluded from the circle of school interests. Like similar organizations in colleges, these clubs are much more temporary in character than the more vital activities.

As to the value of student organizations as an educational agency, three distinct attitudes were taken by our correspondents. A small number—only two out of the thirty replying to the *questionnaire*—consider these societies as entirely alien to the work of the school, and doubt the advisability of their existence in institutions of the secondary grade. Fourteen consider them as legitimate but as quite subordinate, and seem to consider the present condition of affairs quite satisfactory. The remaining fourteen consider them as an essential element in school life, and endeavour by various means to strengthen such associations and render them more efficient.

Mr. Thurston's results should be compared with those just presented. Out of twenty-two definite replies from high schools on the value of school activities, fifteen were favourable in general and seven unfavourable. As we have already noted, debating societies were strongly favoured, while sentiment was equally divided on the subject of athletics. Mr. Thurston concludes that opinions are very diverse respecting the ability of secondary students to run their own clubs, athletic associations, etc., and that there is now comparatively little emphasis put on the value of these voluntary associations in training for democratic citizenship.[*]

There is also a great preponderance of testimony in favour of a close interest in, and supervision of secondary school societies on the part of the school authorities. By supervision is not meant direct interference, but the control of standards through suggestion, and a close watchfulness against degeneration. Many of the most experienced schoolmen favour such societies only when they are supervised. Out of the twenty-five correspondents replying to this question, twenty-one favour systematic watchfulness and supervision, while four believe that the societies should be left entirely to student initiation and control, and that they are only valuable when spontaneous.

In the encouragement of social activities there is one caution which should be continually in mind, and which has been well put by President Sharpless, of Haverford: " It is true that a school without physical

---

[*] Thurston, Henry W. Training for Citizenship in the Public Schools, School Review, vol. vi, p. 577, 1898.

and other outside organizations is not usually a desirable school, and moreover, in this country of the all-powerful boy, might not be a popular or profitable school. But I would like to do something to exalt the really ambitious and promising student from the herd of athletes and musicians in which he is now lost. I would like to make it felt that the real hero is the intellectual rather than the physical leader, and that the much maligned ' grind ' is in many cases the boy with the future. Will not this be in the long run to the great advantage of the athletic interests with which I am in great sympathy? . . . It is lamentable to see the difference with which many excellent and well-prepared students regard their intellectual opportunities. After passing through the secondary school they are to have their reward in the social and athletic activities of college life." *

* Sharpless, Isaac, in School Review, vol. vi, p. 150, 1898.

APPENDIX.

A SELECT CRITICAL BIBLIOGRAPHY ON STUDENT SOCIETIES.

I. STUDENT LIFE DURING THE MEDIÆVAL PERIOD IN EUROPE.

1. COMPAYRÉ, GABRIEL. Abelard and the Origin and Early History of the Universities. Pp. xiii + 315. New York, 1897.

The nations are described in Part II, Chapter II, student life Part IV, Chapters I and II; best popular account.

2. LAURIE, S. S. Lectures on the Rise and Early Constitution of the Universities, with a Survey of Mediæval Education. Pp. ix + 293. London, 1886.

Chapter IX contains a readable sketch of mediæval student life.

3. RASHDALL, HASTINGS. The Universities of Europe in the Middle Ages. Three volumes. London, 1895.

Rashdall's fourteenth chapter contains the most scholarly and reliable treatment of the subject in English. Elsewhere he discusses the nations and colleges.

4. MULLINGER, JAMES BASS. The University of Cambridge to the Accession of Charles I. Two volumes.. Cambridge, 1873, 1884.

Volume I, Chapter IV, is devoted to student life; accurate but less full than Rashdall.

5. LYTE, H. C. MAXWELL. A History of the University of Oxford from the Earliest Times to the Year 1530. Pp. xii + 504. London, 1886.

Material scattered and treatment inferior to Mullinger and Rashdall.

(See under German student life for additional notices of the mediæval period.)

II. STUDENT LIFE AMONG GERMAN-SPEAKING NATIONS.

A. *General, Historical, and Descriptive.*

6. BARNSTEIN, ADOLF PERNWERTH. Beiträge zur Geschichte und Literatur des deutschen Studententhums von der Gründung der ältesten deutschen Universitäten bis auf die unmittelbare Gegenwart, mit besonderer Berücksichtigung des XIX. Jahrhunderts. Pp. vii + 88 + 156. Würzburg, 1882.

Contains the most complete historical sketch; which, however, is very brief, and a valuable bibliography of three hundred and sixty titles, dealing with all phases of German student life.

7. DOLCH, OSKAR. Geschichte des deutschen Studententhums von der Gründung der deutschen Universitäten bis zu den deutschen Freiheitskriegen. Pp. viii + 300. Leipzig, 1858.

The standard German authority. The introduction treats of student life in other European countries.

8. PAULSEN, FRIEDRICK. The German Universities; their Character and Historical Development. Authorized translation by Edward Delavan Perry, and

introduction by Nicholas Murray Butler. Pp. xxxi + 246. New York, 1895.

In Chapter V Professor Paulsen discusses the present forms of German student clubs and their social value. Another translation found in Annual Report of Bureau of Education, 1891–'92.

9. RAUMER, KARL VON. Geschichte der Pädagogik. Two volumes. Vierter Theil. Die deutschen Universitäten. Pp. x + 332. Jütersloh, 1882.

Translated in Barnard's American Journal of Education, Volumes VI and VII. It contains a complete history of student life to the nineteenth century. From 1800 on, the author relates his experience with the Corps and Burschenschaften.

10. ZIEGLER, THEOBALD. Der deutsche Student am Ende des 19 Jahrhunderts. Pp. 240. Leipzig, 1896.

The seventh lecture treats of the duel, the eighth of student clubs; these problems are taken up from a modern pedagogical standpoint.

B. *Special Treatises.*

11. BAYER, EDMUND. Die Entstehung der deutschen Burschenschaft in Sammlung gemeinverständlicher wissenschaftlicher Vorträge. Berlin, 1883.

12. CAROVÉ, FRIEDRICH WILHELM. Entwurf einer Burschenschafts-Ordnung. Pp. 286. Eisenach, 1818.

A manual of the Burschenschaften, containing an elaborate justification of them.

13. DIESTERWEG, F. A. W. Ueber das Verderben auf den deutschen Universitäten. Pp. 76. Essen, 1836.

An attack on the German university system.

14. KEIL. RICHARD und ROBERT. Geschichte des Jenaischen Studentenlebens von der Gründung der Uni-

versität bis zur Gegenwart (1548–1858). Pp. xiv +
662. Leipzig, 1858.

A classic in this field; the most important treatise
which has yet appeared on any aspect of German student
life.

15. MEYER, F. H. Leben und Sitten deutscher Studenten. (Containing Die Studenten, ein Lustspiel von
Christoph Stymmel.) Pp. 100. Leipzig, 1857.

A play describing conditions in 1545.

16. MUTHER, D. THEODOR. Aus dem Universitäts-
und Gelehrtenleben im Zeitalter der Reformation. Pp.
499. Erlangen, 1866.

Contains valuable account of pre-Reformation conditions, with a scholarly analysis of the sources.

17. SCHEIDLER, KARL HERMANN. Ueber das
deutsche Studentenleben und die Nothwendigkeit einer
innern, von den Studirenden selbst ausgehenden Reform desselben. Pp. 96. Jena, 1842.

18. SCHEIDLER, KARL HERMANN. Deutscher Stu-
dentenspiegel als Beitrag zu einer Reform des deutschen Studentenlebens im Geist unserer Zeit und un-
seres Volkthums. Pp. 327. Jena, 1844.

19. SCHMIDT, ERICH. Komödien von Studentenleben aus dem sechzehnten und siebenzehnten Jahr-
hundert. Pp. 35. Leipzig, 1880.

20. SEIFART, KARL. Altdeutsches Studentenleben. Pp. 71. Bremen, 1856.

21. WREGE, REINHOLD. Die Hochquart. Eine Studenten Oepopöe. Essen, 1882.

A burlesque.

22. WREGE, REINHOLD. Das Bilder-Buch eines ar-
men Studenten. Pp. 98. Berlin, 1868.

A collection of sentimental stories.

23. WREGE, REINHOLD. Naturgeschichte des deutschen· Studenten von Plinius dem Jüngsten. Pp. 208. Leipzig.

C. *Descriptions by Foreigners.*

24. BAYNES, A. H. German Student Life. Fraser's Magazine, vol. civ, p. 630.

A clever, well-written account by an Englishman from an English standpoint.

25. BOYESEN, HJALMAR HJORTH. German Student Life. Cosmopolitan Magazine, vol. x, p. 368.

An excellent description of recent developments. Compares German and English student life.

26. HART, JAMES MORGAN. German Universities. A Narrative of Personal Adventure. New York, 1874.

Describes student life in the sixties, compares German and American customs. Best discussion of duelling by a foreigner.

27. HOWITT, WILLIAM. The Student Life of Germany. London, 1841.

Consists of a translation of a treatise by Dr. Cornelius, of Heidelberg; a general encyclopædia of information on the subject, but somewhat diffuse.

28. RUSSELL, JAMES E. German Higher Schools. The History, Organization, and Methods of Secondary Education in Germany. Pp. viii + 455. New York, 1899.

Chapter X describes student life in the German secondary schools.

29. WARREN, F. M. Student Life in Germany. Chautauquan, vol. ix, p. 582.

Brief but thoughtful; contains some general hints of value.

30. WARREN, F. M. The Corps Fuchs and the Rec-

reations of a Corps Bursch. Saturday Review, vol. lvii, pp. 42, 241.

A brief, bright sketch of the recent changes in student customs.

III. Student Life among French-speaking Peoples.

31. KIMBALL, RICHARD B. Romance of Student Life Abroad. Leipsic, 1854.

Deals with student life in Paris during the forties.

32. LEUBA, JAMES H. National Destruction and Construction in France as seen in Modern Literature and the Neo-Christian Movement. American Journal of Psychology, vol. v, p. 496.

Describes the recent student associations founded through the instrumentality of Lavisse.

33. PETERSON, ALICE FESSENDEN. The American Art Student in Paris. New England Magazine, N. S., vol. ii, p. 669.

Contains material bearing on co-operation among art students.

34. STANTON, THEODORE. French University Students. Open court, vol. vii, pp. 38–39.

A brief but excellent general characterization of French student life.

35. SYMONDS, JOHN ADDINGTON. Swiss Athletic Sports. Fortnightly Review, vol. lvi, p. 408.

An account of a Swiss athletic festival.

36. TOLMAN, WILLIAM H. International Students' Associations. Educational Review (American), vol. v, p. 363.

Describes organization in Scotland and France.

37. WARREN, F. M. Student Life in Paris. Chautauquan, vol. ix, p. 406.

Another good characterization, very brief.

38. WHITEING, RICHARD. The American Student at the Beaux-Arts. Century Magazine, vol. i, p. 259.

Describes student customs in the art schools.

39. Flüchtiger Blick in das Pariser Studentleben in the Grenzboten, No. 38, September, 1851, X Jahrgang.

Deals largely with the grisette phase of student life.

40. Student Life in Paris. Household Words, vol. iii, p. 286.

A brief and flippant description of French student life.

41. Athletics in France. The Nation, vol. lxvii, p. 245.

A brief outline of the rise of an athletic type in France.

42. French Athletic Sports. Saturday Review, vol. lxix, p. 694.

A discussion of athleticism among the French lycées.

IV. STUDENT LIFE IN THE ENGLISH UNIVERSITIES.

A. *General, Descriptive, and Historical.*

43. BRISTED, CHARLES ASTOR. Five Years in an English University (Cambridge). Third edition. Pp. 572. New York, 1873.

Written by an American and contains many interesting comparisons of student life in the two countries. Describes conditions in the forties.

44. EVERETT, WILLIAM. On the Cam. Lectures on the University of Cambridge in England. Pp. 390. Cambridge, 1865.

Another American book, inferior to Bristed for details, but aims to be more comprehensive.

45. HUBER, V. A. The English Universities. (An abridged translation from the German, edited by Francis W. Newman.) Three volumes. London, 1843.

Chapter XI, third division, contains some suggestive observations on social life in the English universities.

46. MASSON, DAVID. The Life of John Milton narrated in Connection with the Political, Ecclesiastical, and Literary History of his Time. Six volumes. London.

Chapter IV, Volume I, presents a picture of college life at Cambridge in 1625.

47. MULLINGER, JAMES BASS. [The History of the] University of Cambridge to the Accession of Charles I. Two volumes. Cambridge, 1873, 1884.

Volume II, Chapter V, treats of student life at the close of the sixteenth century.

48. NEWMAN, JOHN HENRY. The Idea of a University Defined and Illustrated. Seventh edition. Pp. xxii + 239. London, 1887.

Lays great stress on the social function of the university.

49. PYCROFT, JAMES. Oxford Memories: A Retrospect after Fifty Years. Two volumes. Pp. 303 + 304. London, 1886.

Diffuse, but contains valuable material on social and athletic affairs.

50. WELLS, J. (editor). Oxford and Oxford Life. Chapters on the Intellectual Life; the Social Life. Pp. 190. London, 1892.

Most comprehensive account of recent conditions. Written with proper perspective.

51. WORDSWORTH, CHRISTOPHER. Some account of the studies at the English Universities in the Eighteenth Century. Cambridge, 1877.

The standard authority on the eighteenth century; merely an undigested collection of facts, with no attempt at narrative.

B. *Briefer Articles on Social Life in General.*

52. DAVIS, RICHARD HARDING. Our English Cousins. Chapter III. Undergraduate Life at Oxford. Pp. 228. New York, 1894.

A clever, popular account.

53. LEHMANN, R. C. In Cambridge Courts. Studies of University Life in Prose and Verse. Pp. 240. London.

A collection of sketches, dialogues, and verses of a humorous nature, giving the flavour of university life.

54. MELLEN, CHASE. Undergraduate Life at Oxford. Outing, vol. xvii, p. 344.

Contains an excellent account of athletic organizations.

55. PARKER, CHARLES POMEROY. Reminiscences of Oxford. Harvard Monthly, vol. ii, p. 127.

Describes social life at Balliol in Jowett's time.

56. PEARSON, NORMAN. Undergraduate Life at Oxford. Lippincott's Magazine, vol. lxxxiii, p. 66.

Calls attention to the social and moral discipline of English university life.

57. PERRY, WALTER C. German Views of Oxford and Cambridge. Macmillan's Magazine, vol. xxxvii, p. 406.

A review of Helmholtz's address on the English university system.

58. Aspects of Modern Oxford by a Mere Don. Pp. 135. London, 1894.

A light, sketchy description of recent tendencies in English university life; contains an account of Oxford journalism.

59. College Life at Cambridge. Westminster Review, vol. xxxiv, p. 456.

An attack on student customs, containing a satirical account of a wine party.

60. Gown and Town Rows at Oxford and their Historical Significance. Dublin University Magazine, vol. lxxi, p. 361.

C. *Articles on Athletics in the English Universities.*

61. GRENFELL, W. H. Rowing at Oxford. English Illustrated Magazine, vol. iv, p. 498.

A fair, general account.

62. LAING, J. W., and BOLTON, W. W. Faculty Control of Athletics at the English Universities. Outing, vol. xxvii, p. 490.

63. LEHMANN, R. C. Rowing at Cambridge. English Illustrated Magazine, vol. iv, p. 507.

64. SHEARMAN, MONTAGUE, and TURNER, R. W. Athletic Sports at Oxford and Cambridge Universities. English Illustrated Magazine, vol. ix, p. 441.

Describes organization and training for track athletics.

65. WINBOLT, S. E. Rowing at Oxford. Atlantic Monthly, vol. lxvii, p. 788.

An excellent brief account of the system of control and training.

66. Boating Life at Oxford. London Society (Magazine), vol. xi, pp. 289, 425, 541.

Contains realistic accounts of social events connected with Oxford athletics.

D. *Articles on Debating Unions.*

67. EVERETT, WILLIAM. The Cambridge Union, Old and New. Vol. iv, p. 40.

An excellent description by an American; contains a brief historical *résumé.*

68. KNATCHBULL-HUGESSEN, E. H. The Oxford Union. Time, vol. ii, p. 146.

Reminiscences of the Union in 1850; presents an excellent view of its inner workings at that time, with criticism of debating clubs.

69. NICHOLSON, EDWARD B. The Oxford Union, a History. Macmillan's Magazine, vol. xxviii, p. 567.

Contains valuable material on the early history of the society.

70. NICHOLSON, EDWARD B. A Night in the Oxford Union. London Society (Magazine), vol. xxii, p. 449.

A realistic sketch of the Union at work.

V. STUDENT LIFE IN THE ENGLISH SECONDARY SCHOOLS.

A. *General, Historical, and Descriptive.*

71. BREUL, KARL. Die Einrichtung und Verwaltung des höheren Schulwesens in England in Baumeister's Handbuch, vol. i, Munich, 1897.

Contains a chapter on student life and a selected critical bibliography of secondary education.

72. CORBIN, JOHN. Schoolboy Life in England: an American View. Pp. viii + 226. New York, 1898.

Written from a pedagogical standpoint; contains in the last chapter a comparison between English and American schools. Describes life at Eton, Winchester, and Rugby. The author has a slight English bias, which does not vitiate his conclusions.

73. LUBBOCK, ALFRED. Memories of Eton and Etonians. London, 1899.

Devoted chiefly to athletics.

74. LYTE, H. C. MAXWELL. A History of Eton College (1440–1875). Pp. 527. London, 1875.

The standard authority; contains many references to rebellions and brutality of manners.

75. MANSFIELD, R. B. (editor). Great Public Schools, by Various Authors. Pp. 344. London.

Contains a history of each public school, with an accompanying chapter on its games.

76. MINCHIN, J. G. COTTON. Old Harrow Days. London, 1898. Contains excellent sketches of headmasters and of school heroes and games.

77. PASCOE, CHARLES EYRE (editor). Everyday Life at Eton, Harrow, Rugby, and other Great Public Schools. Sketched by the Head Scholars. Pp. 324. New York and London.

The most valuable single book on life in the secondary schools of England.

78. PRICKARD, A. O. Life in " Commoners " in Winchester College (1393–1893) by old Wykehamists. Pp. 187. London, 1893.

A number of disconnected sketches.

79. SALMON, EDWARD. Juvenile Literature as it is. Pp. 240. London, 1888.

Chapter IV treats of school stories, characterizing the books of Mr. Hughes, Archdeacon Farrar, Rev. T.

S. Millington, Mr. Ascott R. Hope, Rev. H. C. Adams, and Mr. Talbot Baines Reed.

80. SHARPLESS, ISAAC. English Education in the Elementary and Secondary Schools. New York, 1892.

Chapter V contains an excellent description of the great public schools.

81. WILMOT, E. P. EARDLEY, and STREATFIELD, E. C. Charter House, Old and New. Pp. 295. London, 1895.

Describes many traditional customs and games.

82. Recollections of Eton by an Etonian. Pp. 362. London, 1870.

The story of a typical Eton career, with useful notes on fagging and athletics.

83. Great Public Schools—Eton, Harrow, Charterhouse, Cheltenham, Rugby, Clifton, Westminster, Marlborough, Haileybury, Winchester—by Various Authors. Pp. vi + 344. London.

Contains chapters on games in the different public schools. Another edition of No. 74.

84. School Life at Winchester College, or Reminiscences of a Winchester Junior. Pp.243. London, 1866.

An easy, popular sketch for boys, but contains data on fagging and other traditional customs.

B. *Discussion of Problems.*

85. COOKSON, CHRISTOPHER (editor). Essays on Secondary Education. Public School Athletics, the last essay in the volume by Rev. Lionel Ford. Oxford, 1898.

This essay is a sane, level-headed protest against the extravagances of athleticism.

86. COTTERILL, C. C. Suggested Reforms in Public Schools. Edinburgh and London, 1885.

Chapter II, outdoor exercise, is a description of existing conditions of games in secondary schools.

87. FARRAR, FREDERIC W. The Fall of Man and other Sermons. (Sermon VIII, The History and Hopes of a Public School, preached before Harrow School on Founder's Day, 1859.) London, 1882.

Gives an excellent idea of the public-school spirit.

88. FINDLAY, J. J. Arnold of Rugby: his School Life and Contributions to Education. Cambridge, 1897.

Contains school life at Rugby (Chapter III in Stanley's Life of Arnold), selected sermons preached chiefly in Rugby Chapel, essays on educational topics, and a well-selected critical bibliography.

89. FINDLAY, J. J. Corporate Life and Games in Secondary Schools. Educational Times, vol. lii, p. 28 (January 1, 1899).

Presents the results of a *questionnaire*, with discussion. Relates chiefly to public day schools.

90. FITCH, JOSHUA. Thomas and Matthew Arnold and their Influence on English Education. New York, 1897.

Best brief account of Arnold's work at Rugby.

91. LAWRENCE, P. (Miss). Games and Athletics in Secondary Schools for Girls.

Special Reports on Educational Subjects, (English) Education Department, vol. ii, p. 145.

Resumés recent progress.

92. SHARPLESS, GEORGE. The Organization of Games out of School for the Children attending Public Elementary Schools in the Large Industrial Centres as Voluntarily Undertaken by the Teachers.

Special Reports on Educational Subjects, (English) Education Department, vol. ii, p. 159.

93. STANLEY, ARTHUR P. The Life and Correspondence of Thomas Arnold, D. D. American edition. New York, 1845.

Contains the best account of Arnold's internal reforms at Rugby.

94. THRING, EDWARD. Education and School. London and Cambridge, 1867.

Chapter XVI treats of internal self-government, prepositors, and fagging. Should be compared with Arnold's essays.

95. WOODHOUSE, Mrs. Physical Education in the Sheffield High School for Girls.

Special Reports on Educational Subjects, (English) Education Department, vol. ii, p. 133.

96. Die Missionsvereine der öffentlichen Schulen in England. Deutsche Zeitschrift für Ausländisches Unterrichtswesen. Vol. iv, p. 275.

C. *Articles on British Athleticism.*

97. BRADLEY, A. GRANVILLE. The Prominence of Athleticism in England. Atlantic Monthly, vol. xlix, p. 92.

A violent attack upon British athleticism.

98. EDWARDES, CHARLES. The New Football Mania. Nineteenth Century, vol. xxxii, p. 622.

A somewhat lurid article, dealing with the professional aspects of football.

99. JEYES, S. H. Our Gentlemanly Failures. Fortnightly Review, vol. lxvii, p. 386.

Claims that the present athletic *régime* in English schools produces business incapacity.

100. RICHARDSON, BENJAMIN W. Athleticism in the Scale. Saturday Review, vol. lxxx, p. 167.

A clear and sane protest against athleticism.

101. The Mind and the Body. The Spectator, vol. lxxvi, p. 767.

Points out that athletic interest has increased, while purely intellectual interests have decreased, at the English universities.

102. Professional Football. All the Year Round, vol. lxxiii, p. 558.

A favourable but moderate view of professional football.

103. A Counter-Blast to Exercise. The Spectator, vol. lxix, p. 492.

A mild protest against the prevailing forms of British athleticism.

VI. STUDENT LIFE AT THE SCOTTISH UNIVERSITIES.

104. FRASER, NORMAN. Student Life at Edinburgh University. Paisley, 1884.

Relates the university career of a student of Pietistic tendencies.

105. GRANT, ALEXANDER. The Story of the University of Edinburgh during its First Three Hundred Years. Two volumes. London, 1884.

Appendix S of the second volume contains an account of the student organizations of the university.

106. LEYS, J. Life at the Scottish Universities. National Review, vol. viii, p. 533.

Written from an English standpoint.

107. MASSON, DAVID. Reminiscences of Edinburgh University—Professors and Debating Societies. Macmillan's Magazine, vol. xi, p. 123.

A valuable estimate of the value of debating societies in the university.

108. NICHOL, JOHN.   Scotch Universities, their Friends and Foes.   Fortnightly Review, vol. xl, p. 639.

A useful discussion of the relation of the Scotch universities to national life.

109. RAIT, ROBERT SANGSTER.   The Universities of Aberdeen: a History.   Pp. xii + 382.   Aberdeen, 1895.

Contains incidental references to Scottish student life.

110. The Scottish Universities.   North British Review, vol. xiii, p. 285.

A general view of Scottish education, with a general comparison of the university systems of Germany, England, and Scotland.

111. Life at the English and Scotch Universities: a Contrast.   The Nation, vol. xxi, p. 322.

Contains useful statistics of Scotch student life.

112. North Country Students.   Cornhill Magazine, vol. xxxvii, p. 452.

Diffuse.

113. Scottish University Students.   All the Year Round, vol. xliv, p. 80.

A hostile view, written with an Oxford bias.

114. Student Life in Scotland.   Cornhill Magazine, vol. i, p. 366.

An excellent article; describes debating societies and social life in the universities.

115. Student Life in Scotland.   Blackwood's Magazine (American edition), vol. xxxix, pp. 135, 422.

116. College Life at Glasgow.   Fraser's Magazine, vol. liii, p. 505.

Good account of Scottish student life in the thirties.

117. Scottish Student Life.   Chambers's Journal, vol. lxxi, p. 593.

Gives the history of all the recent movements and changes in Scottish student life.

VII. GENERAL TREATISES BEARING ON AMERICAN STUDENT LIFE.

A. *Works covering the Entire Field.*

118. HALL, B. H. A Collection of College Words and Customs. Pp. 508. Cambridge, 1856.

A storehouse of material, treating of the early periods of American student life.

119. PORTER, NOAH. The American Colleges and the American Public. Pp. vi + 285. New Haven, 1870.

An able defence of existing conditions in American colleges, including the class system.

120. THWING, CHARLES F. American Colleges; their Students and Work. New York, 1883.

Chapter V treats of societies, Chapter VII of journalism. Well written, but not full.

B. *Histories and Reminiscences of Particular Institutions.*

121. BAGG, L. H. Four Years at Yale. By a Graduate of '69. Pp. 713. New Haven, 1871.

A full account of student customs, usages, and societies, well written. One of the most instructive books on American student life.

122. BALDWIN, EBENEZER. Annals of Yale College. Pp. 324. New Haven, 1831.

123. BUSH, GEORGE GARY. The History of Higher Education in Massachusetts. Pp. 445. Washington, 1891.

Contains many useful references to modern student life at Harvard.

124. CLARK, WILLIS G. The History of Education in Alabama (1702–1889). Pp. 281. Washington, 1889.

Describes student life in the South in ante-bellum days.

125. CLEAVELAND, NEHEMIAH, and PACKARD, ALPHEUS SPRING. History of Bowdoin College, with Biographical Sketches of its Graduates (1806–1879). Pp. 905. Boston, 1882.

The standard history of Bowdoin; contains excellent accounts of debating and religious societies.

126. CUTTING, GEORGE R. Student Life at Amherst College: its Organizations, their Membership and History. Pp. 204. Amherst, 1871.

A complete account of all forms of student activity for the period covered. The only book of the kind thus far published in the United States. Probably the most valuable single work for American student life.

127. CUSHING, THOMAS. Undergraduate Life Sixty Years Ago. Harvard Graduate Magazine, vol. i, p. 547.

128. DURFEE, CALVIN. A History of Williams College. Pp. 432. Boston, 1860.

A standard work, with incidental accounts of student life.

129. HITCHCOCK, EDWARD. Reminiscences of Amherst College, Historical, Scientific, Biographical, and Autobiographical. Pp. 412. Northampton, 1863.

Important for the study of the debating society and rise of the fraternity.

130. Lippincott Series on Social Life in American Colleges, in Lippincott's Magazine, vols. xxxix and xl (1887–'88).

Slight and superficial with two or three exceptions; the series runs as follows:

WENDELL, BARRET.   Social Life at Harvard, vol. xxxix, p. 152.

HOPKINS, E. M.   Social Life at Princeton, vol. xxxix, p. 677.

SPENCER, R.   Social Life at Cornell, vol. xxxix, p. 999.

MINOR, J. B., Jr.   Social Life at the University of Virginia, vol. xl, p. 98.

JENKS, A. E.   Social Life at Yale, vol. xl, p. 290.

McDONALD, J. R.   Social Life at Williams College, vol. xl, p. 572.

ROUNDS, R. S.   Social Life at Amherst College, vol. xl, p. 737.

131. MacLEAN, JOHN.   History of the College of New Jersey from its Origin in 1746 to the Commencement of 1854.   Two volumes.   Pp. 414 + 450.   Philadelphia, 1877.

Contains many data on student habits and morals at the beginning of the century.

132. McLAUGHLIN, ANDREW C.   History of Higher Education in Michigan.   Pp. 179.   Washington, 1891.

133. MERIWETHER, COLYER.   History of Higher Education in South Carolina.   Pp. 247.   Washington, 1889.

Contains an interesting description of early Southern student life.

134. MERRIAM, LUCIUS SALISBURY.   Higher Education in Tennessee.   Pp. 287.   Washignton, 1893.

Describes modern conditions at Vanderbilt University.

135. PARKER, LEONARD F.   Higher Education in Iowa.   Pp. 190.   Washington, 1893.

Some incidental references of value.

136. PEABODY, ANDREW P. Harvard Reminiscences. Pp. 216. Boston, 1888.

An interesting description of the old-time relations between faculty and students.

137. PIERCE, BENJAMIN. A History of Harvard University from its Foundation in the Year 1636 to the Period of the American Revolution. Pp. 316. Appendix, pp. 153. Cambridge, 1833.

138. PORTER, JOHN A. (editor). Sketches of Yale Life: Being Sketches, Humorous and Descriptive, from College Magazines and Newspapers. Pp. 288. Washington, 1886.

139. POWELL, LYMAN P. The History of Education in Delaware. Pp. 186. Washington, 1893.

Describes student life in a small college.

140. QUINCY, JOSIAH. The History of Harvard University. Two volumes. Pp. 612 + 726. Boston, 1860.

Valuable for colonial student life. Appendix contains documents showing the habits and customs of the students.

141. Scribner Series on Undergraduate Life in American Universities. Volumes xxi, xxii (1897), Scribner's Magazine.

An able succession of articles, much superior to the Lippincott series. The descriptions of Princeton and Harvard life are particularly good. The titles run as follows:

MARTIN, EDWARD S. Undergraduate Life at Harvard, vol. xxi, p. 531.

ALEXANDER, JAMES W. Undergraduate Life at Princeton, vol. xxi, p. 663.

HOWLAND, HENRY E. Undergraduate Life at Yale, vol. xxii, p. 1.

142. SMITH, BAXTER PERRY. A History of Dartmouth College. Pp. 474. Boston, 1878.

Another standard authority, with incidental treatment of student life.

143. SMITH, CHARLES LEE. The History of Education in North Carolina. Pp. 179. Washington, 1888.

Describes debating societies.

144. START, ALARIC BERTRAND (editor in chief). History of Tufts College, published by the Class of 1897. Pp. 382. Tufts College, 1896.

Treats of student life much in detail. Valuable because it describes many recent experiments with student institutions.

145. STEINER, BERNARD C. The History of Education in Connecticut. Pp. 300. Washington, 1893.

The sections on student life in the history of Yale are excellent epitomes of much longer chapters in the Yale Book.

146. STOREY, MOORFIELD. Harvard in the Sixties. An address before the Harvard Memorial Society. Pp. 24. Boston, 1869.

One of the best descriptions of the old college life.

147. THAYER, W. R. An Historical Sketch of Harvard University from its Foundation to May, 1890. Pp. 66. Cambridge, 1890.

A brief, comprehensive sketch of unusual merit.

148. THORPE, FRANCIS NEWTON. Benjamin Franklin and the University of Pennsylvavnia. Pp. 450. Washington, 1893.

Includes a separate chapter on the history of student organizations within the university.

149. TOLMAN, WILLIAM HOWE. The History of

Higher Education in Rhode Island. Pp. 210. Washington, 1894.

Sketches student life at Brown University.

150. TYLER, W. S. History of Amherst College during its First Half Century (1821–1871). Pp. 671. Springfield, 1873.

Emphasizes the religious life and organizations of the college.

151. WALLACE, GEORGE R. Princeton Sketches. The History of Nassau Hall. Pp. 200. New York, 1893.

Deals with the fraternity problem at Princeton.

152. WELCH, LEWIS SHELDON, and CAMP, WALTER. Yale, her Campus, Class-rooms, and Athletics. Pp. 628 Boston, 1899.

An extended account of all forms of student activity; one of the most valuable recent books.

153. Reminiscences of Scenes and Characters in College by a Graduate of Yale of the Class of 1821. Pp. 229. New Haven, 1847.

154. Sketches of Yale College, with Numerous Anecdotes, by a Member of the Institution. Pp. 192. New York, 1843.

VIII. LITERATURE OF THE CLASS SYSTEM.
A. *College Discipline.*

155. BARTLETT, S. C. College Disturbances. The Forum, vol. iv, p. 424 (1888).

The author holds public opinion largely responsible for student outbreaks.

156. GODKIN, E. L. College Discipline. The Nation, vol. xlviii, p. 154 (1889).

Shows relation between college discipline and the low estimate of college professors by graduates.

157. JORDAN, DAVID STARR. College Discipline. North American Review, vol. clxv, p. 403 (1897).

Author claims that discipline should be reduced to a minimum, that undesirable students should be sent home; the article also treats of hazing and rushing.

158. MCCOSH, JAMES. Discipline in American Colleges. North American Review, vol. cxxvi, p. 428 (1878).

Defends the conservative position; holds that students should be closely watched; touches on hazing and college disturbances.

159. QUINCY, J. P. Coercion in the Later Stages of Education. Old and New, vol. viii, p. 44 (1873).

A plea for a more liberal view of discipline; objects to the recitation marking system and to police duties of professors.

160. SHALER, N. S. The Problem of Discipline in Higher Education. Atlantic Monthly, vol. lxiv, p. 24 (1889).

Treats of the genesis and development of college discipline at Harvard; important.

161. College Instruction and Discipline. American Quarterly Review, vol. ix, p. 283 (1831).

A general discussion; the writer takes a conservative standpoint and opposes all forms of student cooperation.

162. College Discipline. The Critic, vol. i, p. 204 (1881).

Shows the impossibility of a great scholar serving as policeman; the standpoint of the writer radical.

B. *Descriptive of Class Life and Customs.*

163. ALDEN, SAMUEL, and STETSON, CHARLES. The Rebelliard or Rebellion Poem: an Heroic Poem in Five Cantos. Pp. 36. Amherst, 1869.

A burlesque on the students participating in the great rebellion of Harvard.

164. BAGG, LYMAN H. The Bully Club (of Yale). Yale Book, vol. ii, p. 460.

An excellent description of one of the most unique of American student institutions.

165. BUTLER, DANIEL. Commons (at Yale). Yale Book, vol. i, p. 297.

Throws light on the causes of class rebellions.

166. CUSHING, T., and ALLEN, T. P. Town and Gown in Old Times. Harvard Graduate Magazine, vol. viii, p. 15.

A brief account of two early difficulties at Harvard.

167. HALL, BENJAMIN HOMER. Commons (Harvard). Harvard Book, vol. ii, p. 75.

168. LOWELL, JAMES RUSSELL. Class Day. Harvard Book, vol. ii, p. 157.

Important for early history of the class.

169. NORTHROP, CYRUS. Commencement (Yale). Yale Book, vol. i, p. 306.

170. QUINCY, EDMUND. Commencement Day (Harvard). Harvard Book, vol. ii, p. 147.

171. TODD, HENRY ALFRED. Commencement Day (Princeton). Princeton Book, p. 179.

172. WEBBER, SAMUEL. A Narrative of the Proceedings of the Corporation of Harvard College relative to the Late Disorders in that Seminary. Pp. 19. Cambridge, 1807.

Presents the official side in the great rebellion.

173. Don Quixotes at College, or a History of the Gallant Adventures lately achieved by the Combined Students of Harvard University, interspersed by Some Facetious Reasonings—by a Senior. Pp. 20. Boston, 1807.

Another burlesque on the rebellious students of Harvard.

174. Circular (of Students in reference to the Rebellion of 1834). Pp. 12 (1834).

Official presentation of the case for the students.

IX. LITERATURE OF THE DEBATING SOCIETY.

A. *Descriptive.*

175. BAKER, GEORGE P. Debating at Harvard. Harvard Graduate Magazine, vol. vii, p. 363 (1899).

An account of the present method of training intercollegiate debaters at Harvard.

176. BRODT, P. E. Debating Societies at Columbia. Columbia University Quarterly, vol. i, p. 47.

An account of early debating societies at Columbia. The article contains instructive criticism.

177. CAMERON, HENRY C. The American Whig Society. Princeton Book, p. 184.

A brief sketch of one of the Princeton societies.

178. CHAMBERLAIN, D. H. Debating and Parliamentary Practice at Yale; a Speech before the Yale Alumni Association. New York, 1896.

A criticism of the methods of teaching English and coaching debaters then in force at Yale.

179. COE, EDWARD B. The Literary Societies (of Yale). Yale Book, vol. i, p. 307.

Best existing account of the pre-Revolutionary debating societies.

180. Cornell Era, March 30, 1898. Pennsylvania-Cornell debate, 1898. Subject: Reading as a Qualification for Immigrants. Ithaca, 1898.

A verbatim account of an important intercollegiate debate.

181. GARDNER, PERCY. Impressions of American Universities. Nineteenth Century, vol. xlv, p. 102 (January, 1899).

Contains severe criticism of intercollegiate debating from an English standpoint.

182. HOTCHKISS, THOMAS W., Jr. The Secret Societies of Princeton University. Magazine of American History, vol. xxvii, p. 17 (1891).

A fair account of the Princeton societies.

183. JACOBUS, MELANCTHON W. The Cliosophic Society. Princeton Book, p. 201.

A brief sketch of the second Princeton society.

184. JOHNSTON, W. C. The Literary Societies of Yale College. University Quarterly, vol. i, p. 115 (1860).

An excellent account of society rivalry.

185. MILLER, MARION MILLS. Debate in American Colleges. Bachelor of Arts, vol. ii, p. 208.

A brief article of slight importance.

186. PEABODY, FRANCIS GREENWOOD. The Institute of 1770. Harvard Book, vol. ii, p. 341.

An exceedingly brief account of the society which was for many years the chief debating club of Harvard.

187. RINGWALT, RALPH CURTIS. Intercollegiate Debating. The Forum, vol. xxii, p. 633 (1897).

A history of modern intercollegiate debating, with an exposition of present methods.

188. VROOMAN, CARL. College Debating. The Arena, vol. x, p. 677.

An exposition of the purposes of the Intercollegiate Debating Union.

189. College Oratory in the West. Review of Reviews, vol. xi, p. 665.

An account of the Western State oratorical contests, with a characterization of the specehes, and copious extracts.

B. *Principles and Pedagogy of Debating.*

190. BAKER, GEORGE PIERCE. The Principles of Argumentation. Boston and New York, 1895.

A standard manual.

191. BROOKINGS, W. D., and RINGWALT, R. C. Briefs for Debate, with an Introduction by Alfred Bushnell Hart. New York, 1896.

The introduction contains an exposition of the principles of modern intercollegiate debating.

192. CHAMBERLAIN, D. H. The Value of College Literary Societies. University Quarterly, vol. iii, p. 348 (1861).

Somewhat vague.

193. GODKIN, E. L. Collegiate Oratory. The Nation, vol. xxvi, p. 38.

A severe criticism of the rhetorical school of oratory; favours incisive debating instead.

194. HIGGINSON, THOMAS WENTWORTH. Hints on Writing and Speech-making. New York.

195. HOLYOAKE, GEORGE JACOB. Public Speaking and Debate. A Manual for Advocates and Agitators. Second edition. Boston, 1896.

196. MCELLIGOTT, JAMES N. The American De-

bater: Being a Plain Exposition of the Principles and Practice of Public Debate. New York, 1877.

An old and influential manual; now out of date.

197. McELLIGOTT, JAMES N. Debating a Means of Educational Discipline. American Journal of Education (Barnard's), vol. i, p. 495.

A diffuse article representing the old standpoint, but not without suggestions of value.

198. ROBINSON, WILLIAM CALLAHAN. Forensic Oratory; a Manual for Advocates. Boston, 1893.

199. ROWTON, FREDERIC. How to Conduct a Debate. New York.

200. WHATELY, RICHARD. Danger of Debating Societies to Young Men. Bentley's Miscellany, vol. xix, p. 615.

A strong protest, almost a philippic against the debating society.

201. Discussion Classes. Chambers's Edinburgh Journal, vol. x, p. 107.

An excellent *résumé* of the advantages of debating societies.

X. LITERATURE OF THE FRATERNITY SYSTEM.

A. *Descriptive.*

202. BAIRD, WILLIAM RAIMOND. American College Fraternities.

A descriptive analysis of the fraternity system in the colleges of the United States. Fifth edition. Pp. 438. New York, 1898.

The one great authority on this subject. It includes a general sketch of the fraternity system, the history of each society, statistical tables, and a vindication of the fraternity principle.

203. COOK, F. G. The Delta Upsilon at Harvard. Harvard Graduate Magazine, vol. viii, p. 321 (1899).

204. Hasty Pudding Club. Eleventh Catalogue of the Officers and Members—containing a Brief Sketch of the Club and an Index of Names. Pp. 301. Cambridge, 1891.

205. Harvard Book. (History of the Typical Harvard societies by the following authors):

BUSWELL, HENRY FOSTER. Pi Eta Society, vol. ii, p. 409.

CLARK, LESTER WILLIAMS. The Alpha Delta Phi, vol. ii, p. 389.

DANA, RICHARD HENRY. The Phi Beta Kappa Society, vol. ii, p. 343.

DEMING, HORACE EDWARD. The Everett Athenæum, vol. ii, p. 412.

GRANT, ROBERT. The A. D. Club, vol. ii, p. 392.

KIDDER, CAMILLUS GEORGE. The Signet Society, vol. ii, p. 414.

LONGFELLOW, SAMUEL. The Hasty Pudding Club, vol. ii, p. 353.

PERKINS, AUGUSTUS THORNDIKE. The Porcellian Club, vol. ii, p. 348.

WARREN, SAMUEL DENNIS. The O. K. Society, vol. ii, p. 396.

These sketches carry the history of the organizations as far as the late seventies.

206. PACKARD, LEWIS R. The Phi Beta Kappa Society (of Yale). Yale Book, vol. i, p. 324.

207. PIPER, P. F. College Fraternities. The Cosmopolitan, vol. xxii, p. 641 (1897).

A general sketch of the fraternity movement.

208. PORTER, JOHN ADDISON. College Fraternities. Century Magazine, vol. xiv, p. 749 (1888).

An account of the different forms of college fraternities.

209. RANDOLPH, EUGENE H. L. Greek-Letter Societies in American Colleges. New England Magazine, vol. xxiii, p. 70 (1897).

Best general sketch of the fraternities, written from a sympathetic standpoint.

210. THAYER, WILLIAM R. Shall we have a University Club? Harvard Graduate Magazine, vol. iii, p. 468.

Contains an excellent account of the Harvard societies both under the old and the new *régimes*.

211. WHITMAN, EDWARD A. The Pi Eta Society. Harvard Graduate Magazine, vol. iii, p. 486.

B. *Controversial.*

212. AIKEN, E. E. The Secret Society System. New Haven, 1882.

An attack on fraternities in general, and Yale fraternities in particular; intensely partisan.

213. JACOBS, A. B. The Greek-Letter Societies. Detroit, 1879.

214. KELLOGG, H. L. College Secret Societies. Pp. 88. Chicago, 1874.

Another bitter attack; contains considerable data of value.

215. LATHROP, W. W. College Secret Societies. University Quarterly, vol. iii, p. 273 (1861).

A strong argument against the secret-society principle.

216. McCOSH, J., SEELYE, J., ADAMS, H. C., and
22

others. Interchange (on college fraternities). The Academy, vol. ii, p. 372 (October, 1887).

Contains statements of views *pro* and *con* by a number of prominent American educators.

217. Occident Publishing Company. An Account of the Greek-Letter Fraternities in the University of California, republished from the Files of the Occident newspaper. Berkeley, 1883.

An onslaught on the fraternities.

218. PORTER, JOHN ADDISON. The Society System of Yale College. The New-Englander, vol. xliii, p. 377 (1884).

A strong defence of the society system at Yale.

219. SANBORN, ALVAN F. The Advantages of College Fraternities. The Academy, vol. v, p. 386 (1890).

A one-sided plea for the fraternity.

220. WHITE, ANDREW D. College Fraternities. The Forum, vol. iii, p. 243.

A valuable article; favours the fraternity.

221. WHITE, E. E. Report to the Board of Trustees of Purdue University.

A violent attack on the fraternities.

222. Secret Societies in College. The Critic, vol. iv, pp. 109, 137 (1884).

A well-written article, dealing largely with conditions at Yale.

XI. THE LITERATURE OF COLLEGE ATHLETICS.
A. *Descriptive.*

223. CAMP, WALTER, and DELAND, LORIN F. Football. Boston and New York, 1896.

Discusses the game from every possible standpoint,

but with most attention on the technique of training and strategy.

224. Harvard Book. (History of the different branches of athletics by the following authors):

CROWNINSHIELD, BENJAMIN WILLIAM. Boating, vol. ii, p. 191.

HIGGINSON, THOMAS WENTWORTH. The Gymnasium, vol. ii, p. 186.

SANBORN, WILLIAM DELANO. Baseball, vol. ii, p. 268.

225. Princeton Book. (History of the different branches of athletics by the following authors):

SMITH, WILTON M. Baseball, p. 417.

STEWART, DAVID. Football, p. 432.

226. THAYER, FREDERICK W. Harvard's Loss of Athletic Prestige. Harvard Graduate Magazine, vol. i, p. 31.

Describes methods of athletic organization at Harvard.

227. Yale Book. (History of the different branches of athletics by the following authors):

BAGG, LYMAN H. Boating, vol. ii.

BROWN, FAYETTE W. Athletic Sports (track), vol. ii.

BUSHNELL, SAMUEL C. Baseball, vol. ii.

PETERS, JOHN P. Football, vol. ii.

B. *Controversial and Pedagogical.*

228. BOYKIN, JAMES C. Physical Training. Report of the United States Commissioner of Education, 1891–'92, vol. i, p. 451.

An historical sketch of physical education.

229. CAMP, WALTER. Athletic Extravagance in

Training, in Playing, and in Describing. Outing, vol. xxvi, p. 81.

A plea for moderation.

230. DARLING, E. A. The Effects of Training. Harvard Graduate Magazine, vol. viii, p. 21.

A careful study of the physiological effects of training.

231. DAVIS, ANDREW M. F. College Athletics. Atlantic Monthly, vol. li, p. 677.

Contains some suggestions of merit.

232. EMMONS, ROBERT W., 2d. Needed Football Reforms. Harvard Graduate Magazine, vol. iii, p. 318.

A clear statement of the main issues raised by athleticism.

233. GARDINER, A. P. The Graduate Athletic Association. Harvard Graduate Magazine, vol. vi, p. 344.

Treats of the organization of coaching.

234. GODKIN, E. L. Glorification in Athletics. The Nation, vol. lv, p. 406.

Calls attention to the bad results of athletic notoriety.

235. GODKIN, E. L. The Athletic Craze. The Nation, vol. lvii, p. 422.

A pungent criticism of the prevailing methods of athletic training and management.

236. GODKIN, E. L. Athletics and Health. The Nation, vol. lix, p. 457.

A sharp attack on athleticism; claims that watching football games is a poor substitute for moderate exercise.

237. HART, ALBERT BUSHNELL. The Status of Athletics in American Colleges. Atlantic Monthly, vol. lxvi, p. 63.

A history of the problems of athletic organization.

238. HARTWELL, EDWARD MUSSEY. Physical Training. Report of the United States Commissioner of Education, 1897–'98, vol. i, p. 487.

A general history of physical training; criticises American college athletics from the standpoint of scientific physical training.

239. HEMENWAY, AUGUSTUS, and others. Important Suggestions in Athletics, being the Report of the Committee on Physical Training, Athletic Sports, and Sanitary Condition of Buildings. Harvard Graduate Magazine, vol. vi, p. 191.

Outlines the athletic policy of Harvard.

240. JONES, OLIVER S. Morality in College Athletics. North American Review, vol. clx, p. 638.

Contains some suggestive criticism; objects to loafing in connection with athletics and to professionalism.

241. RICHARDS, EUGENE L. Intercollegiate Athletics and Faculty Control. Outing, vol. xxvi, p. 325.

Written from the athlete's standpoint; advises that faculty control be limited to smallest possible extent.

242. RICHARDS, EUGENE L. College Athletics. Popular Science Monthly, vol. xxiv, pp. 446–587.

A thoughtful and suggestive article, with a strong athletic bias.

243. TAUSSIG, F. W. A Professor's View of Athletics. Harvard Graduate Magazine, vol. iii, p. 305.

An article remarkable for its moderation and insight.

244. THAYER, W. R. Class Honours and Athletics. Harvard Graduate Magazine, vol. viii, p. 194.

Shows a close relation between the two. The author exhibits tables of honour men.

245. WALKER, FRANCIS A. College Athletics. Harvard Graduate Magazine, vol. ii, p. 1.

A strong vindication of athletics; this article is republished in the author's educational essays.

246. WHITE, JOHN WILLIAMS. The Constitution, Authority, and Policy of the Committee on the Regulation of Athletic Sports (at Harvard). Harvard Graduate Magazine, vol. i, p. 209.

An account of one of the most interesting recent experiments in athletic organization.

247. WHITNEY, CASPAR (Department of Amateur Sport, in Harper's Weekly).

Contains much intelligent ciriticism of current athletic methods.

248. YOUNG, C. A. College Athletic Sports. The Forum, vol. ii, p. 142.

The author advocates a moderate control of athletics.

249. The Outreachings of Athletics. The Nation, vol. lx, p. 235.

An anonymous correspondent deals with the demoralizing results of college athletics on preparatory schools—noting phases of professionalism.

250. Should Professionals be employed in College Athletics? Bachelor of Arts, vol. i, p. 559.

A strong negative given by a Harvard man, the affirmative position taken by a Cornell graduate.

XII. LITERATURE OF STUDENT SELF-GOVERNMENT.

251. BIGHAM, JOHN. An Instructive Experiment in College Government. Educational Review, vol. iii, p. 162.

A brief and sympathetic account of the Amherst experiment.

252. Bowdoin College. Articles of Agreement between the Faculty and Students of Bowdoin College for the Administration of Justice in the College (1894).

253. SCHURMAN, JACOB GOULD. Report of the President of Cornell University, 1894–'95.

Supports the honour system strongly.

254. FERNALD, M. C. Co-operative Government. Proceedings of the National Educational Association, 1890, p. 685.

An account of the plan of self-government at the University of Maine.

255. GREGORY, JOHN M. An Experiment in College Government. International Review, vol. x, p. 510 (1881).

An excellent sketch of the experiment at the University of Illinois.

256. MCKENZIE, JAMES C. Honour in Student Life. School Review, vol. vii, p. 69 (1899).

A discussion of the honour system in college examinations.

257. PEABODY, SELIM H. An Educational Experiment. Proceedings of the National Educational Association, 1889, p. 539.

An account of the decline and fall of student self-government at the University of Illinois; author's attitude that of hostility to the experiment.

258. SMITH, C. H. Modern Bowdoin. The Congregationalist, June 21, 1894.

Contains a brief sketch of the Bowdoin scheme of self-government.

259. Stanford University. Constitutions of the Associated Students of the Leland Stanford Junior University. Palto Alto, 1896.

Contains the constitution of the student body and all subordinate organizations.

260. STEVENS, W. LE CONTE. Self-Government in Colleges. Popular Science Monthly, vol. xix, p. 697 (1881).

A letter to the editor of the Popular Science Monthly, giving the history of some early experiments in student self-government.

261. Tulane University of Louisiana. Student Handbook (containing the Constitution of the Academic Corps). Revised, 1898.

XIII. LITERATURE OF STUDENT PRESS.

262. Amherst. The Amherst Student. Odd volumes from 1879 to 1896. Amherst.

263. ANDERSON, G. W. College Journalism. Williams's Literary Monthly, vol. i, p. 311 (1886).

An excellent article, indicating the functions of college journalism.

264. BRADLEY, W. A. Undergraduate Publications (at Columbia). Columbia University Quarterly, vol. i, p. 358; vol. ii, p. 27 (1899).

An account of the early student publications at Columbia; an excellent sketch.

265. CARTER, FRANKLIN. College Magazine (at Yale). Yale Book, vol. i, p. 338.

A sketch of Yale journalism.

266. Columbia University Quarterly. Two volumes. New York, 1898–1900.

A graduate magazine, publishing notes and articles of importance on student life.

267. Harvard Graduate Magazine. Eight volumes. Boston, 1892–1900.

A graduate quarterly, publishing important articles on student life, besides an intelligent and compre- · hensive chronicle of student organizations from year to year.

268. Harvard Magazine. Ten volumes. Cambridge, 1854–'64.

A high-class literary and critical magazine published by the students of Harvard.

269. Harvard Monthly. Volumes I to XXVII. Cambridge, 1885–1900.

The present literary magazine of the Harvard undergraduates, representative of the best type of American college journalism.

270. Harvard Lyceum. One volume. Cambridge, 1811.

The oldest college literary magazine which has come down to us.

271. JAMES, HENRY, Jr. The (Harvard) Crimson. Harvard Graduate Magazine, vol. viii, p. 181.

Describes the management, make-up, and influence of the modern college daily.

272. OSBORN, HENRY F. The Princeton Journals. Princeton Book, p. 400.

An historical sketch of Princeton journalism.

273. PERRY, THOMAS SERGEANT. The College Journals (of Harvard). Harvard Book, vol. ii, p. 173.

An historical account of Harvard journalism.

274. Wesleyan. The College Argus. Volumes V to X. Middletown, 1871–'77.

275. Williams. Williams Literary Monthly. Two volumes. Williamstown, 1885–'87.

276. Williams. Williams Literary Quarterly. Five volumes. Williamstown, 1854–'59.

277. Yale. The Yale Literary Magazine. Sixty-four volumes. New Haven, 1837–'99.

The most famous of college literary monthlies.

278. Yale. Yale Courant. Odd volumes from VII to XXXIII. New Haven, 1870–'95.

XIV. LITERATURE OF MISCELLANEOUS STUDENT CLUBS.
A. *Religious.*

279. COOKE, JOSEPH PLATT. The Christian Brethren. Harvard Book, vol. ii, p. 360.

An account of one of the oldest Christian societies.

280. DOGGETT, L. L. History of the Young Men's Christian Association, vol. i, 1844–'55. New York, 1896.

Does not deal directly with college associations.

281. DUFFIELD, JOHN T. The Philadelphian Society. Princeton Book, p. 212.

Corresponded to the societies of inquiry elsewhere.

282. MOTT, JOHN R. The Students of the World united. Some Achievements of the Year 1897–'98 (1899).

Describes the international students' movement of Europe, with account of author's tour and visits to conventions.

283. MOTT, JOHN R. College Young Men's Christian Association Buildings. New York, 1895.

Describes the buildings already erected, and shows the importance of such in the religious life of colleges.

284. MOTT, JOHN R., REYNOLDS, J. B., WISHARD, L. D. The Christian Movement in the Universities of America, Europe, and Asia. Chicago, 1893.

Comparatively obsolete.

285. MOTT, JOHN R., STEVENSON, J. R., ROOT, P.

Report of the Executive Committee of the Student Volunteer Movement for Foreign Missions. Presented, February 23–27, 1898.

Outlines the policy of the movement and summarizes its achievements.

286. RICHMOND, WILLIAM. The St. Paul's Society. Harvard Book, vol. ii, p. 402.

A brief account of an Episcopalian society.

287. SHELDON, GEORGE. The Nassau Bible Society. Princeton Book, p. 227.

A unique Princeton organization.

288. Student Volunteer Movement for Foreign Missions. Official pamphlets by—

EDDY, SHERWOOD. The Supreme Decision of the Christian Student, or the Choice of a Life Work. New York, 1895.

GATES, MERRILL EDWARDS. Christian Missions and the Highest Use of Wealth.

LYON, WILLARD D. The Volunteer Band for Foreign Missions. Chicago, 1895.

Describes the organization and workings of the individual band.

LYON, WILLARD D. The Volunteer Declaration, 1895.

WHITE, J. CAMPBELL. The Self-Perpetuation of the Volunteer Band.

289. TENURE, ARTHUR B. The St. Paul's Society. Princeton Book, p. 231.

290. Young Men's Christian Association. Yearbook of the Young Men's Christian Association of North America, 1897. New York, 1897.

B. *Professional and Industrial.*

291. Federation of Graduate Clubs. Graduate Handbook. Seven volumes (1892–'99).

Introduction to each volume contains an account of graduate clubs. Volume VII much more important than other numbers of the series.

292. STONE, MILTON JEROME, Jr. The Co-operative Society (of Harvard). Harvard Graduate Magazine, vol. i, p. 560.

293. STONE, MILTON JEROME, Jr. History of Co-operation in the United States. Johns Hopkins University Studies in Historical and Political Science, vol. vi. Baltimore, 1888.

Chapters I to II, Co-operation in New England, by Edward W. Bemis, contains accounts of the co-operative stores at Harvard, Yale, and Massachusetts Institute of Technology.

294. CALIFORNIA, UNIVERSITY OF. Proposed New Constitution of the Student Co-operative Society of the University of California. Berkeley, 1894.

C. *Philanthropic.*

295. CALKINS, RAYMOND. Volunteer Charity Work. Harvard Graduate Magazine, vol. iii, p. 323.

An account of the philanthropic activities of the Harvard religious associations.

296. MINNESOTA, UNIVERSITY OF. Actual Experience in making a Living, related by Men who have made their Own Way through the University. Four Essays. 1898.

D. *Musical and Dramatic.*

297. DENNIS, ALFRED L., Jr. Glee and Instrumental Clubs (of Princeton). Princeton Book, p. 412.

298. DWIGHT, JOHN SULLIVAN. The Pierian Sodality. Harvard Book, vol. ii, p. 363.

299. FOOTE, ARTHUR WILLIAM. The Harvard Glee Club. Harvard Book, vol. ii, p. 394.

300. STOECKEL, GUSTAVE J. Music and Musical Societies (at Yale). Yale Book, vol. ii, p. 479.

E. *General Miscellaneous.*

301. HALE, EDWARD EVERETT. The Natural History Society. Harvard Book, vol. ii, p. 385.

302. LOTHROP, SAMUEL KIRKLAND. The Harvard Washington Corps. Harvard Book, vol. ii, p. 375.

303. MERWIN, HENRY CHILDS. Miscellaneous Organizations (at Harvard). Harvard Book, vol. ii, p. 417.

XV. LITERATURE OF WOMEN'S STUDENT SOCIETIES.

304. HILL, MARY BRIGHAM, and EAGER, HELEN GERTRUDE. Wellesley. The College Beautiful. Boston, 1894.

Describes organizations and *fêtes* at Wellesley.

305. RICHARDSON, SOPHIA FOSTER. Tendencies in Athletics for Women in Colleges and Universities. Popular Science Monthly, vol. l, p. 517.

A carefully prepared paper, dealing with the results of Kraepelin.

306. SMITH, L. R. Social Life at Vassar. Lippincott's Magazine, vol. xxxix, p. 841 (1887).

307. STOW, SARAH D. (LOCKE). History of Mount

Holyoke Seminary, South Hadley, Mass., during the First Half Century (1837–1887), 1887.

XVI. LITERATURE OF STUDENT SOCIETIES IN SECONDARY SCHOOLS.

308. COMMONS, JOHN R. The Junior Republic. American Journal of Sociology, vol. iii, p. 281 (1898).

Best sketch of the Freeville experience.

309. FRENCH, C. W. School Government. School Review, vol. vi, p. 35 (1898).

A plea for student self-government, with the constitution of the student association of the Hyde Park High School.

310. McANDREW, W. A. High-School Self-Government. School Review, vol. v, p. 456 (1897).

An account of an experiment at Pratt Institute, Brooklyn, with constitution.

311. MILNER, FLORENCE. School Management from the Side of Social Life. School Review, vol. vii, p. 215.

Discusses the social functions of the class.

312. PEABODY, ENDICOTT. School Patriotism. School Review, vol. ii, p. 502 (1895).

Shows the relation between athletics and the growth of a school spirit.

313. SHAW, ALBERT. The School City. A Method of Pupil Self-Government. (American) Review of Reviews, vol. xx, p. 693 (1899).

An account of the recent schemes for pupil self-government in American schools and high schools.

314. SHARPLESS, ISAAC. What is the Present Consensus of Opinion as to the Most Important Problems

in Preparatory and Collegiate Education? School Review, vol. vi, p. 145 (1898).

Contains a plea for intellectual leadership and protests against excessive athleticism and social activities.

315. SNYDER, Z. X., and others. Report on Normal Schools—The Inner Life of the Normal School. Proceedings of the National Educational Association, 1899, p. 861.

Recognises the value of student societies.

316. THURBER, C. H. High-School Self-Government. School Review, vol. v, p. 32 (1897).

Gives the constitution of the Warren (Pennsylvania) High-School Association, with Comments.

317. THURSTON, HENRY W. An Inquiry relating to Training for Citizenship in the Public Schools. School Review, vol. vi, p. 577 (1898).

Presents the results of *questionnaire*. Section G treats of social education through student societies.

318. Self-Government by Pupils. Appendix H of the Report of the Educational Commission of the City of Chicago. Chicago, 1899.

An account of the system of pupil self-government in the John Crerar Grammar School.

INDEX.

THE END.